William H. Day is Professor of M
at Northeastern Oklahoma State

urpose of this book is to present what should be an obvious
managing a small business, but one which is so frequently
s it impossible that the term *profit* is so closely related to free
hat it is taken for granted? Should businesspeople simply take
after expenses—with some of them rejoicing, some almost
d with some unhappy losers? There appears to be a need to
rofitability more directly. In the many books written, profit
oned in the title, and generally receives only indirect or cursory
Without adequate profit, a business will cease to operate.
this book attempts to put in perspective the broad spectrum of
equired to manage a business, and manage it all profitably.
simply taking what comes out at the bottom line of the operating
managers of small business should be more objective in their
more definitive in their expectations, more resolute in their
tion, and more effective in their task of managing the business

implement the object of this book—putting profit in better
e in the *modus operandi* of small-business people—the book
s early the subject of profit, just as a would be manager assesses
ve business opportunities. Immediately, upon initiating the busi-
hema for profit is presented in a step-by-step procedure whereby
ed or needed profits for the enterprise become involved as a
part of the goals and objectives of the business.
ving brought profit to the fore at the initiatory phase of managing
usiness, the impact of this approach should be carried on throug
er phases: implementing, operating, and futurity. This assume
practice the business operator would relate his activities to th
ss reading," expressed by the profit goal. This book attempts
ize this course of procedure in the chapters presented in each
ases of the business. Someone said, "Increasing your profit is o
s," and it is intended that this book may contribute to such
plishment for the reader.
To give the reader a pragmatic orientation, fifteen case stud
developed which present actual business situations to consid
ts should appreciate the statement of a Harvard University profe
aid, "Wisdom can't be told." This statement underscores the im
and use of the case method as a pedagogical technique. In addi
hancing your practical orientation and "wisdom," they may
ment to your study of managing a small business profitably.
In the Appendix you will find some Learning Experiences, w

MAXIMIZING SMALL BUSINESS PROFITS
with Precision Management

William H. Day

57145

A SPECTRUM BOOK

Prentice-Hall Inc., Englewood Cliffs, New Jersey 07632

Library of Congress Cataloging in Publication Data

DAY, WILLIAM HENRY, 1924—
  Maximizing small business profits with precision management.

  (A Spectrum Book)
  Bibliography: p.
  Includes index.
  1. Small business — Management. I. Title.
HD69.S6D38   658'.022   78-9407
ISBN 0-13-566257-5
ISBN 0-13-566240-0 pbk.

*This Book is Dedicated to My Wife and Our Family—
the Most Important Enterprise in Our Lives!*

A SPECTRUM BOOK

Printed in the United States of America

10 9 8 7 6 5 4 3 2 1

PRENTICE-HALL INTERNATIONAL, INC., *London*
PRENTICE-HALL OF AUSTRALIA PTY., LIMITED, *Sydney*
PRENTICE-HALL OF CANADA, LTD., *Toronto*
PRENTICE-HALL OF INDIA PRIVATE, LIMITED, *New Delhi*
PRENTICE-HALL OF JAPAN, INC., *Tokyo*
PRENTICE-HALL OF SOUTHEAST ASIA PTE., LTD., *Singapore*
WHITEHALL BOOKS, LIMITED, *Wellington, New Zealand*

vi

Preface

The p
approach to
neglected. I
enterprise t
what is left
satisfied, a
deal with
is not ment
treatment.
Therefore,
activities
Instead of
statement,
approach,
determina
profitably
  To
perspecti
introduc
prospecti
ness, a s
the desi
primary
  Ha
a small
the oth
that in
"compa
empha
the ph
busine
accom

were
Stude
who s
tance
to e
enjoy

Being in business for yourself is as American as app
is the American way, for in terms of numbers they re
95 percent of the total number of businesses. And ye
some institutions of higher learning do not teach cou
ship or in how to operate a small business. The main t
on preparing students for employment with big
corporations.
  In practice, little is said and not much encoura
stimulating an interest in developing your own busines
that this important sector of the business community,
American way of life, should have equal time. An enligh
of small enterprise throughout the land could very w
many of our contemporary problems. Instead of expecti
subsidy to supplement the bottom line on the profit an
a more profit-oriented management would accomplish the
their own capabilities. Hopefully, this book may co
managing small businesses more profitably.

were substituted for the usual questions. The Learning Experiences were designed to give students direct involvement in small business situations so they would have better insight and understanding. To enhance that understanding, supplemental study may be pursued with the various materials listed in the Bibliographies.

In the interest of ease in reading the text, it was decided not to change all references to "the businessman" to "the businessperson." The reader will realize that, of course, all points presented in the book will apply to both businessmen *and* businesswomen.

This undertaking could not have been accomplished without the understanding and support of my wife and our family. Their contribution is most appreciated. Certainly my students over the years have in the course of discussions generated many helpful ideas. Many fine instructors, at five universities in particular, plus the many others with whom it has been my privilege to be associated, have all had an impact on my preparation of this book. The helpful assistance of my secretaries Pam Menees, Evonne Snodgrass, and Ruth Bridges in preparing the manuscript is gratefully acknowledged.

WILLIAM H. DAY
Tahlequah, Oklahoma

Contents

THE
INITIATORY
PHASE

1

Assessing
Business
Opportunities

*"Few people recognize opportunity
because it is disguised as hard work"*

Southern Wings[1]

Profitable management of a small business is contingent upon an opportunity which has a profit potential. Business opportunities come in various sizes and shapes, at unexpected times and places. When opportunities come, it is important to be able to assess them as good, bad, or otherwise. This chapter will provide some methods and procedures to use in evaluating opportunities and making important first decisions.

WHAT IS THE BUSINESS OPPORTUNITY?

All that glitters is not gold. Certainly, not all alleged business opportunities are really worthwhile. How can you tell? In a word, by putting a sharp pencil to the proposition. To illustrate, a young man considering a small

---

[1]From Henry L. Sisk, *Management and Organization* (Cincinnati, Ohio: South-Western Pub. Co., 1977), p. 477. Reprinted with permission.

confection business visited his banker, who surprised him by saying, "If you are going into business, why don't you pick a business that will be worthwhile? That small confection business will only yield wages at best, but there are other business opportunities that would provide greater returns for the same time and effort." This provoked the young man to search for a profitable business opportunity.

WHAT KIND OF BUSINESS IS BEST?

The answer to the question is simple. Engage in the kind of business you like, the one which makes you the happiest. Choose the one in which you would put forth the greatest effort and hard work. It may involve merchandise or it may involve services. The choices are many. But if you do not like what you are doing, the probabilities of success and profitable operation are greatly reduced. A good way to find the answer is to first work for someone else in the type of business you think you would like. The experience will be beneficial and will give you a sure measure of whether the business is best for you.

ADVANTAGES AND DISADVANTAGES

Being number one in the operation, calling the shots and making the decisions, is ranked among the top advantages of having a small business. In many instances, the ease of getting into the business may be considered an advantage. It could also be a disadvantage, depending upon the outcome of the venture.

You had best like people and like being with them, because there may be continual direct contacts with customers and employees. For many businesspeople, the contacts provide a great amount of "psychic income" and genuine satisfaction.

The ringing of the cash register may seem like music to your ears as you contemplate the multiplication of sales into rewarding income and profits. Personal efforts correlate fairly well with the compensation received, and you can set the amount yourself rather than have someone else determine your earnings.

Among the disadvantages is the fact that some business operations barely produce a salary comparable to wages paid when working for an employer. Also, there is the risk of losing invested funds and the liability for debts incurred. To a large degree, you have to do everything yourself. That is to be expected in a small business if it is to be profitable. If you hire someone else to do it for you—well, there go the profits! At a small business seminar, one of the speakers described himself as the personnel manager, sales department, accountant, window decorator, advertising specialist, credit section, and janitor, all in one.

Another disadvantage is the long work week, running six days and many nights. But the businessman often says he does not mind when he considers that he is working for himself. If you only want a forty hour a week job, maybe you should get one and forget about being in business for yourself.

HOW TO BEGIN

Assuming you find that the advantages outweigh the disadvantages, your next concern is how to begin. There are two main considerations and a third, outside possibility: (1) purchase a going concern, (2) initiate a new business, or possibly (3) inherit an existing business.

Purchase a Going Concern

Your main interest will be which way it is going. How well is it going? Is it a profitable operation? If not, why not? Can the problems be solved? Profitably? How can you tell?

Make an examination of profitability. Request a preview of the accounting statements. Take time to study them carefully. Use ratios to make comparisons.[2] Check the Dun and Bradstreet operating ratios for

---

[2] A ratio is the proportional relationship between two measures. There are three ways of expressing a ratio: first, by using a colon between the two measures (1:4); second, as a fraction (1/4); and third, as a percentage (25%). For additional information concerning the use of ratios in analyzing business performance, see Chapter 19.

similar businesses. Verify the profits by examining copies of the IRS returns. Yes, ask for them. The business is for sale and you had better be sure of what you are purchasing. Note especially the trends of sales, expenses, and profits. Is the business profitable? How profitable? How much can you realistically expect to increase the profits? If it does not pass the "profit test," forget it.

VISIT THE BUSINESS
If it is a profitable business opportunity, take a closer look by visiting the premises. You may need some help in appraising the relative condition and value of the plant, store, facilities, equipment, fixtures, and inventory. Compare monthly sales volume to monthly purchases. Average the inventory value and stock turnover to be sure the inventory is meeting customer needs. By means of "age analysis" of the inventory a better determination can be made of the relative value to be paid.

Avoid paying too much or buying equipment which may be out of date in terms of being competitive in performance capabilities. Obsolescence of equipment and fixtures is a serious concern in our rapidly changing scene. Another useful check is to examine the owners' insurance policies. Compare the coverage with the value of assets claimed.

ANALYZE THE INTANGIBLES
The seller will probably include in the asking price something for "goodwill." While it may be difficult to ascertain, care should be taken to determine whether the business has earned "goodwill" based upon years of operating successfully and satisfying customers. Has the business in fact incurred ill will because of unwise business policies or bad practices? It would be a good investment of time to inquire of unbiased persons, such as customers, suppliers, other businessmen, bankers, former employees, or others.

Reputation is especially important in the business community. The business may publicly appear to be on the up and up, yet privately be known for unacceptable employment practices, breaches of contract, sharp practices, and other undesirable characteristics which may be difficult to remedy.

Verify the status of leading brands and top merchandise to be sure their continued supply is not in jeopardy. Will the suppliers be willing to continue providing merchandise if you purchase the business? Determine this directly with the suppliers and make the necessary arrangements.

CHECK LEGAL ASPECTS

Be sure the assets being transferred are free of encumbrances such as judg-ments, liens, or pending litigation. There may be possible assignments of assets, commitments, or contractual matters to be investigated. This would be a good assignment for your lawyer.

HOW MUCH IS THE BUSINESS WORTH?

The Bank of America offers a method for arriving at the price of a business. The steps are presented below for your consideration:

> *Step 1.* Determine the tangible net worth of the business on the basis of its liquidation value. (The market value of all current and long-term assets less liabilities.)
>
> *Step 2.* Estimate how much the buyer could earn with an amount equal to the value of the tangible net worth if he invested it elsewhere. . . .
>
> A reasonable figure depends on the stability and relative risks of the business and the investment picture generally. The rate (of return) should be similar to that which could be earned elsewhere with the same approximate risk.
>
> *Step 3.* Add to this a salary normal for an owner-operator of the business. This combined figure provides a reasonable estimate of the income the buyer can earn elsewhere with the investment and effort involved in working in the business.
>
> *Step 4.* Determine the average annual net earnings of the business (net profit before subtracting owner's salary) over the past few years.
>
> This is before income taxes, to make it comparable with earnings from other sources or by individuals in different tax brackets. (The tax implications of alternate investments should be carefully considered.)
>
> The trend of earnings is a key factor. Have they been steadily rising, falling steadily, remaining constant, or fluctuating widely? The earnings figure should be adjusted to reflect these trends.
>
> *Step 5.* Subtract the total of earning power (2) and reasonable salary (3) from this average net earnings figure (4). This gives the extra earning power of the business.
>
> *Step 6.* Use this extra, or excess, earning figure to estimate the value of the intangibles (or "goodwill"). This is done by multiplying the extra earnings by what is termed the "years of profit" figure.
>
> This "years of profit" multiplier pivots on these points. How unique are the intangibles offered by the firm? How long would it take to set up a similar business and bring it to this stage of development? What expenses and risks would be involved? What is the price of goodwill in similar firms? Will the seller be signing a noncompetitive agreement?
>
> If the business is well established, a factor of five or more might be used, especially if the firm has a valuable name, patent, or location. A multiplier

of three might be reasonable for a moderately seasoned firm. A younger, but profitable, firm may merely have a one-year profit figure.

Step 7. Final price = Adjusted Tangible Net Worth + Value of Intangibles. (Extra earnings × "years of profit.")[3]

Here is an illustration showing the application of the above formula step by step:

1. Adjusted value of tangible net worth	$100,000
2. Earning power at 12%	$12,000
3. Owner's salary	18,000
	$30,000
4. Average annual net earnings including owner's salary	35,000
5. Extra earning power of the business (line 4 − lines 2 and 3)	$5,000
6. Value of intangibles based on 3-year profit figure for a moderately well-established firm (3 × line 5)	$ 15,000
7. Final price (line 1 + line 6)	$115,000

Should the earnings in the above example not be sufficient to warrant the payment of goodwill to the owner-seller, then the price for the buyer could be determined on the basis of capitalizing the average annual profit (net earnings after deducting all expenses, including salary for the owner) using the desired rate of return. The price would be calculated as follows:

$$\$25,000 - \$18,000 = \$7,000 \text{ profit}$$
$$\$7,000 \div .12 = \$58,333 \text{ buyer's price}$$

Initiate a New Business

Why initiate a new business? There may not be a going concern available for purchase, or you may not like the conditions offered to make a purchase. Either way, what does it take to launch your own enterprise?

A FEASIBILITY STUDY

Rosy optimism usually characterizes the prospective businessman's attitude toward his new undertaking. To put all the factors, forces, and effects in

---

[3]"How to Buy or Sell a Business," *Small Business Reporter,* 8, no. 11 (San Francisco: Bank of America National Trust and Savings Association, 1969), p. 11. Reprinted with permission from Bank of America.

their proper perspective, an appropriate feasibility study is recommended. Basically, this type of study considers the fundamental constituents that make a market, namely, population plus income data, or "men plus money."

These factors should be carefully researched by a careful market study of potential business in the prime market, with due consideration given to competition. The following questions are suggested by S.B.A. (Small Business Administration) in making an analysis of population:

1. What has been the change in total population in the market area over the past 10 years? (A comparison of census figures will answer this question. Many city and county governments compile population figures on various geographical bases.)
2. What is the current age-group distribution in the market? How has this distribution changed? (In most areas, the age distribution of the population has been changing dramatically.)
3. What is the average family size? (In many consumer-goods businesses, such as a child's clothing store, the size of the average family unit may be more important than total population.)
4. What percentage of the total population or family units are potential customers for your kind of business? (An analysis of the market for specialized goods and services may be the key to evaluating the future of your business.)
5. Will you be depending on a few large-scale buyers? (For example, if you will be selling a product or service to the industrial market, could the loss of one or two large-scale buyers win your volume?)[4]

Income is strategic because it is the means of making demand effective in terms of consumer wants being satisfied. Change in income is a pertinent factor, as are trends in the particular market. These questions will be helpful in analyzing income:

1. What is the total spendable income within the market area? What is the per capita income? What is the distribution of income by income class? (A high-income area is not desirable for all consumer goods and services. For example, one of the largest family-restaurant chains has found that a market area with a mixture of income classifications — low, medium, and high — is better than an area with either low or high incomes.)
2. If you will be selling consumer goods or services, do the consumers in the trading area have a pattern of income and expenditures that will support a high level of business activity? (You need to study past trends and make future estimates.)

---

[4]Verne A. Bunn, *Buying and Selling a Small Business* (Washington, D.C.: Small Business Administration, 1969).

3. What is the level of unemployment in your target area? Is it decreasing? (Unemployment is important because of the direct effect it has on purchasing power and the psychological effect of possible unemployment.)[5]

Competition can have varying effects upon your business depending on its caliber and type. This important aspect of the feasibility study will be facilitated by using the following questions:

1. How many competitive businesses are there within the market area of the business? Where are they located? (The market area in this sense is the trade area in which the business operates. In a retail, wholesale, or service business, this trade area may be rather narrowly defined. For example, the greatest percentage of the total sales volume for a carry-out restaurant will come from a radius of approximately one mile. On the other hand, in a manufacturing or mail-order business, there may be a number of markets—regional, national, and even international.)
2. How many competitive businesses have opened in this market area within the past year? (What is the reason for any increase? Can the market support all of these businesses?)
3. What other kinds of businesses are in indirect competition—that is, deal to some extent in the same kind of goods or services? (The pattern of competition changes rapidly as businesses continue to add lines of merchandise, expand services offered, and create new products and services.)
4. Does poor management of existing firms lead you to believe that you can take away a sufficient part of their business? (This requires firsthand familiarity with such factors in the local situation as high prices, extensive out-of-town purchasing, slow service, high business turnover, poor workmanship, unattractive appearance of business, and high incidence of customer complaints.)[6]

If you have had no experience in putting together a feasibility study, it would be good to secure some assistance through the College of Business or Bureau of Business Research at a nearby university. The undertaking may cost a few hundred dollars, but it could mean thousands downstream if you make a faulty decision in the initiation of a new business.

Inheriting an Existing Business

This is not the usual way to get started in business for yourself. In fact, even the members of business-owning families frequently choose to start their own. For those who decide to perpetuate the family enterprise,

---

[5]*Ibid.*
[6]*Ibid.*

there are special kinds of problems to resolve. It may be a long wait before getting to sit in the driver's seat.

WHAT ABOUT A FRANCHISE?

Entering business by way of a franchise is to do so in a structured and restricted manner. The truth of the matter is that you are not really in business by yourself, but in business with the franchise company. This is not necessarily bad, as many franchisees have been successful and a few have become millionaires. There are pros and cons about franchising. Consider them carefully.

The Pros

First and foremost is the opportunity to become part of a *successful business program*. After much study, research, and experience the franchisor has put it together with the "knowhow" to make it go. The products, procedures, and promotion are provided to build a successful business.

For the established franchise operations, *market acceptance* is a definite advantage. The specially designed building, layout, logo, advertising, and name all contribute to acceptance by the customer in the marketplace.

Another advantage is the *financing,* which is a difficult hurdle for many small businessmen to manage. Once you "qualify" in the mind of the franchisor, when he is convinced you're the one for that particular location. he may do lots of good things to get you started, financial assistance being one of the most important.

Because inexperience is one of the leading causes of failure, most franchise companies obviate this situation by providing *comprehensive training* both for the beginning phase and also as a continuing procedure. In order to maintain the reputation so expensive to establish, the franchisor wants the franchisees to do it the right way.

Finally, there is the advantage of being able to get needed answers from headquarters. Many small businessmen have wished they had an *advisory service* to turn to when problems arose.

The Cons

There are some offsetting considerations to all those good things mentioned above. If one of your main reasons for going into business is to be your own boss, you should be prepared to accept some *loss of independence.* Instead of making all the decisions, you will find that some of the decisions will be made by the franchisor—a lot of things will have to be done the company way.

Franchising is expensive. Depending on the benefits provided, the costs could run high. If you provide the program by yourself, it becomes more reasonable. Nevertheless, not everyone can meet the cost of being a franchisee.

An occasional criticism is the alleged *inadequacy of training.* Promises made before signing the contract are not always fulfilled to the satisfaction of the franchisee. And without the proper training, getting the "knowhow" could be a real disadvantage. You could check this out with other franchisees before getting on board yourself.

If you are seriously considering a franchise business opportunity, it would be well to assess it as you would any other business. Is it feasible? Check it out directly by contacting other franchise holders. You may also want to obtain a report from the local Better Business Bureau or Chamber of Commerce about the franchise promoter. Use your lawyer to check out the details of the contract, and resolve any questions or conditions before you place your signature.

WHICH TYPE OF LEGAL ORGANIZATION TO USE?

Your business may be organized as a sole proprietorship, as a partnership, or as a corporation. While there are various special forms of organization (including the joint-stock company, mining partnership, trust, or partnership association), it is reported that 99 percent of all businesses operate under one of the three basic forms.[7] In resolving which one is best at the particular time, it would be well to utilize the services of your lawyer. As conditions change, the legal form of your organization may also change.

---

[7]H. N. Broom and Justin G. Longenecker, *Small Business Management* (Cincinnati, Ohio: South-Western Publishing Co., 1975), p. 212.

It has been the history of some companies to begin as proprietorships, to expand by means of partnerships, and later to incorporate.

To better understand the implications of your decision, consider the positive and negative aspects of the three forms of organization, listed below.

Positive Considerations of Proprietorship

1. Simple to establish — you begin the business by yourself, and it is a sole proprietorship.
2. Complete authority.
3. No special restrictions by law.
4. Profits belong to owner — no sharing.

Negative Considerations of Proprietorship

1. Unlimited liability of the owner.
2. Limitation of available capital.
3. Life of business depends on life of owner. Business may be terminated at will or upon the death of the owner.

Positive Considerations of Partnership

1. Means of expanding capital for business.
2. Use of limited partners increases the opportunity for acquiring more capital.
3. Provides a method whereby personal capabilities can be expanded and thus enhance the business potential. You may know how to make the product, but have no marketing experience; hence, a partner with sales ability would strengthen the business operations. Plus, two heads will be better than one in resolving many other questions.
4. Division of profits determined by partners.
5. Loss by the business can be deducted from each partner's taxes.
6. Usually, no special legal restrictions beyond those for a proprietorship.
7. Ease of formation with minimal cost.

Negative Considerations of Partnership

1. Profits are divided among partners.
2. Liability to each partner for the actions of other partners affecting the business.
3. Liability for debts of business extends to each partner.
4. Potential conflicts arising from difficulties in human relations.
5. Partnership dissolved by death or withdrawal of partner (except in limited partnership).

In forming a partnership a contract should be drawn, preferably with the assistance of an attorney. The written document, known as *The Articles of Partnership,* should include the following particulars:

1. Identity of the business.
2. Date of organizing the partnership.
3. Purposes of partnership
4. Recognition of all partners by name and address.
5. Site of all business activities.
6. Specified time that partnership is to be effective.
7. Investment by each partner.
8. Basis for distributing profits and losses.
9. Provision for withdrawal or compensation by partners.
10. Responsibility and authority of all partners.
11. Specific required accounting records, and partner accessibility thereto.
12. Basis for dissolution and distribution of assets.
13. Plan for resolving disputes (artibration, if necessary).
14. Special limitations on partners — assuming unnecessary liabilities outside of business.
15. Procedure and means for protecting surviving partners (partner insurance).

The corporation is a creation of the law. It usually consists of three or more owners (depending on state requirements), referred to as stock-holders. Even though the corporation is an artificial being in the law, it may conduct business on a day-to-day basis, own property, enter into contracts, retain liability for debts, and sue and be sued in a court of law. A corporation is created by obtaining a charter from a state and complying with the requirements set forth. Some considerations, positive and negative, regarding the corporation are presented for your consideration.

Positive Considerations of Corporations

1. A corporation has the ability to accumulate capital—through the sale of common or preferred stock, loans (by issuing bonds), reservation of profits from the business, and exchange of assets.
2. Liability is limited to the value of the stock held by each stockholder. However, if the officer stockholders are guilty of fraud, etc., their liability may be extended.
3. Concentrated management, notwithstanding a widespread ownership.
4. Favorable publicity and goodwill may be generated by a large number of owners—stockholders.
5. The length of life for a corporation is established in the charter and is commonly made in perpetuity. Transfer of ownership is facilitated by stock transfers without disturbing the operation of the corporation. Dividing a business among heirs (difficult with a proprietorship or partnership) is accomplished simply by dividing shares of stock.

Negative Considerations of Corporations

1. Depending on the number of stockholders and distribution of shares, the various owners may have little or great influence on the control of corporate operations.
2. Corporation is limited to the activities specified in the charter.
3. Area of operations is geographically limited to the state granting the charter (until permission is granted elsewhere—which means more fees to pay and more regulations to adhere to).
4. Double taxation may pose a drawback.
5. Hired managers usually lack the personal interest and motivation of owner-managers.
6. Special legal restrictions do apply to corporations. Governments require reporting to various agencies, state and/or federal. A corporation is subject to all the civil and criminal matters of the law (as are the proprietorship and partnership). Managers of corporations are subject to the law as regards their conduct in operating the corporation.
7. Many reports to prepare and submit for tax and other reasons. The paperwork increases as the corporation grows.
8. The alleged advantage of limited liability is sometimes obviated in small corporations by requiring the officer-stockholders to guarantee loans and other commitments.

TAXES

Since taxes, particularly federal income taxes, are a major business and personal expense, it is essential to select the most advantageous form of organization. Taxes could be a determining factor between profit and loss for the businessman.

There are basically three forms for income tax purposes. The corporation and partnership are the most common. The taxes in a partnership are based on individual income, as they are in the sole proprietorship. The *Subchapter S Corporation* is the third form, and represents an attempt by Congress to remove tax considerations in the choice of legal form by small businessmen.

In the so-called tax-option corporation, the business may avoid paying income tax if the stockholders elect to report corporation income on their individual income tax returns. In effect, this permits taxation as in a proprietorship or partnership. However, these conditions must be met: (1) The corporation must have less than eleven stockholders; (2) the stockholders must be individuals or estates; (3) the corporation must have only one class of stock; (4) it must be a domestic corporation; (5) it cannot be a member of an affiliated group eligible to file consolidated returns; and (6) no more than 20 percent of its gross receipts may come from passive income (rents, interest, dividends, etc.).

Because of the benefits offered through the Subchapter S Corporation, it should receive careful evaluation. Noteworthy considerations include the following:

1. Income splitting. In a high profit year, a father may give stock to his children to take advantage of his lower income tax bracket without giving up control of the corporation.
2. Shifting income to a lower income year. If the corporation tax year (e.g., starts July 1) is different from the owner's personal income tax year (starting January 1), the dividends may be declared to shift income from high income years in low income years.
3. The benefits of the corporation form of ownership can be enjoyed without the so-called "double taxation."
4. Being taxed as a Subchapter "S" Corporation may be elected and terminated at will. This makes possible the use of the Subchapter "S" Corporation taxation during years when it is an advantage and not during years when it is not an advantage.[8]

---

[8]Bruce Goodpasture, "Danger Signals in a Small Store," *Small Marketers Aids,* No. 141 (Washington, D.C., Small Business Administration).

The final decision as to which form of organization to select should be made after consultation with experts in law, tax, and accounting. Since your choice may have a direct impact on profit maximization, it is an appropriate facet of assessing a business opportunity.

SUMMARY

If you want to manage a small business profitably, first be sure of the possibilities. Assess the business "opportunity" with great care. Is it the best kind of business for you? How should you begin? Is the business or proposition worth the price? Could a franchise be a possibility? Will you operate as a proprietor, partner, or corporation? Should you use the Subchapter S "tax-option" corporation?

Getting started is the difference between getting somewhere and nowhere.

2
Establishing Business Goals and Objectives

*If you know where you are going
you can plan how to get there.*

W. H. Day

DEFINING OBJECTIVES

The above quote is a succinct expression of the function of objectives —
the purpose of activities, the course to follow, the goal to be attained.
Defining objectives is the key to planning. Different kinds of plans arise
out of different kinds of objectives.

Davis[1] provided a comprehensive classification of objectives together
with an explanation of their interrelationships. The primary objective is
what Davis calls the *service objective,* an expression of the *"raison d' être"*
of the business. *Personal objectives* involve the interests of management
and employees. *Collateral social objectives* relate the business to its environment and consider the obligations arising from this relationship. It would
be a good investment of your time to codify the various specific objectives

---

[1]Ralph C. Davis, *Industrial Organization and Management* (New York: Harper and
Brothers, 1940), pp. 23-29.

of your business. Carefully defined objectives provide helpful guideposts to better chart the course of operations and render the required decisions along the way.

To determine your primary service objective, ask yourself why you are engaged in business. What is the basic purpose of your undertaking? You should consider the interests of your personnel, wages, bonuses, fringe benefits, and the extent to which they can be satisfied presently and in the future.

It would be helpful, when you are approached by different groups in the community (the chamber of commerce, service clubs, churches, schools, etc.), for you to have predetermined the scope of your business activity in these areas — the collateral social objectives of your business.

Another class of objectives, namely, secondary objectives, have to do with the effective and economical accomplishment of the various primary objectives mentioned. Basic decisions need to be made with reference to the amount of product quality, the level of customer service, and the funds for community endeavors, to name a few. For example, will you provide a box for the customer's merchandise? Will the box have a fancy wrapping, or will you convey the purchased item in a paper sack?

In writings about business objectives the idea of profits is sometimes treated as an almost automatic reward for effective accomplishment of primary objectives. For example, if you effectively manufacture and market bicycles, you should make a profit. Perhaps?

> *When a businessman says he is going to make all the profit he can . . . how much is that?*

Two reasons why businesses are not more profitable are:

1. Businesspeople do not determine how much profit to make; they fail to set a profit goal; they never plan how much profit to achieve.
2. Those who develop a plan fail to activate and implement the plan to a successful fruition.

HOW TO DETERMINE
THE PROFIT OBJECTIVE

Having dealt with objectives from the standpoint of company policy, the next consideration is setting *operational* objectives. One of the keys to planning operations is the *profit goal*, which can be expressed as a return

TABLE 2-1
YOUR COMPANY: Balance Sheet—December 31, 19____

Assets

Current Assets:			
Cash	$ 6,673		
Accounts Receivable	52,184		
Inventory	88,402		
Prepaid Expense Items	978		
Total Current Assets		$148,237	
Fixed Assets:			
Equipment and Machinery	$72,400		
Building	44,500		
	$116,900		
Less Reserve for Depreciation	22,850		
Net Fixed Assets		94,050	
Total Assets			$242,287

Liabilities

Current Liabilities:			
Accounts Payable	$49,438		
Notes Payable	3,000		
Miscellaneous Payables	3,372		
Total Current Liabilities		$55,810	
Long-Term Liabilities:			
Mortgage Payable		22,674	
Total Liabilities			$78,484
Net Worth (owner's equity)			
Capital Stock	$150,000		
Retained Earnings	13,803		
Total Net Worth			$163,803
Total Liabilities plus Net Worth			$242,287

Source: Adapted from Tate, Megginson, Scott, and Trueblood, *Successful Small Business Management* (Dallas, Tex.: Business Publications, Inc., 1975), p. 419.

on investment, as net income on sales, or as a total dollar figure. Regardless of how you choose to express your goal, the important thing is to have a target for aiming business operations. The profit goal should not be some "pie in the sky" chosen for the sake of putting down a figure, but a carefully set target that is obtainable through efficient operations.

To assist you in planning a profit goal, a practical procedure will be presented item by item. The balance sheet (Table 2-1) and income statement (Table 2-2) will facilitate explaining the planning procedure. Assume these records represent your company.[2]

Decide the Desired Profit Goal

According to the balance sheet (Table 2-1) there is an investment of $150,000 (capital stock) plus retained earnings of $13,803, making a total investment (total net worth) of $163,803. You could have invested these funds in stocks or bonds for a return ranging from 5 to 10 percent — without the risks and responsibilities of operating a business. What would be your profit goal if you desired a return on your investment at the rate of 7%? The answer is $26,208, based on the following calculation:

$.07 \times \$163,803 = \$26,208$

Unless you make provision for payment of taxes on earnings, your profit will be reduced accordingly. At an estimated tax rate of 30%, the $26,208 desired profit represents 70% of the total sum needed *before* income tax. Dividing $26,208 by .70 equals $37,440 — the amount needed before income tax. (The tax estimated at 30% would be $11,232. $37,440 minus the tax equals the desired profit after taxes — $26,308.) You have accomplished item one: set profit goal at $37,440.

HOW TO CALCULATE
THE OPERATIONAL PROFIT

Project a Sales Target

A sales forecast is strategic to planning business operations. There are several methods suggested for making a sales forecast, and there is some variance in their complexity and sophistication. Many factors must be taken into consideration, including. economic conditions, market demand, competition, product positioning, pricing, and promotion

---

[2]For additional information about profit and loss statements and balance sheets please see Chapter 4.

program. Helpful information can be obtained (usually at the beginning of a new year) from various business publications and organizations who project expectations for business.

Analyzing the performance trend of your company is a good place to begin the projection of a sales target. The factors mentioned above will be useful in understanding past performance and setting future goals. One approach is to set a percentage increase over the previous year. Let us assume that after you have carefully evaluated the question of future sales your estimate is a 7 percent increase over last year. Taking the net sales of your company to be $440,235, as shown on the income statement (Table 2-2), multiply by 1.07 to secure the sales forecast — $471,051.

TABLE 2-2
YOUR COMPANY: Profit and Loss Statement — January through December 31, 19____

Gross Sales	$447,207	
Less Returns and Allowances	6,972	
Net Sales		$440,235
Less Cost of Goods Sold		259,739
Gross Profit		180,496
Operating Expenses:		
Advertising	9,250	
Building Services	4,940	
Delivery	5,850	
Depreciation*	6,100	
Interest	2,223	
Insurance*	5,500	
Maintenance	1,630	
Office and Supplies	6,375	
Rent*	6,000	
Salaries	91,567	
Sales Promotion	3,600	
Taxes and Licenses	4,374	
Utilities	5,512	
Miscellaneous	500	
Total Expenses		$153,421
Net Income Before Taxes		$27,075
Less Income Taxes		12,251
Net Income After Taxes		$14,824

*Fixed-cost expense items

Source: Adapted from Tate, et al., *Successful Small Business Management,* p. 422.

Estimate Expenses to Achieve Sales Target

Historical expense data from past operations will prove helpful in projecting expenses. Table 2-3 lists the expenses of your company for last year and the estimate of new expenses based on the 7% in sales. The cost of goods runs about 59% of sales. Expenses such as depreciation, insurance, and rent are usually carried forward as fixed amounts. Other expenses will increase in line with the percentage increase in sales volume. There may be some items, such as advertising, which will be increased more as a

TABLE 2-3
Operating Expense Projection

Item	Last Year	Next Year
Cost of goods	$259,739	$277,921
Advertising	9,250	10,898
Building Service	4,940	5,286
Delivery	5,850	6,200
Depreciation*	6,100	6,100
Interest	2,223	2,379
Insurance*	5,500	5,500
Maintenance	1,630	1,744
Office and Supply	6,375	6,821
Rent*	6,000	6,000
Salaries	91,567	97,977
Sales Promotion	3,600	3,852
Taxes and Licenses	4,374	4,680
Utilities	5,512	5,898
Miscellaneous	500	535
TOTAL	$413,160	$441,851

*Fixed-cost expense items

Source: Adapted from Tate, et al., *Successful Small Business Management*, p. 444.

means of reaching the sales target. A special increase should be made to cover the continual inflation affecting the costs of doing business. After careful consideration each item of expense would be listed.

Calculate your operating profit by subtracting the total estimated expenses from the estimated sales income. The result is your estimated operating profit before income taxes, $29,200 ($471,051 − $441,851).

Analyze the Variance Between
Operating Profit and Profit Goal

The operating profit, $29,200, is $8,240 less than the desired profit, $37,440. Seldom if ever do the two planned profit figures equate. Therefore, some additional planning is necessary to ascertain the best means for reducing the difference.

HOW TO EVALUATE EXPENSE
DATA, SALES VOLUME, AND
BREAK-EVEN POINT

As you proceed to estimate expenses, bear in mind the characteristics of fixed, variable, and semi-variable types. Figure 2–1 illustrates graphically the behavior of the three kinds of expense. The lines shown are subject to kinks in them—as in the case of materials reflecting a quantity discount beyond a certain quantity, utilities reflecting the change in type of equipment (e.g., expanded telephone lines and equipment), or rent reflecting the acquisition of additional space for expansion. However, within a given scale of operations the behavioral characteristics noted do apply.

Expense Allocation

Table 2–4 illustrates the separation of fixed and variable expenses in order that the sums of each may be used in subsequent calculations. Some expenses as noted are part fixed and part variable, and should be separated accordingly. (Table 2-4 appears on page 26.)

Project Profit at Selected
Sales Volumes

With total fixed and variable expenses estimated, it is possible to calculate marginal income per dollar of sales income, which is necessary in projecting profit at different sales volumes. First, the total marginal income is derived by subtracting variable expense from sales income (Sales income − variable expense = total marginal income: $471,051 −

Figure 2-1.
Graphic Illustration of Differences Among Variable, Semi-Variable, and Fixed Expense Behavior.

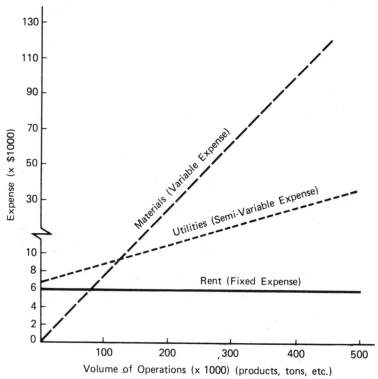

$361,418 = \$109,633$). Second, the marginal income per dollar of sales income is derived by dividing total marginal income by the sales income (Total marginal income ÷ sales income = marginal income per sales dollar: \$109,633 ÷ \$471,051 = .233). The remaining .767 of the dollar of sales income is the variable expense per dollar of sales income; it is used in projecting profit at selected sales volumes, as shown in Table 2-5.

Determine Break-Even Point

The break-even point is where total income equals total expense. You must reach that point in operations to cover expenses; but there is no profit. A break-even chart is presented in Figure 2-2. In addition to

TABLE 2-4

Expense Item	Total Estimated Expenses	Fixed Expenses	Variable Expenses
Cost of Goods	$277,921		$277,921
Advertising	10,898		19,898
Building Service	5,286	$5,000	286
Delivery	6,260		5,260
Depreciation	6,100	6,100	
Interest	2,379		2,379
Insurance	5,500	5,500	
Maintenance	1,744	1,000	744
Office and Supplies	6,821	3,400	3,421
Rent	6,000	6,000	
Salaries	97,977	45,000	52,977
Sales Promotion	3,852		3,852
Taxes and Licenses	4,680	4,000	680
Utilities	5,898	4,433	1,465
Miscellaneous	535		535
TOTAL	$441,851	$89,433	$361,418

Total Marginal Income = Sales Income − Variable Expenses
= $471,051 − $361,418 = $109,633

Marginal Income per Sales Income Dollar = $109,633 ÷ $471,051 = .233/Sales Income Dollar

TABLE 2-5

Sales Income	Fixed Expense			Variable Expense	Profit
$345,000	$80,433	.767 × 345,000	=	$264,615	($48.)
$350,000	$80,433	.767 × 350,000	=	$268,450	$ 1,117
$375,000	$80,433	.767 × 375,000	=	$287,625	$ 6,942
$400,000	$80,433	.767 × 400,000	=	$306,800	$12,767
$425,000	$80,433	.767 × 425,000	=	$325,975	$18,592
$450,000	$80,433	.767 × 450,000	=	$345,150	$24,417
$475,000	$80,433	.767 × 475,000	=	$364,325	$30,242
$500,000	$80,433	.767 × 500,000	=	$383,500	$36,067

$$BEP = \frac{Fixed\ Expense}{MI/SID} = \frac{80,433}{.233} = \$345,206$$

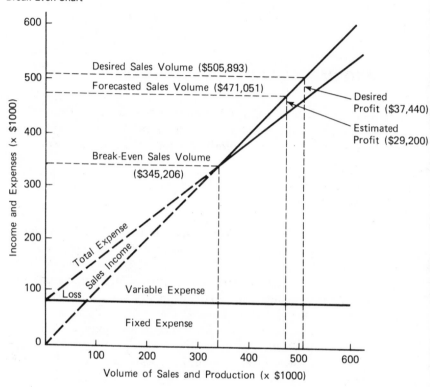

Figure 2–2.
Break-Even Chart

determining the break-even point, you will want to check the sales income level in order to reach desired profit. Using the data from Table 2-5 you can prepare a break-even chart. The break-even point is calculated by dividing fixed expense by the marginal income per dollar of sales income: fixed expense ÷ marginal income per dollar of sales income = break-even point.

$80,433 ÷ .233 = $345,206

To determine the sales income necessary to provide desired profit, you add the desired profit to the fixed expense.

($80,433 + $37,440) ÷ .233 = $505,893

The total sales target will be achieved with greater certainty when the time span is reduced from annual to monthly, weekly, or even daily sales targets. (Monthly sales, $42,158; weekly sales, $9,729; daily sales, $1,405.)

HOW TO IMPROVE OPERATIONAL PROFITS

The profit goal desired in our example, $37,440, is above the estimated profit from projected operations by a sum of $8,240. Plan to implement the achievement of the desired profit, $37,440. What are the most feasible alternatives?

Lower Expenses

A fact often overlooked by businessmen is that each dollar of expense reduced adds one dollar to profit, whereas each additional dollar of sales only adds a fractional contribution to profit. Therefore, if expenses can be reduced without adverse affect upon operations, this could be a significant means for increasing profits. To illustrate: using a variable expense, how would a 2% reduction raise profits? The answer is $36,528. The 2% reduction would raise the marginal income from .233 up to .2483 (.767 × .02 + .233 = .2483). Increase in profit at $471,051 × .2483 − $80,433 = $36,528. This alternative is promising, providing the variable cost reduction can be realized.

Raise Unit Sales Volume

Assume you could raise sales $20,000 with an increase of $4,000 in advertising expenses. How much would this alternative raise profits? Answer: ($20,000 × .233) = $4,660. However, subtracting the cost of advertising, $4,000, would leave a net increase of $660. Not as attractive as the previous alternative.

Modify Price

There are a number of factors to consider before undertaking this alternative. The price could not be reduced above 23.3%, as this would irradicate the sales income. Before you move, anticipate competitor behavior. Below is an example of what could happen with a 5¢ change on the price with volume changes of 10% and 5%.

	Unit Sales	×	Price	=	Sales Income	Profit
	471,051		$1.00		$471,051	$29,322
+ 10%	518,156		.95		492,248	34,261
+ 5%	494,603		.95		469,873	29,047
− 10%	423,946		1.05		445,143	23,285
− 5%	447,498		1.05		469,873	29,047

Add Profitable Products or Services

Before doing so, make a careful analysis of profitability and assure yourself that the income will exceed the expense enough to warrant the risk.

Compare Material and Merchandise Costs

Periodically, it is good practice to verify costs from existing suppliers by soliciting and comparing bids from other suppliers. Be sure to use identical specifications.

Obtain Lower Costs Through Subcontracting

Do not be surprised if a subcontractor can save you money. Even large corporations take bids from subcontractors, compare them with inhouse costs of production, and sub out work when doing so is more profitable.

Combination Approach

Do not limit yourself to any one of the alternatives above. Perhaps the best way to maximize profits is to consider a combination of the above alternatives, where practical.

HOW TO IMPLEMENT THE PROFIT PLAN
TO ATTAIN THE OBJECTIVE

After careful analysis of the foregoing items for profit planning, a decision should be made. Your judgment will be put to the test. Remember to consider that could mean a loss of sales income and market share, and an adverse impact on competitors. Reduction of expenses may result in employee layoffs or curtailment of customer services. Whatever your decision, project the estimated results in the form of a projected profit and loss statement. Assume you made a decision to reduce expenses by 2%: the results are illustrated in Table 2-6.

TABLE 2-6
YOUR COMPANY: Planned Profit and Loss Statement—For the year 19____

Sales Income		$471,051
Less:		
Cost of Goods Sold	$277,921	
Other Expenses (reduced 2%)	+ 159,672	
		− $437,592
Net Profit before taxes		$ 33,459
Less Taxes (30%)		− $ 10,037
Net Profit after taxes		$ 23,422
Return on Investment		14.30%

Source: Adapted from Tate, et al., *Successful Small Business Management,* p. 452.

SUMMARY

To manage a small business profitably, set goals and objectives to guide your planning and operational efforts. The most strategic goal is the profit objective. Determine your profit objective after careful consideration of the sales forecast, the impact on expenses, and the resulting operating targets. Break-even analysis should prove helpful; but allow for changes that may occur to modify expected results. Use every practical means to maximize operational profits—lower the expenses, raise the unit sales volume, compare material and merchandise costs, obtain lower costs through subcontracting. A combination of the foregoing may be the key to maximizing profits. Implement your plans and achieve profitable operation.

3

Professional Assistance and Information Sources

"To profit from good advice requires more wisdom than to give it."

J. Collins

PROFESSIONAL ASSISTANCE

Unlike the large business, which is usually well staffed with specialists, the small businessman must make some arrangements for expertise in his affairs. Some professionals who could be helpful in meeting particular needs will be discussed.

Bankers

Among the best informed persons on local business conditions are the bankers. A banker's knowledge may provide useful information and may lead to other means of assistance. Keep in close touch with the bankers, but do not rely entirely on a single source for information or assistance. Maintain, strengthen, and perpetuate good business relations with bankers.

Lawyers

A businessman needs legal advice at one time or another. To illustrate the areas in which a lawyer can be helpful, Theodore Voorhees identified the following six situations:

1. If a business is incorporated, the entrepreneur may need advice about directors and stockholders meetings, dividends, rights of stockholders, and so on.
2. Relationships with employees may require legal services in labor negotiations, proceedings from the National Labor Relations Board, and boards of arbitration and all other matters involving industrial relations.
3. The entrepreneur may need advice about anti-trust violations by his suppliers or about Robinson-Patman Act questions in sales to customers.
4. The company may encounter difficulties in its relations with the public — such as collection claims and claims for personal injury, property and product liability. Somewhat less frequent are claims for libel, slander, defamation, false arrest, and malicious prosecution.
5. The legal problems of taxation — federal, state and local — are faced almost daily by all business concerns.
6. There are other highly specialized fields of legal advice, such as patent, copyright and trademark, Security and Exchange Commission Financing, and practice before government agencies such as the Interstate Commerce Commission.[1]

Lawyers' assistance may transcend the matter of legal questions and include such functions as business advisor, a negotiator, and acting as an interface with the financial community, a sounding board for ideas, or as a defender, should the occasion demand it.

Someone said that nothing is so expensive as a second-rate lawyer. In selecting a lawyer you should not be motivated by the least-cost approach. Quality will pay dividends in the end, and will bear the cost necessary to provide it. Some of the best leads for obtaining a good lawyer will come from other businessmen. You may inquire what lawyer they are using or what lawyer they may have dropped. What are the customary fees that they have been paying for legal services? Does the lawyer seem to have good connections in the business and financial worlds? Does the lawyer come through well as an effective business advisor? What are his negotiating skills? Don't settle for the usual offhand answer, "He's one of the best lawyers in town."

---

[1]Theodore Voorhees, "Selecting a Lawyer for your Business," *Management Aids,* no. 8 (Washington, D.C.: Small Business Administration, 1962), pp. 66-73.

Remember that suggestions from large businesses or bankers are not likely to be very helpful, because their interests are not the same as those of a small businessman. Someone else suggested that the local bar association is a waste of time, that you might just as well look in the Yellow Pages.

The selection of the right lawyer for your business is a very important decision, and deserves all the time and effort it may require to obtain the best possible choice. You will not want to settle on the first lawyer recommended or the first lawyer interviewed that seems right. Try to interview at least the top three or four prospects. This will give you a better opportunity to see the types of lawyers available, and the additional contracts will be well worth the time and experience.

Carefully plan the interview with your prospective lawyer, and take along some questions which you have predetermined. You may well ask some of the questions discussed with a small businessman who is one of his or her other clients. One of the things to clarify is whether or not there is either present or possible future conflicts of interest. Another important thing to settle is the amount of time the lawyer has available to handle your business. For what fees and on what basis he or she will handle your business? Would he or she be willing to assist you in the collection of delinquent accounts? What is the range of his or her experience? Has the lawyer worked with matters of financing, incorporating, labor relations, etc.?

In making your decision, be willing to use your intuition as well. Ask yourself whether you like the individual. Do you think you could work together effectively to plan strategy and negotiations? Does he appear to be as tough as you would like? How well will he represent you in dealings with people? Do you have a feeling that he will take a genuine interest in your business affairs? It is well to select your lawyer early as legal advice will be needed and perhaps a better choice can be made without being under the gun of some legal problem.

Insurance Agents

The matter of handling business risks is discussed later in the text. One of the special kinds of assistance needed in a small business is in the matter of insurance. Because this is a rather technical field, the small businessman should seek out the services of a competent and reliable agent. Most agents are more than willing to evaluate insurance needs of small businesses and to recommend a package. Because insurance is a competitive business, it will be well for you to investigate various agents and make comparisons as to coverage, cost, and convenience before deciding which agent and company will best serve your insurance needs.

Accountants

Whether you decide to employ an independent accountant or a certified public accountant, he should be able to render valuable assistance where business records are concerned. A well-trained accountant may also give valuable assistance in making financial decisions. While most accountants are competent in setting up a standard bookkeeping system and in providing the necessary balance sheet and income statements required for business operations, it is essential to the small businessman to have the accountant explain fully the system designed to insure understanding for maximizing effective utilization of that system. As in selecting a lawyer, it would be advisable here to consider the recommendations of other businessmen, to contact several accountants personally, and to check references and other information before making a decision.

Business Consultants

Selection of consultants should be done with the same discretion that has been recommended in selecting the other specialists discussed. Good consultants are well worth their cost in resolving problems such as the following:

1. A "one-shot" problem, such as solving a specific operating problem like setting up an advertising campaign or design a plant layout.
2. A business appraisal, such as a periodic check-up of the business ,with recommendations for increasing overall effectiveness.
3. A feasibility study — for example, an objective evaluation of a nonrecurring problem such as where to locate a new store or which data processing equipment to install.[2]

Suggestions have also been made by the Small Business Administration for selecting a qualified consultant:

1. Clarify in your own mind exactly what you want the consulting firm to accomplish.

---

[2]David R. Mayne, "Specialized Help for Small Business," *Small Marketers Aids,* no. 74 (Washington, D.C.: Small Business Administration, 1961).

2. Obtain information on the services offered and the general reputation of the consultant from your business friends, accountant, banker, or attorney. Ask the consultant for recent references on comparable assignments.

3. If it is a large consulting firm, talk to the men who will actually be assigned to work on your project. See if they are specialists in your problem area(s) and determine if they are the type of individuals with whom your company could work effectively.

4. Insist on a written proposal from each consulting firm interviewed that outlines what the work will cover, how the work will be performed, how long the study will take, whether a written report will be submitted, an estimate of the total cost, and how much time the principals of the consulting firm will spend on the assignment.

5. See if the consultant will put his recommendations into effect if your own people are not qualified to implement them. Get a written agreement about the cost of implementation. For example, will the consultant only instruct your people, or will he install the recommendation?

6. Finally, do not be hesitant to discuss cost, and beware of the high-pressure salesman offering a low-cost *packaged* survey.[3]

Tax Consultant

Because of the complicated nature of taxation on business, a tax consultant is highly recommended. An expert in this field will more than pay his costs through savings in tax payments. In addition, he will be able to monitor or act as an auditor on the firms' recordkeeping done by the regular bookkeepers or accountants. Having the right answers in regard to taxes, in view of the many taxes presently confronting the businessman, can easily mean a worthwhile profit differential.

INFORMATION SOURCES

Government

A wealth of information is available at no cost to small businessmen. Much of this information will be found in local libraries as publications of the federal government, and the source of the information can be obtained by referring to the publication entitled *U.S. Government Publications, Monthly Catalogue*. This is usually available in local libraries or can be

[3]*Ibid.*

obtained from the Superintendent of Documents, Government Printing Office, Washington, D.C. 20230. The U.S. Department of Commerce is the principal agency for distribution of government publications.

It would be well for a small businessman to become acquainted with the local Department of Commerce field office, to learn of the vast amount of information available to assist him in his operations. Useful information may be found in the *County and City Data Book,* which presents information on county, state, and region, including standard metropolitan statistical areas. Data on employment and payroll by industry groups will be found in *County Business Patterns,* based on data supplied by the Social Security Administration.

A monthly publication providing a list of materials available and of interest to businessmen is the *Marketing Information Guide.* By consulting *The Directory of National Trade Associations,* a small businessman can secure information about the types of associations, their locations, names of officers, and information about data published by the association.

The U.S. Department of Commerce's *Survey of Current Business* provides articles and special data on the conditions of the economy — such as national income, industry production, gross national product, population, prices, and employment.

Some small businessmen may be interested in dealing with the federal government on a business basis, and will find useful information in the *Synopsis of Proposed Procurements and Contracts Awards Information.* This publication lists proposed procurements by the federal government offices. Additional information may be had by referring to *The United States Government Advertiser* and *Commerce Business Daily:* These two publications provide further details about federal purchasing and sales of surplus property.

BUREAU OF CENSUS

Periodically, the government provides valuable information to businessmen through the publications of the *Bureau of the Census.* Much useful information can be derived from the *Census of Population:* This is provided every ten years, and is an enumeration of all people of the United States by state, county, city, and metropolitan area, and by census tract designations in larger cities. Population is broken down by classifications according to sex, age, citizenship, race, education, county of birth, marital status, occupation, income, and employment status. During the intervening period between censuses, population data are provided in the publication *Current Population Reports,* sometimes referred to as the P-28 series.

Census data provide information on customer location, purchasing power, employment and marital status, age, sex, race, and the trend in market population (increasing or decreasing).

Another publication with useful information is the *Census of Housing,* also provided every ten years. *The Census of Housing* supplies information on dwelling units—the year built, rent paid, number of rooms, type of occupancy, race of occupant, mortgage status, type of water supply, type of toilet, heating equipment, bathtub or shower availability, heating and fuel, kitchen sinks, radio and television ownership, cooking fuel, and type of financing. In cities of over 50,000 population the information is provided on the basis of city blocks. Such facts about the market can be of utmost importance in making decisions for the small businessman.

The *Census of Business* reports data in terms of a *Census of Wholesaling, Retailing and the Service Trades.* This publication provides considerable information about competitive business, including the number of stores by line of business, volume of sales, amount of payroll, number of employees, sales on credit, accounts receivable, and sales by line of merchandise. In addition, data are provided on sales according to class of customer, size of firm, and size of sales, and the data include levels on inventory and operative expenses.

For those businessmen who are involved in industrial markets, the publication *Census of Manufacturers* is especially helpful: It provides information from 500 industries covering 6,500 commodities. Those businessmen involved in agriculture will find that *The Census of Agriculture* is of particular help: It lists the number of farms, acreage in production by crop, number of fruit trees, presence of electricity and running water, presence of telephone, and the age and sex of farmers, for each county in the United States.

The Statistical Abstract of the United States, an annual publication, provides useful information on industrial, social, political, and economic aspects of the United States. By referring to the "Bibliography of Sources of Statistics" in *The Statistical Abstract,* a businessman can determine which agency he should contact or which publication would contain detailed information on any specific problem he may be researching.

SMALL BUSINESS ADMINISTRATION

Various government departments have rendered assistance programs for small business from time to time. It would be well to check current programs of assistance as provided by the Commerce Department, the Department of Health, Education and Welfare, the Department of Labor, and the Office of Minority Business Enterprise. The principal government effort to assist small business has been through the Small Business Administration, activated in 1953. S.B.A. is best known for the assistance rendered in the form of loans to small business. Management assistance is provided through the service of field representatives, available in the eighty-two offices located throughout the United States, Guam, and Puerto Rico. Special consulting programs have been funded to assist the small businessman, and details can be secured through S.B.A. Another means used is the ACE program for providing consulting assistance. ACE stands for Active Corps of Executives and is staffed by experienced volunteers providing free consulting over a broad spectrum of business. ACE is one of S.B.A.'s special programs. Another program offered through S.B.A. is SCORE, the Service Corps of Retired Executives, organized into chapters in various cities and towns. These retired retailers, wholesalers, manufacturers, educators, lawyers, engineers, accountants, and others are available for consulting assistance to small businesses.

S.B.A. has also made an effort to provide management training through courses, conferences, and workshops, usually co-sponsored by colleges or business and civic organizations. Unfortunately, the small businessman is often too involved with daily responsibilities to attend such meetings. Thus, those in greatest need of the information are usually least able to attend.

Another form of S.B.A. assistance comes through the Procurement Center Representatives in major government procurement agencies, who assist in placing contracts with small businesses to fill federal government needs. This program, known as "Set-Aside Contracts," provides small business the opportunity to supply goods and services on contracts involving billions of dollars. S.B.A. field offices assist small businessmen in making the necessary information available on the S.B.A. assistance programs.

There is further abundance of information available from S.B.A. A series of pamphlets is published under each of the following titles: *Management Aids for Small Manufacturers; Technical Aids for Small Manufacturers;* and *Small Marketers Aids.* Separate publications treating miscellaneous subjects pertinent to small business management are also provided by S.B.A. In addition, research studies on small business problems have been subsidized by grants from the S.B.A.

PATENT INFORMATION

Many small businesses have innovation as their *raison d'être,* and innovations may be patentable through the U.S. Patent Office. A useful source of new product ideas will be found in the U.S. Patent Office registry of patents available for license or sale, which also gives the name and address of the patent owner. *Government Owned Patents,* another publication of the Patent Office, describes thousands of government-developed products and processes which U.S. citizens can use on a royalty-free basis. Another publication, *Dedicated Patents,* provides data about patents which have been dedicated to the public by the owners and thus can also be used on a royalty-free basis. The official *Gazette,* published by the Patent Office, enables an individual to keep up with the latest developments in the field of patents. If complete information is not available in your local library, write directly to the Department of Commerce field office or to the Commissioner of Patents, U.S. Patent Office, Washington, D.C. 20005.

In addition to the foregoing federal sources of information, data may be obtained through state and local governments. The data may not be in published form, but the various government offices within the state can usually provide useful information such as tax data, license requirements, automobile registration, sales tax statistics, unemployment, school enrollment, marriages, deaths, and births. Directories published in most states provide useful information about manufacturers, wholesalers, and other types of business within the state. If one decides to pursue this possibility, *The Monthly Check List of State Publications* issued by the Library of Congress may serve as a guide. Other useful sources are the city directories and poll lists. Much information can be obtained about individuals from these publications.

Someone said that being aware of the environment is the first step toward business success. Another recognized fact is that the only constant thing in a manager's life is change. Therefore, if the businessman does not notice the changes around him, he cannot possibly keep up with them.

Trade Associations

Trade associations endeavor to promote the well-being of businesses in a particular state or industry. One of their aims is to assist the group of member firms in activities which would be too costly for the individual firm. There is much sharing of information, on an anonymous basis, and this statistical information on operations can be helpful to the small businessman comparing his firm's operations with those of the other members in the trade association. Such comparisons can pinpoint areas of weakness, as well as those of strength.

Various reports and trade journals are published by these associations, which also sponsor conferences, workshops, seminars, and other meetings of benefit to their members. Trade shows are often organized and promoted for the benefit of members. Usually, the services rendered by and benefits received in trade associations far outweigh the expenses of association dues and membership fees.

The Encyclopedia of Associations, published by Gale Research, and the *Directory of National Trade Associations,* published by the U.S. Department of Commerce, supply detailed information about trade associations.

Directories

One of the best-known directories in the United States is the *Thomas Register of American Manufacturers.* A detailed classification of more than 50,000 manufacturers by product and region is found in *MacRae's Blue Book.* An often neglected source of information is the classified telephone directory. This source can be obtained in most cities of the United States from the local Bell Telephone Company office. It is an easy and inexpensive means of obtaining numbers, names, and addresses of possible customers or dealers. Of further interest to the small businessman is the possibility of yellow-page advertising for developing his business potential.

Questions concerning labor relations problems at the federal and state level can be answered with information from the *Prentice-Hall Labor Service* and the *Commerce Clearing House Labor Law Reports.* These publishers also provide tax information, in the *Prentice-Hall Federal Tax Service* and in the *Commerce Clearing House Federal Tax Guide Reports.*

On the subject of advertising, *Standard Rate and Data Services* gives extensive information, including advertising rates for printed and broadcast media. For similar data pertaining to newspapers and magazines, use the *N. W. Ayer and Son's Directory.*

Dun and Bradstreet publish useful information in their *Middle Market Directory* and *Million Dollar Directory.* The former reports information on firms with a net worth of $500,000 to $1,000,000; the latter on firms with a net worth of over $1,000,000. Information is given by line of business, geographically, and alphabetically; it may prove useful for measuring market penetration in terms of prospects and actual customers, for locating new customers, defining territories, and for reducing selling time and costs by planning sales calls more efficiently. Another Dun and

Bradstreet publication, *Key Business Ratios,* covers 125 different lines of businesses.

To check on the credibility of insurance companies before purchasing insurance for a small business, it would be helpful to refer to *The Spectator,* a reference source usually available in public libraries.

To assist in the buying function, the *New York Manual of Resident Buying Offices, Phelon's Resident Buying Book,* and *Sheldon's Retail Trade* are useful sources to help put small businessmen in touch with resident buyers or buyers of department stores and specialty stores. These publications can usually be found in the larger public libraries.

Newspapers and Periodicals

It may go without saying that the business information in the daily newspaper, and particularly in the local daily newspaper, is useful. Of further interest is the insight and valuable information which may be obtained by reading the *Wall Street Journal* and/or *Barron's,* two of the leading newspapers that deal primarily with business.

A habit of reading some of the recognized business magazines will help keep you up to date on business developments. One well-known publication in this field is *Business Week.* Another is *Sales Management,* which also publishes an annual "Survey of Buying Power" issue each July (giving information on cities and counties of over 10,000 population in the United States, Canada, and Mexico).

Additional Sources

Libraries are well stocked with business textbooks that will help the small businessman expand his knowledge of particular areas of interest or help him solve special problems that present themselves. Many of the references cited in this text would be helpful, supplementary reading materials.

In addition to the government sources, there are a number of quasi-public sources, including libraries, port authorities, better business bureaus, metropolitan planning commissions, chambers of commerce, and universities.

In making effective use of libraries, it is suggested that contact be made with the reference librarian, who is well informed on the resources of the library. The often overlooked value of library resources was humorously reported by a corporation that spent ten thousand dollars to collect information which was available for free in the library, from a 35¢ government publication. Remember to inquire about an inter-library loan: When the desired source of information is not available in the local library, it might be obtained within a reasonable time from adjacent libraries.

The local university may be another valuable resource. Establishing contact with the Bureaus of Business and Economic Research may prove valuable for published information or assistance with problems requiring research and consultation. Also useful will be the publications of the Bureau of Business Research, which provides analysis, insight, and comment about business conditions within the immediate area. *The Directory of University Research Bureaus,* available in many libraries, can be very helpful in facilitating contact with various university organizations.

Local planning commissions are a reservoir of much useful information. They accumulate data which have a bearing on the future developments of the area, and are particularly helpful in providing the information. Chambers of Commerce can be very helpful in providing the information to the small businessman. Through membership in the Chamber of Commerce, the small businessman will have a more complete exposure to the ways that the Chamber of Commerce can be of assistance to him in his business.

Remember that the suppliers with whom you are dealing may be a source of valuable information and assistance. Special information may be obtained from them with regard to your marketing program and promotional strategy. Customers are another valuable source of information, sometimes overlooked. Customer surveys may generate information that will help the businessperson to form a more profitable operation. In the business community, noncompeting businessmen can be of great help and assistance, as can well-informed real estate personnel, members of planning commissions, and credit bureau managers.

SUMMARY

Our modern world is characterized by a high degree of specialization. Small business requires one to be a generalist, to perform in many roles. It is being a generalist and performing many of the functions personally that is essential to reaching a satisiactory bottom-line figure (net profit) on the profit and loss statement.

Small business requires a fine sense of balance in deciding what is essential and nonessential with regard to employing help. While trying to be frugal, a small-business person must not be "pennywise and pound foolish," as the old saying goes. There are alternatives to be considered in the matter of employing professional assistance, which may be vital to insuring profitable business operations. In fact, professional expertise may be the primary means of increasing the profitability of your business. Therefore, secure the desired quality of assistance, but use it only as necessary — a part-time commitment may suffice at the outset. As a rule, professional assistance will pay for itself over time.

Another characteristic of our modern world is the wealth of information. The volume of available data continues to multiply, as does the amount of time needed to research the information. Considering the multitudinous tasks of being an entrepreneur, it becomes all the more essential to know precisely what kind of information is available, to screen your reading material and separate the chaff. The main thing is to keep abreast of the items pertinent to your enterprise. Profitable operation depends on effective use of knowledge gained from professional assistance and information sources.

4

The Company Information System

"Knowledge is Power."

Francis Bacon

A wealth of information which can be generated within the firm, and it can be strategic in making profitable decisions. Because of the growing complexity of business, it becomes all the more important for the small business to develop a system for internal information. Information in a management context may be defined as meaningful material which conveys knowledge useable by the recipient. To be useable by the recipient, information must —

1. Meet the needs of the recipient. It must aid him in what he is trying to accomplish.
2. Be accurate. If the data is to be valuable to the recipient, they must be collected and processed in a manner that renders them accurate to the user.
3. Be available at the proper time. If the information is not available when needed, it is worthless.
4. Be in the proper place. If the information is not in the right place when needed, it will not be worthwhile.
5. Be in the proper form. If the material is not in a usable form or one easily adaptable by the recipient, it is worthless.

6. Be understandable. Is the material clear? Do the words mean to the user what they are supposed to mean? Is there a problem of misunderstanding?[1]

Not all facts and figures are information. In many large companies, reports and papers are distributed which fail to meet the criteria noted above: In many cases, the information is useless for management purposes. It costs just as much to collect, process, retain, and distribute meaningless data as it does to produce valuable information. Therefore, the challenge to the small businessman is to develop and distribute the essential information for the operation of his business, at the same time keeping the cost to a bare minimum and eliminating useless facts and figures.

To justify the expense of generating information, three important functions should be met:

1. Tell the story of what has happened.
2. Explain why it happened.
3. Suggest solutions to problems and indicate hitherto overlooked opportunities.[2]

Strategic information produced by internal sources can prove effective in dealings with the Internal Revenue Service, in applying for loans at banks, and in detecting potentially profitable or unprofitable operations.

The kinds of information needed by a manager of a small business are facts about such things as cost, prices, sales, productions, markets, inventories, personnel, customers, equipment, plans, and taxes. The non-managerial personnel need information about policy, work instructions, deadlines, schedules, work change notices, and evaluation reports.

An effective small businessman should be able to answer the following questions, but may be unable to do so unless he has an effective information system:

What is the cash balance in the business?

What is the amount of the accounts receivable?

How much money has been invested in the business?

Should the business be relocated?

What is the amount of operating expenses for a particular period?

Are the operating expenses increasing or decreasing?

---

[1]George R. Terry, *Office Management and Control,* fifth ed. (Homewood, Ill.: Richard D. Irwin, Inc., 1966c.), p. 4.

[2]From *Small Business Management: Concepts and Techniques for Improving Decisions* by John V. Petrof, et al. Copyright © 1972 by McGraw-Hill Book Co. Used with permission of McGraw-Hill Book Company.

Figure 4-1.
An Information System. *Source:* George R. Terry, *Office Management and Control,* seventh ed. (Homewood, Ill.: Richard D. Irwin, Inc., 1975c.). Reprinted with permission of the publisher.

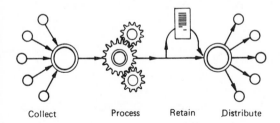

Collect   Process   Retain   Distribute

Which is the most important operating expense?
Are we selling the right kinds of product?
Who are the best customers?
Who is our best salesman?

There has evolved in the study of this subject a so-called information management concept. In this concept, as depicted in Figure 4-1, a system requires four basic operations.[3] Information must be collected, processed, retained, and distributed in an efficient manner.

COLLECTING INFORMATION

The following activities represent the primary internal sources from which needed information is generated:

ACTIVITY	*INFORMATION NEEDED*
Purchasing	Vendors' kits, quotations, prices, delivery dates
Receiving	Receiving reports, inspection
Stockroom	Stock on hand, due in, location, availability
Production	Processing time, orders, waiting time
Sales	Orders, sales analyses, prices
Delivery	Date, carrier information, bills of lading
Billing	Customer, merchandise, price

---

[3]Terry, *Office Management,* p. 6.

| Collection | Credit, invoice, discount |
| Disbursing | Payroll, accounts payable, taxes[4] |

The challenge lies in collecting the proper data and information.

PROCESSING INFORMATION

Careful thought should be given to converting the information collected into a usable form. The means employed in data processing will vary, and may range from a clerk with pencil to an electronic computer system.

Table 4-1 suggests eight elements to be utilized in processing data, giving reasons for each and the results expected.

RETAINING INFORMATION

It is important to know what information to retain and to have it available when needed. In all probability, a vertical paper file will be utilized for retaining the information in a small business, although some businesses are now making use of computer memory units by contract with data processing firms. In either case, it is important that the information be available in the proper form to be utilized when needed. A decision must be made on what information to retain and how long the information will remain pertinent to the management task.

DISTRIBUTING INFORMATION

For information to be utilized, it must be put into the hands of those who need it, in time for its intended use. It is best to distribute information only to those who need it, and to avoid sending it to other personnel, wasting their time with reading material that is not of their concern.

---

[4]*Ibid.*

TABLE 4-1
The Basic Elements of Processing Data

Basic element of data processing	Why performed	Results in:
1. Reading	To interpret data by going over characters, words, and symbols	Awareness of data existence
2. Writing, typing, card punching, or paper-tape perforating (frequently called *input*)	To facilitate processing by putting data on or in medium, i.e., alphabetical or numerical marks on paper, holes in paper, magnetic areas on tape, and magnetic ink on paper	Start of data processing
3. Recording or printing (frequently called *output*)	To obtain results of processing, the data—in medium form for processing purposes—are converted to form easily read by a human being, if not already in that form	End of data processing
4. Sorting	To classify data	Data being related to one or more bases
5. Transmitting	To disseminate data	Data availability for specific purpose and place
6. Calculating	To manipulate data mathematically	Numerical data being added, subtracted, multiplied, or divided
7. Comparing	To check data for accuracy and completeness	Quantitative and qualitative inspection of data
8. Storing	To retain or keep data	Data being available when needed

Note: The meaning of each of the following terms, frequently used in office management, is included in the above listing: "Interpreting" (usually associated with element 2 or 3) is imprinting the meaning of the punched holes in a punched card on that card. "Reproducing" (usually associated with 2) is duplicating an exact copy of a punched card. "Collating" (usually associated with 4 is merging sets of related data into a single set. "Segregating" (usually associated with 4) is separating sets of related data into several sets.

Source: George R. Terry, *Office Management and Control,* fifth ed. (Homewood, Ill.: Richard D. Irwin, Inc., 1966c.) p. 8. Reprinted by permission of the publisher.

KINDS OF INTERNAL INFORMATION

Information essential to effective decision making can be derived from three major categories: accounting records, production records, and sales records. Additional information may also be obtained relative to customer, competitors, advertising, publicity, personnel, labor unions, and government.[5]

Records from Accounting

Accounting information is regarded by some as the language of the businessman. The operator of a small business has several options to consider in providing basic accounting records. He may elect to keep the accounting records himself, depending on his experience and knowledge of accounting procedures. He may decide to employ an accountant to establish the system; then, after his own training, take over and conduct the accounting himself. Or, he may elect to engage a professional accountant to operate the system on a fulltime basis.

Whichever option the manager elects, it is imperative that the accounting system be clearly understood and closely monitored, so that the businessman may remain knowledgeable about the conditions reflected by the accounting records. Regardless of the processes used to accumulate the data of various transactions in the business, these data should be recorded in a book known as a journal. The journal transactions are later summarized in a book of accounts, the ledger. Using the debit and credit method of recording, the ledger should balance with the sum of the debits equalling the sum of the credits. Various statements are then prepared from the figures of the ledger, to guide the manager in operating the company.

RECORDS OF CASH

All transactions involving cash receipts and disbursements should be recorded in a cash-receipts journal. For example, when a sales transaction is made for cash, the records should be made debiting the cash and crediting the sales, with the result of a reduction in merchandise inventory. When a charge customer makes a payment, the customer's account is credited in the accounts-receivable ledger: the net result in the transaction is to increase cash and decrease accounts receivable.

Use of a checking account is recommended as a good way to keep cash records: all receipts are deposited in the checking account when checks are written to cover all expense items (exception those handled

---

[5]John V. Petrof, et al. *Small Business Management,* p. 61.

in a petty cash fund). Cancelled checks provide receipts that may be useful for proving payments or for substantiating expense items for tax authorities.

Items of less than five dollars are usually handled through a petty cash fund. A record is made of establishing the petty cash fund, and an amount suitable for the needs of the business would be provided in the cash register, to cover daily, miscellaneous expenses of a minor nature. Each time a transaction is made, a petty cash receipt is filled: the information on the receipt is used to charge the proper expense accounts. When the petty cash fund has been depleted, a reimbursement check is written to replenish the fund.

RECORDS OF PURCHASES

The primary purpose of a record of purchase is to insure that bills for purchases on credit are paid on time, to preserve the credit rating of the businessman. If you set up a bill file with a section for every day of the month, bills received can be filed according to their due dates — which insures the taking of cash discounts provided by the vendor. This sets up a routine so that checks can be made daily. To avoid the possibility of double payment, paid bills should be marked with the date of payment and filed alphabetically.

Suppliers usually offer credit options that allow the businessman to either get a discount by paying within the discount period or to take a longer period of time, without discount. A businessman might be inclined to disregard a ten-day discount of 2%, without taking time to consider what the annual equivalent of a 2% discount for ten days represents. A common term of sale is 2/10 net/30. When the bill is paid within ten days, a 2% discount is allowed: this means that if the bill is not paid within ten days the businessman will be paying 2% for an additional twenty days of credit. By dividing 20 into 360 days of the year, we find there are 18 such periods; and multiplying these by the rate of 2% yields an annual interest of 36%. Since businessmen are usually able to borrow at less than 36% interest, it would be to their advantage to borrow money, if necessary, in order to take the discounts on accounts payable. Businessmen who fail to do this may be paying exorbitant interest rates for short-term funds.

RECORDS OF EQUIPMENT

It is good business to keep a record of purchased equipment to be used by the business. A record should be set up to include the following information: date purchased, net cost for cash payment, down payment for installment purchases, monthly payments due, balance due, annual depreciation, record of repairs, and maintenance cost.

RECORDS OF DEPRECIATION

Depreciation is the means for a business to decrease the value of its assets as they are used over a period of time. It is necessary for the businessman to select the best method of computing depreciation for his particular business. Two common and simple methods used are straight-line depreciation and accelerated depreciation. Depreciation is considered an operating expense of a business, although it is a noncash expense (it does not require immediate outlay of cash to cover the expense of the accrued period). Money was expended when the asset was purchased. Depreciation provides a method of charging off a specified sum for a period of the life of the asset, thus reflecting the current value of the item.

Because depreciation reduces taxes payable, it contributes to the cash flow in the company. If the company is not earning any profit, the depreciation is merely an expense that does not require an outlay of cash, and thus reduces the actual cash loss.

Straight-line depreciation can best be explained with an example:

Suppose the original cost of an electric typewriter is $600.00 and the estimated trade-in or salvage value at the end of its estimated life is $50.00 by subtracting the $50.00 from the $600.00, we get the amount to be depreciated $550.00. The typewriter has an estimated life of ten years, so the annual depreciation will amount to $55.00 ($550.00 divided by 10 equals $55.00 per year).[6]

Accelerated depreciation methods have been adopted widely since their use was permitted for income tax purposes in 1954. Under these methods a larger share of the asset cost is charged during the early years of the asset's life.

Support for accelerated depreciation hinges on the fact that assets are most valuable when new and they rapidly decrease in value as they become older. As time passes, better equipment is invented, sometimes making existing equipment obsolete even before its functional life span has been exhausted. Mechanical efficiency and performance tend to decrease with age, and maintenance costs tend to increase. Under accelerated depreciation, the maintenance costs are lower when depreciation costs are

---

[6]*Ibid.*, p. 64.

high, and vice versa: this tends to level the overall cost of operation, since maintenance costs go up as the equipment ages.

While there are many accelerated depreciation methods, the best known is the sum-of-years'-digits method. As an example, if a piece of equipment has an estimated useful life span of five years, the numbers 1 through 5 are added in the following manner: 1 plus 2 plus 3 plus 4 plus 5, equalling 15.[7] The depreciation rate for each year is expressed as a fraction in which the denominator is the sum of the years (15) and the numerator is the number of years *remaining* in the life of the equipment.

An allowance should be made for the estimated salvage value after which the depreciation for the first year would be 5/15 of the cost, and for the second year 4/15, and so on. An example will help to clarify this. Assuming the cost of a lathe is $1,000 and its salvage value is $100, the amount to be depreciated would be $900. Using the estimated life of five years, the depreciation schedule under the sum-of-years'-digits method is:

First year :	5/15 times $900 equals $300.00
Second year:	4/15 times $900 equals $240.00
Third year :	3/15 times $900 equals $180.00
Fourth year :	2/15 times $900 equals $120.00
Fifth year :	1/15 times $900 equals $ 60.00
	$900.00 Total

Use of the accelerated method makes it possible to write off approximately two-thirds of its estimated life. The straight-line method would only allow one-half the cost to be depreciated during each half of its estimated life. The accelerated method increases the operating cost on paper while reducing actual cash outlays to the tax collector. This approach will decrease tax liability and may prove beneficial to the businessman with limited funds.

RECORDS OF ACCOUNTS RECEIVABLE

This record is kept in conjunction with the sales that are made on credit. It essentially represents a record of money due the company for sales transactions that have been made and not fully paid for. Services which operate on a strictly cash basis would not find it necessary to keep an accounts receivable record. Detailed discussion on the extension of credit by a business is discussed in a later chapter.

---

[7] *Ibid.*, p. 65.

PROFIT AND LOSS STATEMENT

Sometimes called the income statement, the profit and loss (P & L) statement provides a summary of business activities for a given period of time and indicates whether a profit or loss was made from operations. The normal time period is a year, though in some operations income statements are prepared on a quarterly or even a monthly basis. The example below illustrates the essential information provided in the profit and loss statement:

Sales	$100,000	100%
Cost of goods sold	$ 60,000	60%
Gross Margin (gross profit)	$ 40,000	40%
Operating expenses	$ 30,000	30%
Net income before taxes	$ 10,000	10%

The P & L statement gives an indication of the score for the time period reported, as far as the business activity is concerned. While this information is beneficial by itself, the value can often be multiplied by a careful comparison of previous periods reported on P & L statements. It is well to examine the differences in the bottom-line figures (profits or losses), the causes for the changes as indicated in the operating expenses, cost of goods sold, or even modifications in sales income. From the analysis it will be apparent that some factors are controllable while some are uncontrollable, and each will have to be treated accordingly. Obviously, where items are controllable corrective action should be taken to remedy any undesirable trends. Uncontrollable factors, such as increases in wages or material costs, might suggest that the selling price may have to be elevated in order to maintain a profitable operation.

For new businesses especially, and for those desiring a greater degree of control on operations, it is recommended that the P & L statement be prepared more often than annually to keep close tabs on business operations.

The profit and loss statement is a vital source of information concerning business operations. It is also invaluable to the manager of a business seeking to borrow money or finance equipment purchases. It will help the prospective lender to perceive the ability of the business to pay its debts out of its current operations. The lender wants to be assured that sufficient funds will be available to service a new debt incurred by the company.

BALANCE SHEET

The balance sheet, unlike the P & L statement, portrays the condition of the business as of a given date. The term "balance sheet" is derived from the situation in which total assets, "balance," are equal to the total liabilities plus owner's equity. This could be interpreted as meaning that the assets possessed by the firm were financed either through ownership or through borrowed funds. Like the profit and loss statement, the balance sheet is affected by the business transactions of the firm. To illustrate the format and the essential items in a balance sheet, the following example is provided:

Cash (on hand, in bank)	$11,100	Accounts Payable	$ 2,000
Accounts receivable	$ 1,550	Notes payable within	
Inventory	$11,900	one year	$11,500
Current Assets	$24,550	*Current Liabilities*	$13,500
Furniture & Fixtures	$13,200	Long-term notes	$14,000
Equipment	$13,500	Owner's equity	$23,750
Total Assets	$51,250	*Total Liabilities*	$51,250

The balance sheet presents information on how much cash is available, how much inventory is on hand, the amount of receivables from customers, and the amount the firm owes its creditors.

Useful information is derived from each balance sheet. The information is increased in value when analyzed along with previous balance sheets to indicate trends underway in the business operations. For example, it is well to examine the owner's equity section to indicate whether earnings are increasing or the position is that of a loss. The information provided by the balance sheet is important in that it shows the financial condition of the company at a given point in time. A manager should keep constantly apprised of this information.

Records from Production

The production function is to provide merchandise for sale to customers, either by manufacturing or by acquisition through buying. In either event, the data generated is important in preparing accounting statements: it can range from a rather simple statement of facts to a complex source of information, depending on the needs of the particular business.

RECORDS OF MATERIALS

A primary concern in production activity is the amount of materials used and the labor involved. Usually, materials are handled on the basis of beginning inventory plus materials purchased, less the ending inventory. An example of such a statement follows:

Beginning Inventory	$25,000
Purchases	$15,000
Material Available for Sale	$40,000
Less: Ending Inventory	$25,000
Cost of Inventory Sold	$20,000 [8]

The information "cost of inventory sold" is transferred to the profit and loss statement, and may be provided monthly, quarterly, or yearly, depending upon the needs of the business. It is required by law (in connection with the tax reports) that a physical inventory be taken at least once a year. Depending on the nature of the business, it may be supplemented periodically. If monthly statements are to be used, the ending inventory of the previous report is entered as the beginning inventory for the succeeding period, to preclude the necessity of having to constantly take physical inventories.

RECORDS OF DIRECT LABOR

The principal concern with direct labor is that it be separated from indirect labor: this is facilitated by the use of cost reports, which show the amount of time charged to each particular job as direct labor. The purpose in separating direct and indirect labor is to facilitate a more accurate determination of profitability for particular products in manufacturing operations.

RECORDS OF INVENTORY

Inventory records are important, especially those involved with production, marketing, and accounting. The importance is underscored by the legal requirement of the Internal Revenue Service, which makes an annual physical inventory mandatory. Accurate records are essential to calculate the cost of goods sold and subsequently, the actual profit or loss from operations.

---

[8]*Ibid.*, p. 72.

RECORDS OF INSPECTION

A record of inspection is a barometer of efficiency in production operations. Any indication of decline in quality should be met with prompt corrective actions to insure satisfactory products for sale. Inspection records may be helpful when tracing back any complaints of customers with regard to quality.

RECORDS OF SCHEDULING

Scheduling involves assigning production activities in line with a time frame. Production schedules provide a means of implementing plans for production and a means of controlling the actual production process. The production schedule becomes a guide on how many employees will be necessary to produce a certain number of items during a given time period. The reports related to the production schedule include some indication of personnel performance, the machine hours run, machine hours available, maintenance performed, tool costs, and reworked parts. Further explanation of the production function will be taken up in a later chapter.

Records from Sales

Sales transactions are usually the beginning of most business records. There is a certain amount of flexibility in gathering information about sales transactions. Unlike accounting records, which are more or less standardized, sales records can be modified and developed in order to gather and classify the type of information desired by the particular company. Sales data are frequently the source of information necessary for obtaining solutions to certain business problems.

SALES SLIPS

The sales slip, sometimes called the sales invoice, is designed to provide the information required for each particular business. An example is given in Figure 4-2, showing a typical format.

Information from sales invoices may provide the name and location of the customer, sex and age, product description, dollar value of sale, name or identifying number of sales person, terms of sale, date or period when sale was transacted, and further information such as manufacturer, size, color, etc.

Figure 4-2.
Sales Slip. *Source:* Petrof, Carusone, and McDavid, *Small Business Management* (New York: McGraw-Hill Book Company, 1972). Reprinted with permission of the publisher.

Salesman_____	How sold_____	Date_____
Name_____	Sex_____	Age_____
Address_____		

Quantity	Item	Price	

For those businesses transacting operations strictly by cash, information can be derived by keying certain information into the cash register. In a supermarket, for example, it is very simple to keep a record of sales under the headings of meat, groceries, produce, and bakery.

SALESPERSONS' REPORTS

Much useful information can be derived from reports of salesmen and dealers. These people are in constant contact with customers and competitors, and are in a position to supply useful information concerning customer preferences, long-range product plans, and activities of competitors. Figure 4-3 shows a particular salesman's report.

A variety of information can be solicited from the salesperson, including which products sell best, how the salesperson spends selling time, expense information by salesperson, and pertinent information about customers and competitors. Actually, there is no limit to the scope of information from sales records that can materially assist in making decisions regarding sales operations. It would be helpful to know which items are selling rapidly and should be reordered, and which items are not selling and should be marked down and promoted for disposition. Geographical differences in purchasing patterns would be helpful information, as would listings of successful and unsuccessful dealers.

Figure 4-3.
Salesman's Weekly Report. *Source:* Petrof, Carusone, and McDavid, *Small Business Management* (New York: McGraw-Hill Book Company, 1972). Reprinted with permission of the publisher.

Salesman_____ Date_____

1. Call Report

Date	Company	Name of contacted individual	Location	Time in			Prod-ucts sold	Other activities performed
				Travel	Wait	Selling		

2. Competitive Activity Report

Date	Company	Competitor	Type of competitor product used	Reasons	Possible sales volume

3. Expense Report

Date	Mileage	Meals	Lodging	Miscellaneous	Total
Total					

Other Types of Information

In addition to the basic types of internal information already discussed (from accounting, sales, and production), there are other areas of the business that represent information sources which can prove helpful in making profitable management decisions.

ADVERTISING AND PUBLICITY

It would be advisable to keep copies of all advertising run by the company, including radio, T.V., newspaper, etc. This would facilitate review, so that improvements might be effected. The same is recommended in respect to publicity.

COMPETITORS

Various means are available for obtaining information about competitors: salespersons, customers, press clippings, dealers, suppliers, trade publications, and competitors' advertisements. Certainly, information should be kept available and up to date on any competitor who is in a position to take action that would affect your business.

CUSTOMERS

Whether the number of customers is large (as in the retail trade and service business) or the number is small, including large purchasers (as in the case of industrial business), the appropriate records about customers will be valuable in better satisfying their needs. The fact that information about customers is gathered by other businesses should be reason enough to consider this an important facet of business.

GOVERNMENT

Changes in local, state, and federal laws affecting personnel will be of importance to the business. In fact, any legislation which has a bearing on business operations should be readily available for reference. It would be highly advisable to keep abreast of current developments ot prospective legislation which might call for persuasive action to be taken by businesspersons as a group.

LABOR UNIONS

Some businesses are not directly involved with union relations insofar as personnel are concerned. However, it would be advisable to keep informed from articles in the press and other information sources about union activity in the particular area.

PERSONNEL

Performance of personnel, good or bad, should be a matter of record: when it comes time for promotions, reductions, changes in compensation, etc., the facts will be readily available, and you will avoid having to rely on memory. The minimal personnel record would be an application form, along with such back-up information as educational records and letters of recommendation. In the progressive business firm, this information would be supplemented by periodic personal evaluations and reviews.

SUPPLIERS

Some companies rate suppliers, as part of an objective effort to know the best sources of materials and merchandise. Prime considerations include performance on quality, service (delivery), and price, although any one of these factors may be given more relative weight. It is advisable to keep records of noteworthy efforts as well as of problem situations, to insure fairness in the treatment of vendors.

SUMMARY

Review your system of internal information in the light of the data and material presented. Does your internal system collect, process, retain, and distribute the essential facts needed for effective operation? Does your internal information system provide adequate and sufficient records to assemble the necessary data from accounting, production, and sales? Does your internal information system include advertising and publicity, competitors, customers, government, labor unions, personnel, and suppliers?

The internal information system should be tailored to meet the needs of your business. Beware of those who would impose a standard system imported from another company. To make profitable decisions, you must understand the system, how it operates, and how to effectively use the data generated. Always bear in mind that the record should help in managing the business. Do not become a servant of the system; have the internal information system as your helpful servant. Modify as necessary to insure that you receive the pertinent information desired. Control expenses by terminating the information which is superfluous.

In conclusion, the secret to obtaining information from internal sources is to assign responsibility to insure that the information will be forthcoming.

5

Legal
Requisites

*"It is more important
to do the right thing
than to do things right"*

Peter Drucker

To maximize profitability of a small business in the long run, it must be
managed legally. Some individuals, practitioners and students alike, have
the mistaken notion that in order to make a profit in business it is necessary
to cheat, trim the corners, bypass the regulations, be illegitimate, or be
downright illegal. Such tactics will come to nought. Someone said you
can't be saved in ignorance, and this certainly applies to the law. In regard
to legal matters, a good policy is to utilize a well-selected lawyer for assistance. The suggestions to follow in the matter of selecting a lawyer have
been discussed earlier in this text.

Two philosophies have dominated in the enactment of legislation to
govern business in the American economy. The first view, projected in the
antitrust legislation days of Teddy Roosevelt, was to "promote competition."
The Clayton Act and the Federal Trade Commission Act were also enacted
in support of this philosophy.

During and after the Great Depression of the 1930's, with intense
competition ensuing, legislation was enacted to prevent "unfair competi-

tion." While a number of laws would fit into this category, at the head of the list would be the Robinson–Patman Act of 1936. Now, we'll take a closer look at the impact of some legislation, with regard to particular subject areas.

COMPETITIVE PRACTICES

The Federal Trade Commission monitors the practices of business to ensure the maintenance of competition. Some examples of unfair trade practices which have been cited by the FTC include the following: price cutting for the purpose of eliminating competition; secret rebates; boycotts, misbranding; competitive spying; disparagement of competitors' goods; use of misleading names; false and misleading advertising; bait advertising; bribing patronage; forced-line selling; pirating employees; selling used items as new; merchandising by lot or chance; and offering "fake" buying advantages.

Two programs of the FTC are of particular interest for the small businessperson. The first, the Division of Trade Practice Conferences, endeavors to write rules which interpret the laws enforced by the Commission in their application to particular industries. The second program, the Division of Discriminatory Practices, investigates complaints of unfair practice and consults with small business owners regarding applicability (to their own problems) of laws administered by the FTC.

The Sherman and Clayton Acts are federal legislation that apply only to interstate commerce. Most states have legislated similar laws for the regulation of intrastate commerce. If you are contemplating an action or procedure which involves a question of legality, it would be advisable to have your lawyer check the matter first and be sure that compliance with both federal and state laws is assured.

PRICE MEASURES

Price becomes the center of many competitive struggles, and has consequently become the subject of regulation. The efforts to regulate price can be classified in four particular areas: price cutting, price fixing, price discrimination, and resale-maintenance.

Price Cutting

Price cutting has been used as a weapon for eliminating competition. If the practice is allowed and competition is destroyed, an excessively high "monopoly price" could result. While consumers tend to benefit in the short run from lower prices, they would pay dearly in the long run through the higher prices.

Price Fixing

The motive behind price fixing is different than that behind price cutting. It is the result of collusion among competitors in an effort to establish certain price levels. The practice is not limited to fixing uniform prices, but also involves the illegal establishment of "indirect" methods of fixing prices—including agreements to maintain uniform discounts, methods of calculating markup, charges for delivery, and other practices affecting prices of competitors.

In those states where antitrust laws are not yet enacted, price fixing is practiced. It is not uncommon to find uniform prices among local businesses in the service trades, such as barber and beauty shops, automobile repair shops, dry-cleaning establishments, and others.

Price Discrimination

Under the law, the Robinson–Patman Act of 1936, it is illegal to discriminate in price between goods of like grade and quality to different buyers in competition. The burden of proof is on the seller, who must justify price differences with explanations such as variance in cost of manufacture, in selling, or in handling the merchandise. A seller is permitted to charge different prices to different buyers where the object is to meet the reduced prices of competition in the market place.

Also specified under the law as being discriminatory, were pseudo-brokerage fees paid to the buyer who was not acting as a "legitimate broker." The Robinson–Patman Act also forbids the paying of allowances for advertising and sales promotion which are not equal on a proportional basis to all customers, based on the services actually rendered by the buyers. This is intended to preclude discrimination or unfair competitive practices on the part of sellers of merchandise.

The law places the burden of proof on the seller to justify price differentials; and any buyers who participate knowingly in such illegal price discrimination are equally liable under the law with the seller.

Resale-Maintenance

This topic covers the so-called fair-trade statutes that were in effect from the 1930's to the contemporary period. However, in the late 1940's and during the 1950's the attitudes of the courts began to turn away from fair-trade laws. The abandonment of the laws by such companies as General Electric and Sunbeam did much to stop their continued use. These large manufacturers recognized that fair-trade pricing was hindering their efforts to have volume production. In order to supply the growing discount-house operations they emerged with a new attitude about fair-trade. Some of the devices used to bypass fair-trade regulations included inflated trade-ins, non-fair-traded articles given free with each purchase at fair-trade prices, and sales tickets made out at fair-trade prices accompanied by an unrecorded cash refund, just to mention a few. It is almost impossible for a government regulatory body to control all such evasionary practices.

Certainly, legal devices cannot substitute for competent management when it comes to insuring profitability of business operations. Attempts by businessmen to insure profits by means of the law have not been successful over the long run. The more sure method is rendering a genuine satisfaction of consumer needs by efficient conduct of business activities.

LABOR LAWS

Labor law, as it has developed, addresses itself to five broad categories: 1) protective legislation covering women and children; 2) regulations covering wages, hours, and working conditions; 3) fair employment practices; 4) economic-security legislation; and 5) settlement of labor disputes.[1]

---

[1]Clifford Baumback, et al., *How to Organize and Operate a Small Business* (Englewood Cliffs, N.J.: Prentice-Hall, Inc., 1973), p. 496.

Women and Children

The employment of children is specifically covered under the federal Fair Labor Standards Act as follows:

1. Children between sixteen and eighteen years of age may not be employed in occupations defined as "hazardous" by the Department of Labor.
2. A child under sixteen years of age is not permitted to work unless (a) he is employed by a parent or guardian in an industry other than mining and manufacturing or one defined (above) as being "hazardous"; and (b) he is at least fourteen years of age and has a temporary permit to work issued by the Department of Labor.

While the above limitations apply only to those firms engaged in interstate commerce, most legislation enacted in the states imposes the same kind of limitations, with only slight variations for those firms engaged in intrastate commerce.

The protective legislation pertaining to women refers to the following three areas: special working conditions, "equal pay for equal work," and "equal opportunity." Legislation covering the first area has been enacted at the state level only. These laws require that special facilities be provided, and they regulate night work and industrial "home work."

The Equal Pay Act of 1963 followed a pattern which had been established in a number of states that require employers to pay equal wages to men and women doing equal work on those jobs requiring equal skill, effort, and responsibility, and performed under similar working conditions. It is permissible to have differentials in compensation between male and female jobs only where the differences in job content can be demonstrated. The Federal Civil Rights Act of 1964, and similar state enactments, provide that merit increases in promotions cannot be denied on the basis of sex only.[2]

Wages, Hours, and Working Conditions

Minimum hourly wages are specified for employees under the Fair Labor Standards Act of 1938, covering most firms engaged in interstate commerce. Another requirement of the Act specifies that employers must

---

[2]*Ibid.*, p. 500.

compensate employees at "time-and-a-half" for employment in excess of forty hours per week. No maximum working hours are specified; however, the overtime provision is intended to keep the working hours from exceeding the forty per week. Of special interest to small-businesspeople is the provision that under certain terms of agreement with employees an exemption from the overtime provision of the Act may be arranged. This provision would be particularly significant for those firms involved in a highly seasonal business. A waiver may also be obtained on the overtime provision for employers signing labor agreements that guarantee a specified number of working hours per year (within a range of 1,840 to 2,240 hours).

Another point of interest to small-business people is the fact that not all employees engaged in interstate commerce are covered by the federal Fair Labor Standards Act. The exceptions include: the employees of retail stores and service establishments whose annual gross volume of sales or receipts is less than $250,000; outside salesmen,; and executive, administrative, and professional personnel.

When a small business is involved in a government supply contract, it must comply with the provisions of the Walsh-Healy Act of 1936. Under the provisions of the Act, those firms whose government contracts exceed $10,000 must pay the "prevailing wage rates": thus, the minimum wage would vary from one industry to another and from one locality to another. Also, hours worked in excess of eight hours per day or forty hours per week must be compensated at the rate of time-and-a-half, based on whichever yields the highest compensation.

Small business firms which do not come under the Federal Fair Labor Standards Act will most likely be regulated by a similar minimum-wage requirement enacted by the state where the business is domiciled. Similarly, the working hours for women and children and for male workers in hazardous occupations will also be specified by most state laws.[3]

Time-off-for-voting laws provide for paid time to enable employees to vote where they have insufficient time before and after work.

Fair Employment Practices

Compliance will be required under the Federal Civil Rights Act of 1964 or the various Fair Employment Practice (FEP) Laws with regard to racial discrimination. The usual procedure under the state laws provides

---

[3]*Ibid.*, p. 499.

that complaints of discrimination be brought before the prescribed administrative agency, which attempts to resolve the problem through conciliation. Should this procedure fail, a formal decision would be rendered enforceable by the state courts. The matter is kept confidential up to the point of conciliation. However, when a formal decision is rendered it becomes a matter of public record. Under the federal law the commission only conciliates the differences between the complaintant and the employer (or union): the members of the commission cannot make a binding decision. Refusal by the employer (or union) to comply with the judgement may result in the commission bringing a suit in the federal district court. A jurisdiction of the federal law includes firms and unions functioning in interstate commerce, with a proviso that states with FET laws will be given a priority of jurisdiction for sixty days.

Economic-Security Laws

The purpose of this legislation is to minimize losses in employee income that result from industrial accidents, involuntary unemployment, or occupational diseases. Provisions are also made for hospital and medical care and some income after retirement. The various state workmen's compensation laws usually afford protection to the workers from income loss connected with industrial accidents and occupational diseases. All of the states provide legislation to cover employees in intrastate commerce, and federal legislation covers civil service employees. The particular provisions of your state laws should be checked to insure appropriate response. The Federal Social Security Act of 1935 and the Employment Security Amendments of 1970 should be checked to ascertain the obligations of employers with regard to the payment of required taxes. By means of a merit-rating or experience-rating system, many states provide that employers with low labor-turnover rate may pay a progressively lower tax.

A small-business person should pay particular attention to the obligations specified under the Social Security Program. It is mandatory that a social security tax be paid and that an annual report be rendered, whether you hire employees or are self-employed. It is required that you file and pay your self-employment tax with your federal income tax, using Schedule C with the 1040 form. The filing of this information is required whether or not you have any income tax liabilities.

A social security account number is also mandatory. Do not confuse your account number with the identification number required of employers. When you employ one or more persons in covered employment you must have an identification number. This number may be obtained by filing a form SS-4 at the nearest office of the Social Security Administration. Your assigned identification number should appear on all social security records, tax returns, and correspondence.

Settlement of Labor Disputes

The significant legislation involving the settlement of labor disputes include: the NLRA (National Labor Relations Act), known also as the Wagner Act of 1935; the Labor Management Relations Act of 1947, known as the Taft-Hartley Act; and the Landrum-Griffin Act, passed in 1959. From a highly favored position for labor expressed through the Wagner Act, the pendulum has swung more in favor of the management side through the passage of the Taft-Hartley Act. Finally, the Landrum-Griffin Act gave consideration to the rights of the individual members as a means of protecting them from undesirable union authority.

Should you be confronted with a labor dispute, *don't run scared.* While it is true that labor has certain rights, there are also rights pertaining to management. Secure a competent labor lawyer and prepare to deal with the issue at hand. If your labor contract provides for arbitration, which seems advisable, you may be negotiating through the use of an arbitrator to resolve some of the labor disputes.

ADVERTISING

The Federal Trade Commission regulates advertising under the Wheeler-Lea Law. The Food, Drug, and Cosmetic Act specifies requirements regarding labeling of products, which are enforced by the Federal Trade Commission. Truth-In-Lending regulations as they pertain to advertising of credit terms are also enforced by the FTC. In addition to this federal program of regulating advertising, several states have enacted legislation to regulate false and misleading advertising.

CONSUMER CREDIT LEGISLATION

The principal legislation that a business must be concerned with in regard to consumer credit is outlined in the Fair Credit Reporting Act of 1971 and the Truth-In-Lending Law of 1969. The federal statutes are enforced by the Federal Trade Commission. Also, several states have established maximum rates which can be charged in financing consumer credit. In either case, understanding and compliance with the law is recommended.

PRODUCT CONTROL

Numerous acts have been passed for the purpose of controlling various products. Some of the practices to be controlled include misgrading of goods, dispensing of patent medicines as "cure-alls," food product adulteration, and improper labeling of clothing. For reference, please check the provisions of the following acts: Food, Drug, and Cosmetic Act of 1938; the Wool Products Labeling Act of 1939; the Fur Products Labeling Act of 1951; the Federal Flammable Fabrics Act of 1953; the Textile Fiber Products Identification Act of 1958; the Hazardous Substances Labeling Act of 1960; the Fair Packaging and Labeling Act of 1966; and the Consumer Product Safety Act of 1972.

LICENSING AND PERMITS

Legal requisites for conducting your business may necessitate obtaining certain licenses or permits from either state or local governments. Some permits, such as health permits, apply to employees. Some permits, such as city business permits, are issued for purposes of taxation. Before initiating your business, you should check and determine what licenses and permits are required to conduct business. Another detail worthy of checking is whether or not licenses and permits for a specific business will transfer when the business is being acquired.

Other regulations and restrictions which are enforced locally pertain to the use of business premises, alleys, joining side walks, parking spaces, store signs, wiring, plumbing, heating, delivery equipment, and similar items.

Besides regulations, there may be established social controls among businessmen in a particular area or community, which relate to hours of operation, acceptable types of advertising, the "going" rate of pay, prices and pricing practices, and the normally expected community services. While these items do not have the force of law, they are nevertheless effective in regulating business practices in a so-called unwritten or informal way.

OSHA

Since the late 1960's small-business people have had more contact with the federal government as a result of the Equal Employment Opportunity Act and the Environmental Protection Agency Legislation, as well as other laws and executive actions involving wages and price controls. These actions have increased regulation and the cost of doing business.

A further extension of regulation by the federal government came as a result of the enactment in 1970 of the Occupational Safety and Health Act (OSHA). The Act covers virtually every employer and employee in the United States. However, the Act is perhaps the least understood, most complex, technical, and comprehensive of recent government regulatory efforts. The purpose of the legislation was to protect the American worker at his place of work.

Compelling reasons for the passage of the Act are suggested by voluntary reports by members of the National Safety Council. Summation of the report data indicated that in 1971 there were 14,200 deaths from accidents on the job; 2,200,000 disabling injuries (out of 7,000,000 total injuries); and 9.3 billion dollars lost in wages, insurance, property damage, and medical expenses.

Another concern was the increasing rate of accidents between 1961 and 1970 reported by the Bureau of Labor Statistics. The increase in disabling injuries per million man hours increased from 11.8 to 15.2, for an increase of 29%, between 1961 and 1970. The U.S. Public Health

Service estimated 390,000 persons had contracted occupational diseases during the year of 1970.

The enactment of the legislation sent inspectors into the field to check for violations and unsafe conditions. Figures released by OSHA showed that 32,701 inspections were conducted in fiscal 1971, and that 23,231 citations were issued alleging 120,861 violations of the standards. The result of the inspections and finds generated considerable pressure upon congressional representatives from small-businesspersons at home. In writing on the subject, Jack R. Nicholas, Jr. summarized the objections to OSHA by small-businesspersons as follows: 1) fear of citation and finds without warning; 2) lack of information on safety and health standards; and 3) excessive record and reporting requirements.[4]

Information is available for small-business operators through the U.S. Government Printing Office. Knowledge is power, and it would seem advisable for the small-business operator to become informed about this legislation so that appropriate action may be taken for conformity. It is reassuring to know that help is on the way to abate the major objections to OSHA as voiced by small business people.

TAXES

Payment of taxes has become a complex responsibility. Expert advisory help is recommended to avoid the possibility of forgetting a tax payment or neglecting some technicality or deduction. The owner-manager of a business has evolved into both a tax agent and a tax debtor: an agent, because of withholding and paying taxes owed by others; a debtor, because of paying taxes which are due by himself and the business.

A businessperson has the following major tax-withholding respon-sibilities:

1. *Sales Taxes.* The imposition of sales taxes by state and local governments is almost universal. The small business firm becomes a tax agent in collecting the required taxes and transferring them to the proper government office.
2. *Social Security Taxes.* Again the small business is a tax agent, and must deduct the specified contributions from employees' salaries in making pay-

---

[4]Jack R. Nicholas, Jr., "And Then There is Big Brother," *MSU Business Topics,* (Washington, D.C.: The American University, 1973, pp. 57-64).

ments of social security taxes. Again the deductions are forwarded periodically to the appropriate government agency.

3. *Income Taxes.* By means of an authorization which the employee signs, in which the number of allowable deductions are specified, amounts are withheld from earnings and passed on to the government by the employer at specified periods of time.

As a debtor, the small business must pay taxes. The major kinds are listed below:

1. *Local Taxes.* Various taxes are imposed by local entities, school districts, towns, and counties. Real estate taxes and personal property taxes are examples. The various licenses and permits are a form of taxes, though not so recognized by the small-business person.

2. *Unemployment Taxes.* Those firms employing four or more employees are required to pay both federal and state unemployment taxes on the salaries and wages of employees. The amount of the tax rate is generally related to the previous unemployment record.

3. *Federal Excise Taxes.* These taxes are levied on the sale or use of some items and in the case of some occupations. A tax is commonly leveled on certain motor fuels, a highway use tax on trucks which use federal highways, and an occupational tax on retail liquor stores.

4. *Income Taxes.* The amount of income tax paid to the federal government by a business is related to the earnings and the legal form of organization. The amount for corporations is 22 percent of all net income, plus a surcharge on the taxable income over $25,000. The individual business person must pay personal income taxes on either the earnings of the proprietorship, partnership earnings, or corporate salaries and corporate dividends. The payment of income tax has also been extended to some states and cities.

The Self-Employed Individual's Tax Retirement Act

Before the passage of the Self-Employed Individual's Tax Retirement Act in 1962, small business proprietors or partners were denied the opportunity of participating in tax-favored plans because they were not classified as "employees." In effect, this act makes sole proprietors and partners employees for the purpose of establishing employee pensions and profit-sharing plans. The purpose of the law is to enable small-business persons to establish a pension, and it provides that deductions for this purpose may be deducted for federal income tax purposes. These following major provisions will help familiarize you with the law:

1. The plan providing benefits to a self-employed person must be a written program specifying definite arrangements of all required provisions to qualify at the time the plan is initiated. While the self-employed person may be the only person covered by the plan at the beginning, the plan must include all the provisions relating to the participation of employees who may become eligible in the future.

2. The plan by which the owner-employee participates must provide benefits for all full-time employees who have worked for the company a total of three or more years.

3. The maximum annual contribution that can be made to the plan for the benefit of an owner-employee is $2,500 or 10% of the earned income for the year, whichever is smaller. As a tax deduction the owner-employee may deduct the entire contribution providing it does not exceed the stated maximum.

4. In order for the owner-employee to be covered by the plan, it is necessary that employees' rights under the plan must be nonforfeitable at the time the contributions are made for their benefit.

5. For distributions to be made under the plan it is required that the participant reach age 59 years and 6 months, becomes disabled, or dies. They may not commence later than age 70 years and 6 months.[5]

For full particulars relating to the various methods and conditions pertaining to the law, a careful check should be made.

Tax Influence on Decisions

The expansion of taxation on business has elevated the importance of careful business planning. Numerous management decisions are affected because of the wide diversity of taxes. To point up some of the relationships of taxes to business decisions, the following examples are provided.

INFLUENCE ON INITIAL DECISIONS

A question of taxation is paramount in deciding which legal form of organization to utilize. The effect of taxes should be anticipated with regard to processes, products, or prices prior to making the change. The implications of taxes should be carefully determined prior to making decisions: failure to do so may substantially lessen the profitability of business operations.

---

[5]Baumback, et al., *How to Organize and Operate a Small Business*, p. 508.

INFLUENCE ON LOCATION DECISIONS

Location decisions may be modified appropriately based upon the rate of taxation or the tax concessions offered. Substantial tax savings over many years may be obtained by making the proper location decision, which will add materially to the profits of a company.

INFLUENCE ON FINANCIAL DECISIONS

The comparative amount of income tax required as a corporation, a partnership, or a proprietorship will have an impact upon the financing decisions. This is particularly true where the firm is endeavoring to grow from retained earnings. The most profitable arrangement for maximizing funds for reinvesting purposes would depend upon the size of the business income and the tax bracket involved.

When borrowed funds are used for financing, the interest paid may be deducted for income tax purposes. The use of equity financing does not permit a deduction from income for the cost of the capital obtained. Decisions made with regard to leasing or buying also result in differences of allowable expense for computing taxable income. Another tax consideration involves the contributions made to charitable organizations, which provide another means of reducing tax payment.

INFLUENCE ON DEPRECIATION METHODS

There is a choice permitted among various alternative rates of depreciation. It is important that the small-business person consider the implications of depreciation with regard to the tax bill for the firm, as it relates in turn to the question of profitability. To accelerate depreciation is often advisable for the small firm both from a tax as well as profit standpoint.

INFLUENCE ON DIVIDENDS

Because the owners of small business corporations are advised to pay individual taxes on dividends received, the question of taxes affects the decision on dividend policy. The tax question with regard to undistributed earnings may also affect the decision with regard to dividend policy. Further considerations with regard to dividend policy involve the payment of cash versus stock or property dividend, and the time for declaring dividends.

INFLUENCE ON INVENTORY

It would be well for the small-business person to study the various methods of inventory evaluation permitted by the IRS from the standpoint of the tax question and the resulting profitability of operations. Once the decision is made, it should be consistently followed.

The services of a competent tax consultant may be profitable from the standpoint of capitalizing on legal tax avoidance. Knowledge is power, and the expert on taxation can frequently generate sizable savings for the small business firm from knowing the law and the permissible tax savings. Tax evasion is illegal, and the penalties for dishonesty should be a deterrent.

BANKRUPTCY

A condition of bankruptcy exists in a business when the total amount of all liabilities exceeds the total value of assets: in other words, when there are not sufficient assets to pay all the debts. From a technical standpoint, the business is not bankrupt until it is declared to be bankrupt. The declaration is usually made by the courts as a result of two possible procedures: (a) voluntary bankruptcy, which is initiated by the owners of the business, or (b) involuntary bankruptcy, which is instituted by creditors of the business. When bankruptcy is declared by the court, a trustee is usually appointed to dispose of the assets and divide the receipts according to a specified list for distribution. The services of the trustee are compensated by deducting his fee from the funds acquired before they are distributed to creditors. The question of liability arises in cases of bankruptcy; and the rule requires that sole proprietors and general partners assume unlimited liability, whereas stockholders in corporations have liability limited to the extent of their investment in the corporation.

Your attention is called to Section XI of the Bankruptcy Act, which sets forth provisions for settlements without bankruptcy proceedings. Where cases justify this procedure, the life of the business is spared; and there are stipulated requirements not present under voluntary settlements. With this federal law, settlement plans can be provided without the unanimous agreement of all creditors that is required under a voluntary plan.

Usually, the debtor takes the initiative in action before the court, by suggesting a plan for extension, a prorata cash settlement, or some combination. The court may then appoint a receiver to manage the business, or leave it in the management of the debtor under court supervision. The proposed plan is usually evaluated by auditors and appraisers to determine acceptability. The creditors are usually given the opportunity to participate in negotiations, and have the opportunity to vote on acceptance or rejection of the final plan. When obligations are met by the debtor as specified in the court-approved plan, he or she is discharged from further obligation. Other old liabilities need not be paid out of further earnings of the business. It is to the debtor's advantage to use this plan, as it provides for the possibility of continuing to operate the business as a going concern. Also, creditors may net a greater return by such an arrangement, rather than by forcing liquidation through bankruptcy proceedings.[6]

Being declared a bankrupt attaches an undesired stigma, whether the debtor is a dependently employed consumer or a small-business person. In any event, bankruptcy proceedings should be initiated only as a last resort when other possibilities for resolving difficulties are inadequate.

MAINTAINING LEGAL OPERATIONS: BUSINESS LAW AND THE BUSINESSMAN

Legal Counsel

In dealing with all matters pertaining to legal requisites of the business, it is advised that competent legal counsel be utilized to insure legality and to accomplish the best interests of a firm.

Contracts

Many small-business persons are not aware that there is involvement in some form of contract, written or verbal, almost daily. While a contract is an agreement, or meeting of the minds, not all agreements are contracts. To be a valid contract, the following requirements must be met:

1. Agreement — the offer must be accepted as offered
2. Competency of contracting parties

---

[6]*Ibid.*, p. 504.

3. True consent — contract made freely without duress
4. Legal objective — agreement must not be in conflict with public policy
5. Consideration — the seller must receive something of value
6. Proper form — some contracts must be in a form specified by law in order to be enforceable (e.g., to be enforceable, contracts for the sale of real property must be in writing)

PRECAUTIONARY MEASURES—
BREACH OF CONTRACT

While it is true that there are certain rights of recourse in the event a contract is breached, there are also precautionary measures that may be taken so that it is not necessary to rely exclusively on legal action. For instance, a creditor-seller may arrange for the use of certain security devices: as in the case of installment credit transactions, there is a provision for a chattel mortgage or a conditional sale arrangement. Mortgages in real estate transactions serve in like manner.

MECHANICS LIEN

This type of claim against property serves to protect material suppliers or contractors by providing a lien against the property, should the owner or tenant default in payment for either the material or the construction labor. The same procedure would apply involving a repair firm working on machinery or equipment.

ATTACHMENT

An attachment is used to preclude the removal or disposal of property necessary to satisfy a legal claim. Attachments may be made against debtors' bank accounts or certain property or inventory that may be involved.

STATUTES OF LIMITATIONS

The purpose of this type legislation in various states is to encourage creditors to be prompt in initiating action involving unpaid claims. A small-business person should be aware of the particular statutes of limitations, and avoid loss through failure to take action promptly.

BULK SALES LAWS

This type of legislation has been enacted in some states to preclude the possibility of a debtor defrauding a creditor or creditors through the secret sale of an entire business prior to legal action being taken by a creditor to assist in collection of debts. Bulk sales laws preclude such behavior by requiring that selling of business inventory must be preceded by written notification to the creditors involved. Failure to comply makes bulk sales fraudulent and void with regard to creditors.

PROCEDURE FOR BREACH OF CONTRACT

Having examined the precautionary measures, there still remains the rights of one party to a contract in the event the other party does not fulfill the provisions of the contract. To obtain satisfaction in the matter, the following steps may be initiated: 1) collect damages from the non-performance of the contract, 2) require performance of the contract, and 3) discharge the contract. When you perceive difficulty with regard to the execution of a contract in which you have entered, it is well to take counsel with your legal advisor and be guided by his judgement about which course to pursue with regard to having the contract satisfied.

AGENCY

Business is frequently transacted by means of an agent. The purchase of insurance, the procurement of equipment and materials, and the acquisition of real estate are usually accomlished through the use of agents. Normally business proceeds as though the transactions were being accomplished with the principal who the agent represents. Because the appointment of agents is usually by means of a contract, the law of contracts does apply to agency. It becomes important, therefore, to understand clearly the limits of authority delegated and defined insofar as the agent's duties and responsibilities are concerned.

If you elect to use an agent in the conduct of your business, you incur certain obligations and liabilities. You become liable to compensate the agent for his services as well as to pay for expenses incurred in the discharge of his duties. Any losses sustained by the agent in the execution of his duties must also be indemnified by the principal. Furthermore, as a principal you would be liable to a third party for the performance of any contracts made by the agent wherein he acts according to the scope of the authority granted. Liability of the principal is also maintained for any fraudulent, negligent, or wrong acts committed by the agent while performed within the scope of the agency granted.

As a principal using an agent, you should be knowledgable about the obligations and liabilities that pertain to the agent. For example, the agent must accept the orders and instructions of the principal, use prudence and care in the discharge of his duties, and act in good faith. The agent becomes liable when exceeding the stipulated authority or when causing damage to the third party resulting from exceeding the authority granted — except and unless the principal ratifies the act, and in such case the principal assumes liability thereby. Obviously, the appointment and use of agents in a small business is a matter for serious concern. Because of the inherent dangers involved, extreme care should be exercised in selecting agents. The delegation of authority and responsibilities should be carefully considered and explicitly prescribed.

Uniform Commercial Code

The federal government establishes the rules governing *interstate* commerce between the states. Historically, each state has had the responsibility for establishing the laws governing *intrastate* commerce. Over the years since 1890 efforts have been put forth to unify the rules concerning the conduct of commerce under more uniform laws. The success of this effort culminated in the publication of the first Uniform Commercial Code in 1952. It was later revised in 1958; and, with the exception of Louisiana, all states have adopted the Uniform Commercial Code.

It would be helpful to the small businessman to be cognizant of the provisions of the Uniform Commercial Code as it pertains to the following areas of law: 1) sales, 2) commercial paper, 3) bank deposits and collections, 4) letters of credit, 5) bulk transfers, 6) warehouse receipts, bills of lading, and other documents of title, 7) investment securities, and 8) secure transactions, sales of accounts, contract rights and chattel paper.

Leases

The implications of operating with a lease are of utmost importance to the small-business person. Involvement in leasing presents a wide range of possible problems. Some of the pertinent considerations when dealing with a lease include the following:

1. *Contracts to build.* The owner agrees to construct a building according to the tenant's specifications on a lease-back arrangement.

2. *Percentage leases.* The landlord receives his income as a percentage of the business income of the lessee. Particular attention should be directed to the specific clauses within the percentage lease.

3. *Fire and casualty insurance.* One of the clauses which is common in a lease for a store tenant is the requirement that the landlord maintain fire and casualty insurance on the property. It is well to check to insure that the amounts of insurance will be adequate for the restoration of the building for use by the tenant in the event of a fire or some casualty incident.

4. *Repairs.* Repair clauses are noted for inevitably producing struggles between the parties of the lease with regard to obligation. Therefore, great care should be exercised in executing a lease, and particular attention directed to the specifications concerning repairs.

5. *Rent escalation.* Landlords may attempt to increase rent by including a provision in a lease whereby any increases in taxes or operating expenses are shifted to the tenant. Obviously, these matters should be negotiated and settled before the signing of the lease.

6. *Competing neighbors.* This subject, of course, is aimed at protecting a tenant from competition which might arise from future tenants of the landlord. It would be in the best interest of the small-business person to specify clearly the type of competing neighbors as tenants.

7. *The shopping-center leases.* Items of particular interest in the lease would include the subjects of common areas, the combined attraction of customers, and the specific description of premises, all of which should be clearly understood by the small-business person and carefully negotiated before signing the lease.[7]

Negotiable Instruments

Promissory notes, drafts, trade acceptances, and ordinary checks usually possess those characteristics which qualify them as negotiable instruments. The term *negotiable* means transferable from one party to another, and these instruments are normally used in the place of money. Because the possession of a negotiable as a *holder in due course* does not provide the defenses possible in an ordinary contract, it becomes incumbent upon the small-business person to secure instruments which are prepared so as to render them fully negotiable. The general requirements for a negotiable instrument are listed below:

---

[7]Excellent supplemental material on the subject of leases may be found in Milton R. Friedman, "Selected Problems in Store Leasing," *The Practical Lawyer,* XV, no. 8 December 1969, pp. 41–57, and Benjamin Pollack, "Clauses in a Shopping Center Lease," *The Practical Lawyer,* XVI, no. 5 (May 1970), pp. 31–44.

1. It must be in writing and signed by the maker of drawer.
2. It must specify the amount to be paid.
3. It must be payable "to order" or "to bearer."
4. It must contain an unconditional promise or order to pay a certain sum in money.
5. It must be payable on demand or at a fixed rate or at a determinable future time.
6. It must specify the drawee with reasonable certainty when the instrument is so addressed.

When a negotiable instrument is to be paid on a specific date, it should be presented for payment at a reasonable hour on that date. Should payment be dishonored, the holder should take immediate steps for protection by formally and immediately notifying any endorsers.

WHAT ABOUT BAD CHECKS?

Profitable operation of a small business can be adversely affected by and through excessive losses from bad checks. This potential problem can be controlled through establishing effective check-cashing procedures and efficient collection practices. The small-business person should be familiar with the following types of checks which are circulated: personal checks, two-party checks, payroll checks, government checks, counter checks, and traveler's checks.

Personal Checks. An individual prepares a personal check by making it payable directly to the small business. The important thing is positive identification for all personal checks. One of the best means of identification is the photograph, which is now being affixed to driver's licenses in many states. Compare the signature on the driver's license with the signature on the check. To make positive identification, additional aids are credit cards, membership cards, etc.: these are useful as comparisons with the driver's license and the check.

Two-Party Checks. A two-party check is a check made out to the individual and endorsed for the purposes of being honored or cashed by a small business. Some small businesses post a sign "No two-party checks accepted." Because of the possibility of the check being stolen or being forged, it is generally not advisable for a small business to accept a two-party check, unless the small-business person is knowledgable about the parties involved.

Payroll Checks. These checks compensating employees are usually designated "payroll check" on the face and have the amount of payment imprinted by machine. The same identification procedures should be followed as with personal checks. Because of the possibility of theft of payroll checks, it is not recommended that out-of-town payroll checks be cashed by a small-business person.

Government Checks. The source of these checks may be from local, state, or federal government. The checks may be drawn for the purposes of making payment for wages, pensions, welfare allotments, tax refunds, social security payments, and veteran's benefits. Thieves have been known to specialize in stealing government checks. Some banks will not cash a government check unless the person is known and has an account in the bank. The small-business person should take notice and require positive identification before cashing a government check.

Counter Checks. With the advent of modern data processing, the use of counter checks has been minimized. However, where they may be utilized, the small-business person should not honor a counter check unless he knows the customer.

Traveler's Checks. Traveler's checks are provided by a number of firms and banks to those persons not desiring to carry large sums of money, particularly when traveling. The procedure calls for the buyer to sign each traveler's check in the presence of the bank representative, and a second signature is placed below the original signature at the time the check is cashed. This procedure facilitates comparison of two signatures to identify the owner. As a safety measure, the small business should not accept a traveler's check unless the second signature is affixed at the time of cashing and the signature compares favorably with the original signature.

Small business firms are advised not to cash money orders, as they are usually purchased for payment of obligations by mail and not for the purpose of direct transactions.

It would be helpful if the small business observes the following additional items when cashing checks:

1. Old dates or post-dated checks
2. Any difference in the written and the numerical amount on the check
3. Erasures and written-over amounts
4. An address of the customer and the bank
5. Proper endorsements
6. That the check is properly signed by the drawer.

A sound business procedure is to stamp on the backs of all checks received for cashing the notation "for deposit only," along with the name of the business. The procedure prevents checks from being cashed if lost or stolen.

WHAT TO DO ABOUT BAD CHECKS?

A small-business person may not be in business long before encountering one of the following types of bad checks: insufficient funds, closed account, no account, or forgery.

Insufficient Funds. Normal procedure in handling a check return marked "insufficient funds" is to resubmit a second time after notifying the customer. This procedure usually facilitates collection on such checks. However, when these checks do not clear the bank it becomes the responsibility of the small-business person to collect. When the small business-person is unable to collect, the alternatives are (1) to resort to a direct effort to collect, (2) to utilize the services of a collection agency, or (3) to proceed with prosecution in the courts. In the last case, it would be well to check the law to determine the proper procedure. In most states the business-person is required to send the check writer a registered letter and to wait from five to ten days for payment before initiating a suit.

Closed Account. A check marked "closed account" may be the result of the person changing banks and forgetting an outstanding check; or the bank may have closed the account because of too many overdrafts; or it could be an outright case of fraud by the check writer. In any event, collection should be attempted before resorting to prosecution.

No Account. Unfortunately, when a check is returned from a bank and marked "no account" the possibility of collection is remote. In most cases this indicates intentional fraud by the check writer. It is possible that the check writer may have changed banks and written a check on the wrong bank: therefore, an attempt should be made to contact the person before turning the matter over to the police.

Forgery. When forgery has been determined in connection with a check, the police should be notified immediately. If the case involves a U.S. government check, the field offices of the U.S. Secret Service should be notified. Because forged checks are worthless, it is futile to attempt collection.

Additional Legal Considerations

COPYRIGHTS

A copyright is the means of protecting the rights of authors, composers, designers, or artists, as provided by the Federal Copyright Law. The length of protection runs for twenty-eight years from the date of first publication, and may be renewable for an additional twenty-eight years.

PATENTS

Unlike the copyright, a patent may not be renewed. It runs for a period of seventeen years, affording protection to inventors. It is recommended that a reliable patent attorney be retained to assist a small-business person in obtaining a patent. By making improvements on the original patent, it is possible for a small-business person to extend the control of the item for an additional seventeen years.

TRADEMARKS

A trademark can be an effective means for distinguishing the products of a small business. Whether the trademark be a word, figure, or symbol, it may provide useful identification and be a feature in advertising efforts. Trademark infringement has been known to occur. To be protected, registration may be facilitated under federal law. The registration of a trademark is set to last for a term of twenty years, and may be renewed for additional twenty-year periods as needed. A registered trademark may become a valuable asset in the future. Any infringement should be contested.

ACTS INVOLVING LIBEL

The small-business person should exercise care with regard to being subject to charges of libel. One area of particular concern is the matter of correspondence concerning credit and the use of collection letters. A good rule to follow in credit correspondence is to confine the communication to the facts. The following tests are recommended as a means of checking messages intended for debtors:

1. Are the statements true? (If not, obviously they should not be made.)
2. Is the debtor being accused of dishonesty, unfairness, or lack of integrity simply because he has failed to pay his debt? (He might not have the money to pay it.)
3. Is the debtor being accused of unwillingness or refusal to pay the debt simply because payment has not been forthcoming to date?
4. Is the debtor being accused of failure, refusal, unwillingness to pay, or even of slowness of paying all his debts, or his debts to others, where the writer does not have proof of these accusations? (Such accusations, if false, might tend to injure the debtor's credit standing.)[8]

---

[8]Credit Research Foundation, National Association of Credit Men (ed.), *Credit Management Handbook* (Homewood, Ill.: Richard D. Irwin, Inc., 1958), p. 499.

SUMMARY

Knowledge is power, and the small-business person should exert reasonable effort to gain an understanding of the more important laws to insure profitable operations. The matter of business regulation, taxation, and business law have become complex fields requiring extensive training and experience. Therefore, it is highly recommended that the small-business person obtain and utilize cmpetent counsel on matters pertaining to regulation, taxation, and law. It should prove helpful to the small-business person to subscribe to a tax-reporting service, such as the Prentice-Hall Service, and to supplement this study by consultation with special assistants.

THE
IMPLEMENTING
PHASE

6

Funding
Business
Requirements

"Ready money is Aladdin's lamp."

Lord Byron

Someone said it takes money to make money. Certainly, it takes money to operate a business. Insufficient capital is recognized as a major cause of failure in small businesses. It is paramount that some means be devised whereby the capital needs of the company can be carefully ascertained and provided. The reason some small businessmen come up short on funds is their failure to consider all of the needs for capital when starting a business. For example, there are the ongoing costs each month to maintain the family while the business is generating sufficient volume to meet expenses and supply a livelihood. There is also the necessity to finance the sales to some customers in order to secure business; to extend credit necessitates additional capital.

To assist you in making a careful plan of your financial needs, the accompanying checklist (Fig. 6-1A, B, and C) is provided. After working through each of the items listed on the checklist and totaling out the cash requirements, you should have a much more complete indication of financial needs in funding a business enterprise.

Figure 6-1a & b.
Capital Needs Worksheet. *Source: Checklist for Going into Business* (Washington, D.C.: Small Business Administration, 1973), p. 7.

	Estimated Monthly Expenses		
Item	Your estimate of monthly expenses based on sales of $ _____ per year	Your estimate of how much cash you need to start your business (See column 3.)	What to put in column 2 (These figures are typical for one kind of business. you will have to decide how many months to allow for in your business.)
	Column 1	Column 2	Column 3
Salary of owner-manager	$	$	2 times column 1
All other salaries and wages			3 times column 1
Rent			3 times column 1
Advertising			3 times column 1
Delivery expense			3 times column 1
Supplies			3 times column 1
Telephone and telegraph			3 times column 1
Other utilities			3 times column 1
Insurance			Payment required by insurance company
Taxes, including Social Security			4 times column 1
Interest			3 times column 1
Maintenance			3 times column 1
Legal and other professional fees			3 times column 1

Item	Your estimate of monthly expenses based on sales of $_____ per year	Your estimate of how much cash you need to start your business (See column 3.)	What to put in column 2 (These figures are typical for one kind of business, you will have to decide how many months to allow for in your business.)
Miscellaneous			3 times column 1
Starting Costs You Only Have to Pay Once			Leave column 2 blank
Fixtures and equipment			Fill in Figure 10-2 and put the total here
Decorating and remodeling			Talk it over with a contractor
Installation of fixtures and equipment			Talk to suppliers from who you buy these
Starting inventory			Suppliers will probably help you estimate this
Deposits with public utilities			Find out from utilities companies
Legal and other professional fees			Lawyer, accountant, and so on
Licenses and permits			Find out from city offices what you have to have
Advertising and promotion for opening			Estimate what you'll use
Accounts receivable			What you need to buy more stock until credit customers pay
Cash			For unexpected expenses or losses, special purchases, etc.
Other			Make a separate list and enter total
Total Estimated Cash You Need to Start with		$	Add up all the numbers in column 2

Figure 6-1c.
Fixtures and Equipment Worksheet. *Source: Checklist for Going into Business* (Washington, D.C.: Small Business Administration, 1973), p. 12.

List of Furniture, Fixtures, and Equipment

Leave out or add items to suit your business. Use separate sheets to list exactly what you need for each of the items below.	If you plan to pay cash in full, enter the full amount below and in the last column.	If you are going to pay by installments, fill out the columns below. Enter in the last column your downpayment plus at least one installment.			Estimate of the cash you need for furniture, fixtures, and equipment
		Price	Downpayment	Amount of each installment	
Counters	$	$	$	$	$
Storage shelves, cabinets					
Display stands, shelves, tables					
Cash register					
Safe					
Window display fixtures					
Special lighting					
Outside sign					
Delivery equipment if needed					
Total Furniture, Fixtures, and Equipment (Enter this figure also in Figure 10-1 under "Starting Costs You Only Have to Pay Once.")					$

The funds necessary to embark on a business venture are usually obtained from equity capital supplied by the entrepreneurs, from debt capital in the form of borrowed funds, or from both. The type of organization formed in starting has a direct impact on the means of generating capital. If you have decided to operate as a sole proprietorship, for example, the amount of equity capital will be confined to your savings account or other resources which can be converted or used in raising funds. If you decide on a partnership, then you may raise the amount of capital available through the joint resources of the partners.

If your decision is to operate as a corporation, another avenue for raising equity capital will be through the sale of stock in the corporation. Follow the rule of supplying 50% or more of the financial requirements as equity funds. After determining the funding requirements for your particular business, you may be prepared to modify your decision as to operating as a proprietorship. If it appears necessary to borrow more than 50% to supply the needed funds, it may be far better to seek a partner or to consider a corporate form of operation. Excessive borrowing handicaps a business: earnings must be used to make the monthly payments and to pay interest.

According to Gardiner G. Greene, you should use the "OPM" formula in funding the requirements of the business.[1] He advocates incorporation as the *modus operandi*, regardless of business size. Rather than commiting personal funds and adding on, he suggests that such funds be held in reserve: if something should go wrong, it may be difficult to retrieve personal funds committed to the firm. By the way, the "OPM" formula means "Other Peoples' Money." Our next concern is to examine where these funds may be found.

SOURCES OF BUSINESS CAPITAL

Trade Credit

Capital can be raised for the business by utilizing trade credit effectively in the purchase of inventory, equipment, and supplies. Some small businessmen are reluctant to negotiate for better credit terms

---

[1]Gardiner G. Greene, *How to Start and Manage Your Own Business* (New York: Mentor Book Co., 1975), pp. 14–19.

because they fear the risk of creating the impression that they are marginal operations lacking financial substance. It is just good business to negotiate for the best terms possible. And, without paying additional interest, thirty, sixty, or ninety days may be arranged. These arrangements will not be automatic, but must be initiated; and you are encouraged to make such arrangements. Carefully managed trade credit is one of the most inexpensive sources of capital, since it does not require interest payments.

Investment Banks

This source endeavors to bring together those who need funds and those who have funds to lend. Primary determinants involve the present financial requirements, market potential, and projected status for approximately two years. Unless your business has the expectation of being national or regional within two years, the use of the investment banker is not a viable consideration.

Insurance Companies

Insurance companies have traditionally done debt financing, but more recently they are demanding equity purchasing warrants to be included as part of the total package. You can go directly to the insurance company or contact the agent, an investment banker, or a mortgage banker representing the insurance companies to negotiate financing arrangements.

Commercial and Industrial Financial Institutions

These organizations usually represent higher financing costs than do other alternatives. However, the funds may be more accessable. Assistance is usually provided in the form of loans on fixed assets leased on purchase arrangements, on accounts receivable financing, and on factoring arrangements on accounts receivable. Commercial finance companies emphasize collateral as a basis for the loan, whereas banks emphasize net worth.

In the case of factoring, now considered a proven credit financing tool, the financing company purchases the accounts receivable outright, guarantees its clients against credit losses, and performs account checking, bookkeeping, and credit services.

Commercial Banks

The usual loans extended by commercial banks are for short-term capital needs. Many of the loans are for thirty, sixty, or ninety days. In fact, commercial banks lend more short-term funds than any other type of financial institution. The maximum length of time on loans extended by commercial banks may range up to five years, but loans do not usually exceed three years. There are cases where the banks do participate with Small Business Administration guaranteed loans for longer periods of time. Commercial banks dispense money in several ways: by traditional bank loans, installment loans, lines of credit, by discounting accounts receivables, and by discounting installment sales contracts.

How do you establish a line of credit? The answer is to start borrowing money. It is a real advantage in business when you can walk into a bank and borrow $10,000 on your signature. To do this on your first visit is most unlikely. However, a proprietor of a men's store explained one evening that he was able to borrow entirely on his signature because of his successful borrowing over many years. It began when he started selling Oxford men's clothes out of a suitcase on a COD basis. He decided that he needed to be able to borrow money to pay the COD charges, so he approached his banker: he was able to borrow $50 for thirty days. He paid it on the day it was due, and two weeks later borrowed $100 for sixty days. It too was paid on time. He continued borrowing and raising the amount of the loan over the years, and now he can borrow large sums on signature only. Begin establishing your line of credit now. It will pay off someday as a valuable asset.

Vendors

Firms who sell merchandise to a business will usually finance the purchase of these goods for short periods of time — thirty to ninety days. However, such terms are not automatic; you will have to make arrangements for these considerations. Extended dating permits the sale of the merchandise before payment is required, thereby facilitating the capital requirements of the business. Most vendors are willing to give consideration to suggestions which provide a viable means for financing inventory requirements.

Equipment Manufacturers and Distributors

To facilitate sales and encourage the purchase of equipment, manufacturers and distributors still offer a financing program. It is not uncommon to have a loan arranged in the form of an installment sales contract. The manufacturer will either carry the note or discount the installment sales contract with a financial institution. Some of the more common items financed by manufacturers and distributors include machinery, equipment, display fixtures, cash registers, and various office equipment.

Factors

In their role as financial specialists, factors provide business funds by discounting accounts receivables. Factors either purchase the accounts receivable or discount accounts receivable. On the discounting basis, they lend a certain amount of money based on their analysis of the accounts receivable, to be turned over as collateral until the debt is satisfied. The remaining collections are debts of the business firm.

When accounts receivable are purchased outright, the factor makes an analysis of the collectability of the accounts and pays the business a percentage of the total amount. Subsequently, either the factor or the business collects the amounts with the funds going to the factor.

Sales Finance Companies

This source of capital can be used by selling a customer on an installment sales contract. Afterwards, you take the sales contract and have it purchased by a sales finance company. As a matter of practice, the business is given the full face value of the contract. The profit to the sales finance company is provided in the form of interest carried on the contract.

The practice known as "floor planning" is used in the retail automobile trade and in the retail sales of larger appliances. Under the floor planning arrangement, the sales finance company arranges for the purchase of the dealer's stock of merchandise. The dealer pays the sales finance company interest on the loan until the merchandise is sold. When the merchandise is sold, the dealer turns the contract over to the sales finance company and receives the full amount of the purchase. Subsequently, the sales finance company collects the principal and interest in monthly installments paid by the customer. The merchandise involved serves as collateral to the sales finance company until the loan is fully paid.

Insurance Companies

Long-term loans may be secured from insurance companies to facilitate the purchase of fixed assets. This extension of funds to businesses is a means of providing investment opportunities for insurance companies. However, insurance companies are regulated by state and federal agencies which control the type of loans permitted, with due regard to protecting policyholders. Insurance companies are usually selective in dealing with small businesses, and extend loans to those with high value collateral that can be pledged to insure the repayment of the loan. Apartment buildings and shopping malls are typical bases for loans extended by insurance companies.

Private Investors

Some individuals are willing to provide capital, providing they can earn a higher rate of interest than available through savings accounts or savings and loan associations. However, the rate that they charge is usually above most financial institutions. Because the rate of interest charged is comparable to that required by small loan companies on consumer loans, you should check other possible sources to compare the cost. A further warning: be sure that you are dealing with respectable people; avoid getting involved in crime or with those who are indulging in usurious practices.

The Small Business
Investment Corporations (SBIC)

These corporations are privately owned financial institutions, licensed, regulated, and promoted by the Small Business Administration, which is an agency of the federal government. The procedure for loans by these corporations are specified by S.B.A. Loans or guarantees of loans can be arranged through the S.B.A. to fund small businesses. An SBIC must have a minimum initial investment of $150,000. Those with larger investments may exceed a million dollars. Loans or guarantees may be obtained in conjunction with the S.B.A. equivalent to twice the SBIC's paid-in capital. The maximum is 7.5 million dollars. The SBIC funds are used to make loans for longer than five years to small businesses, or may be invested in small businesses. In the latter situation, they are prohibited from obtaining controlling interest in the businesses. Where investments are made in small businesses, the SBIC usually extends consulting services to the business firms to protect their investment.

MINORITY ENTERPRISE SMALL BUSINESS
INVESTMENT CORPORATIONS (MESBIC)

The MESBIC program was established in 1969 by S.B.A. to assist minority enterprises. Since 1969, the MESBIC have increased to over seventy throughout the country, and have a total profit capitalization in excess of 34 million dollars. These funds can be matched with low-cost government loans to provide a basic pool of over 90 million dollars in direct assistance to businesses owned by minority members. These investments can trigger as much as 500 million dollars in funding from conventional sources.

MESBIC are privately managed venture capital corporations. They are chartered and licensed by the S.B.A. in each state to operate on a national level, providing sources of capital and management assistance. Here is a source of venture or expansion capital for business firms owned or operated by socially or economically disadvantaged members of minority groups — including blacks, the Spanish-speaking, American Indians, Orientals, Viet Nam era military veterans (honorably discharged), the handicapped, and others. These businesses must be owned at least 50% by socially or economically disadvantaged Americans. Under the special provisions of MESBIC financing, it would certainly be well to utilize this special source of capital.

Small Business Administration (S.B.A.)

The Department of Commerce established this agency in 1953 to help promote small businesses. The various activities of the S.B.A. have been discussed earlier in the text. The prime concern here is financial assistance to small businesses. Basically S.B.A. engages in the following types of loans:

1. Direct and immediate participation loans
2. Loan guarantees
3. Pool loans
4. Economic opportunity loans
5. Development company loans
6. Disaster loans

Under the S.B.A. program, there is no direct competition with financial institutions in making loans. When you can obtain sufficient money through private institutions by yourself, the S.B.A. is precluded from making a loan. In some situations, the S.B.A. will participate in making a loan in conjunction with a private lending institution.

Quite commonly, the S.B.A. participates in loan guarantees wherein 90% of the loan to the financial institution is guaranteed, with a maximum of $350,000. The lending institution lends the money, and the S.B.A. guarantees a specific percentage for repayment. Should the borrower default on the loan, the S.B.A. then reimburses the lending institution the amount of the loan guarantee.

Should you desire to cooperate with other small businesses in pooling resources for acquiring raw materials, inventories, equipment, etc., it is possible to coordinate such a loan through the S.B.A. by forming a corporation representing the various small businesses. This is a worthwhile arrangement, should your business qualify according to the circumstances specified.

Funds are extended to disadvantaged persons under the caption Economic Opportunity Loans. Those qualifying have insufficient income for the needs of the family and are unable to qualify through other lending institutions at reasonable terms. The maximum under this provision is $25,000, with a maximum term of fifteen years. These are high-risk loans with almost no collateral, primarily designed to assist disadvantaged persons.

SUMMARY

The purpose of considering the various sources of capital available is to acquaint you with the variety of funding possibilities, so that each can be explored according to the needs of your business. Rather than deciding on a specific source of capital, the best solution may be a combination of two or more.

Keep in mind that there are two basic kinds of capital required for operating a business: (1) short-term capital to provide working capital, customer credit, and merchandise inventory, and (2) long-term capital to provide land, machinery, furniture, buildings, fixtures, etc. The sources usually specialize in one kind of capital or another, either short term or long term. Therefore, it is necessary to structure the financial needs so that appropriate arrangements with sources will insure adequate funding for the total financial requirements of the business.

When shopping for money it pays to look around. Check the various financial sources. Visit more than one banker. Compare the offers. Choose the best alternative. When you borrow, be sure the amount is adequate. It may be more difficult to raise the loan at a later date. Only spend what you need; remit the coverage as a payment on the loan.

7

The Location Decision

"This is the right place!"

Brigham Young[1]

Where should your business be located? This question may be regarded as the key problem to be solved, and the answer is strategic to maximizing profits. Sometimes the question involves a single location to be analyzed without alternatives. At other times the solution is a matter of selecting the best answer from among numerous alternatives. There are many considerations involved in making a wise location decision. For simplification the subject will be treated first in terms of general factors, second in terms of specific site considerations, and finally in terms of those who can give assistance in resolving the question. Remember that haste makes waste: this decision is worth the time it will take.

---

[1]From B. H. Roberts, *History of the Church*, Vol. III (Provo, Utah: Brigham Young University Press, 1948), p. 224. Reprinted with permission.

GENERAL FACTORS—
REGION, STATE, CITY, AND TOWN

Many factors must be considered in deciding on the location of your business. What is your location preference? There are some businessmen who have a strong preference as to where they desire to do business. If you have a strong preference, the question of which region or state or city or town may already be decided. If your decision is to do business near home, capitalize on the advantages: utilize your knowledge of local conditions, supplemented by businessmen who may assist. Analyze your potential customers, including friends and relatives. Being a home-owner, you should be able to establish the necessary credit. Before you make your final decision, perhaps it would be well to ascertain whether or not the basic considerations for selecting a particular region are favorable and compatible with your preference.

Geographical Restraints

There are certain small businesses—such as automotive repair, clothing, food, or drugs—which will not be restricted on a geographical basis. However, by the very nature of the particular business, certain locational considerations may be restricted: a fishing dock must be located on the water; a boat repair business must be near the water; and, naturally, you will find greater potential for winter sports, Ski-doos, and ice skates in the northern climates than in the sunny South.

Availability and Cost of
Raw Materials

If your planned operation involves the use of heavy raw materials, it becomes imperative for economic reasons to locate near the source of raw materials. Will your planned business be affected by this question? In considering both the market and the source of raw materials, it is sometimes necessary to make a compromise decision.

Labor Considerations

What are the labor requirements for the business? Do the jobs require skilled, semi-skilled, or unskilled labor? Are there sufficient numbers in the proposed area? What will be the distances that employees will be required to travel? If highly skilled labor is required, the business location may be dictated by the location of such personnel.

Labor costs frequently represent a high proportion of total operating costs. Therefore, it should be carefully considered in terms of the different areas under consideration. In addition to the cost of labor, the history of labor relations with other businesses in the area should be checked, as should the question of labor productivity. Some businesses are relocating in the South, particularly in rural areas, for reasons of labor costs, employee attitude, and productivity.

Market Proximity Versus Transportation Costs

Manufacturers are perhaps more concerned about these factors than are distributive businesses. An evaluation for choosing a region should give consideration to the accessibility of the market. The prime concern involves the question of transportation cost of the finished product. When transportation costs run high, it is perhaps advisable to locate the operation as near to the market as possible, to maximize competitive position as well as profitability.

ADDITIONAL FACTORS

1. Competition, domestic and foreign
2. Land costs plus site preparation
3. Railroad facilities present and future
4. Taxes
5. Disposition of waste materials
6. Costs of water, electricity, and other municipal facilities
7. Environmental considerations
8. Minority group employment

Selection of City or Town

Some cities are more eager than others to attract new businesses. This may become more apparent if you consider alternative cities as potential location sites. Special inducements are often extended in terms of reduction of taxes, of utility rates, and even of land costs or site preparation expenses. Beyond the inducements, ascertain the city's trend. Is the city experiencing an increase or decrease in population? What are the reasons for the change? Striking differences in rate of growth in population can be ascertained from the Bureau of Labor Statistics.[2]

While it may be informative to receive comments from local businessmen, it is advisable to corroborate the information with census reports published by the Department of Commerce and with the biennial report "County Business Patterns."

Sometimes a decision of location may involve a site between two cities or towns. The use of Reilly's Law of Retail Gravitation may prove helpful in determining how far customers will drive for the particular product or service offered by the business.[3] This law is based on two factors: the population of the competing towns, and the distance between each of the towns. The size of a community trade area varies inversely with the town's population and directly with the distance between two towns, according to Reilly's Law.

An illustration will demonstrate the application of Reilly's Law in providing an inter-city location: Towns X and Y are forty miles apart. The population of X is 30,000 and the population of Y is 70,000.

$$\text{Breaking point in miles from town Y} = \frac{\text{Distance between X and Y}}{1 + \sqrt{\dfrac{\text{population X}}{\text{population Y}}}}$$

$$= \frac{40}{1 + \sqrt{\dfrac{30,000}{70,000}}}$$

[2]Bureau of Labor Statistics Bulletin 1370-9, *Employment and Earnings: State and Areas* (Washington, D.C., Bureau of Labor, 1930-1971).

[3]Wroe Alderson, *Marketing Behavior and Executive Action* (Homewood Ill.: Richard D. Irwin, Inc., 1957), p. 342.

$$= \quad 1\sqrt{\quad + \quad \frac{\frac{40}{.429}}{\frac{40}{1.655}}}$$

$$= \quad 1.655$$

Location from town Y = 24.2 miles

The kind and amount of competition in a given city should be carefully considered. Also, the quality of competition is an important dimension of concern. Are the existing businesses providing customer satisfaction? Is there an opportunity for a new competitor?

Information showing the average population required to support a given type of business can be determined on either a national or regional basis. Using such data in making comparisons in a given city will help to give a clearer insight regarding competition. Nothing will be more helpful than visiting the cities and examining your prospective competitors firsthand.

Does the city have the type of personnel with desired skills? What are the wage scales that will have to be paid? What is the record of labor relations? A community with a record of peaceful relations is to be desired over one besieged with continual labor disputes. Does the community have a good economic base in terms of other diversified industries, so that it avoids the problem of severe seasonal and cyclical business fluctuations? Does the city have the necessary customers and suppliers of essential services? Will satisfactory police and fire protection, streets, water, other utilities, street drainage, and public transportation be provided? Is the local tax structure reasonable and satisfactory? Have you checked local ordinances that may be restrictive on business operations?

Other considerations which may be of importance to you and your employees involve the matter of churches, schools, recreational facilities, advertising media, clubs, and restaurants.

OPPORTUNITIES IN SMALL TOWNS

You may be inclined to snub the idea of locating in a small town. However, there are many operators of highly profitable small businesses located in small towns. In fact, over 40 percent of the nation's total business is done in towns with under 5,000 population, in the following business categories:

general stores, feed and seed stores, farm implements, high-bred seed corn, filling stations, and hardware stores.[4]

Lunch counters, drug stores, and variety stores are typical of businesses which do as well in small communities as in large communities. Stores selling office and school supplies, cameras, furs, and books are likely to be missing in a small town; but the merchandise is likely to be sold in the small town in other stores.

Because payroll is normally the largest expense item for retail stores, many small retailers employ few if any employees. In such cases, rent becomes the major operating cost; and, according to occupancy expense data compiled by Dun and Bradstreet, the advantage favors small towns over large towns.

The small town may offer another advantage: because of size, it may not meet the minimum standards of large chain organizations. This would preclude some rather severe competition. In the absence of chain competition, opportunities for the independent are wide open. The increasing concern for the "crisis of the cities," with insurmountable problems of welfare, transportation, pollution, and crime, point to brighter prospects in the future of small town locations.

SPECIFIC SITE CONSIDERATIONS

Zoning and Restrictive Ordinances

One of the first questions to be answered concerns the legality of using the site for the purposes intended. Despite what people may say, check with the zoning commission to verify that the zoning classification of the property expressly provides for the type of use. At the same time, check if there are restrictive ordinances pertaining to activities of the business. It is more likely that a manufacturing business will be affected by such ordinances than will distributive or service businesses. If the proposed site cannot be used in a legal way, there is not much point in spending additional time evaluating additional considerations.

---

[4]Clifford M. Baumback, et al., *How to Organize and Operate a Small Business* (Englewood Cliffs, N.J.: Prentice-Hall, Inc., 1973), p. 143.

Comparative Analysis

It is both difficult and ineffective to try to keep all the different site factors in mind. A more sure approach would be to devise some means for facilitating comparisons of the various factors pertaining to each site. Determine the factors to be compared and the criteria for comparison, and set up *a work sheet* to record the factual information. Each location could then be ranked on the basis of individual factors, thus providing a more objective evaluation for determining the best location.

A form which could be helpful in evaluating significant cost factors is provided in Figure 7-1. Using a numerical value for each location and weighing the different factors according to their importance should simplify making the decision. Recording the essential information on a work sheet will be far more effective than trusting it to memory. By rank-

Figure 7-1.
Location Cost Analysis Worksheet for Manufacturers. *Source:* Adapted from Broom and Longenecker, *Small Business Management* (Cincinnati, Ohio: South-Western Publishing Company, 1975), p. 251. Reprinted by permission of the publisher.

Cost Item	Location A	Rank	Location B	Rank	Location C	Rank	Location D	Rank

Materials
  Fuels
  Raw Materials
  Supplies								

Operating Costs
  Labor
  Rent (or
    Depreciation)
  Electric
  Gas
  Water
  Sewer
  Telephone
  Insurance
  Others								

Taxes
  Income
  Payroll
  Property
  Others								

Transportation
  Raw Materials
  Finished Products								

ing objectively each of the factors, the best location will usually become more readily apparent.

Using a map can be particularly helpful in gaining perspective about the different locations under consideration. This would be true for analyzing locations in different areas or regions as well as for specific sites within a given city. Regional maps will facilitate comparison of general territory, cities, population, lakes and rivers, highways, and railways. City maps are useful in comparing: downtown business districts, primary and secondary shopping areas, parking lots and parking meter areas, routes, major highways, primary streets, secondary streets, one-way streets, railways (sidings for projected sites), competitive locations, residential areas (including employee residential areas), airports, trucking and rail terminals, and others. Zoning maps would also be helpful. By visiting the local zoning commission or planning agency, maps could be examined, noting particularly the planned and approved building projects, both business and residential. Proposed changes in highways, projected subdivisions, and shopping centers can be important in evaluating future developments affecting your location decision.

How to Determine the Specific Site

The nature of the business itself will dictate the general considerations. For example, manufacturing enterprises are usually located in industrial parks or areas nearby. Wholesale businesses are closely aligned with transportation facilities and terminals. Retail locations are determined by specific considerations within broader choices, such as the primary or central business area of the community, neighborhood, or sub-business center. The last may include shopping centers, which themselves vary in their size and the nature of tenants—regional shopping center, community shopping center, or neighborhood shopping center.

Another dimension of this question involves the nature of goods being marketed: specialty goods, shopping goods, or convenience goods. A determination should be made as to whether or not it would be advantageous to be in close proximity to competitive businesses.

ECONOMIC CONSIDERATIONS

There may be some locations priced beyond your means. In determining the suitability of a site, some guidelines should be set with regard to the ability to pay—within the estimation of projected occupancy cost in relation to the estimated volume of income for the business. When it is apparent that the cost of occupancy for a particular location is beyond your means, evaluate the next alternative, keeping in mind the objective of obtaining the best affordable location.

RETAIL SITE CHECKLIST

The Small Business Administration has provided the following checklist,[5] which will be useful in evaluating a particular site for retail stores. As noted, the suggested rating is based on a plus (+) for desirable, minus (−) for undesirable, and zero (0) for neutral. By this objective approach to the analysis of alternative locations for a store location, the best location should become more readily apparent.

	Rating $(+ , - , 0)$
I. *City or town*	
A. Economic considerations	
1. Industry	
a. Farming	_____
b. Manufacturing	_____
c. Trading	_____
2. Trend	
a. Highly satisfactory	_____
b. Growing	_____
c. Stationary	_____
d. Declining	_____
3. Permanency	
a. Old and well established	_____
b. Old and reviving	_____
c. New and promising	_____
d. Recent and uncertain	_____
4. Diversification	
a. Many and varied lines	_____
b. Many of the same type	_____
c. Few varied lines	_____
d. Dependent on one industry	_____
5. Stability	
a. Constant	_____
b. Satisfactory	_____
c. Average	_____
d. Subject to wide fluctuations	_____

[5]Checklist for locating a store. *Source:* Small Business Administration, *Small Business Location and Layout* (Washington, D.C.: U.S. Government Printing Office).

6. Seasonality
   a. Little or no seasonal change   _____
   b. Mild seasonal change   _____
   c. Periodical — every few years   _____
   d. Highly seasonal in nature   _____

7. Future
   a. Most promising   _____
   b. Satisfactory   _____
   c. Uncertain   _____
   d. Poor outlook   _____

B. Population
   1. Income distribution
      a. Mostly wealthy   _____
      b. Well distributed   _____
      c. Mostly middle income   _____
      d. Poor

   2. Trend
      a. Growing   _____
      b. Large and stable   _____
      c. Small and stable   _____
      d. Declining   _____

   3. Living status
      a. Own homes   _____
      b. Pay substantial rent   _____
      c. Pay moderate rent   _____
      d. Pay low rent   _____

C. Competition
   1. Number of competing stores
      a. Few   _____
      b. Average   _____
      c. Many   _____
      d. Too many   _____

   2. Type of management
      a. Not progressive   _____
      b. Average   _____
      c. Above average   _____
      d. Alert and progressive   _____

   3. Presence of chains
      a. No chains   _____
      b. Few chains   _____
      c. Average number   _____
      d. Many well established   _____

   4. Type of competing stores
      a. Unattractive   _____
      b. Average   _____
      c. Old and well established   _____
      d. Are many people buying out of community? _____

D. The town as a place to live
    1. Character of the city
        a. Are homes neat and clean or rundown and shabby?   _____
        b. Are lawns, parks, streets, etc., neat, modern, attractive?   _____
        c. Adequate facilities available   _____
            (1) Banking   _____
            (2) Transportation   _____
            (3) Professional services   _____
            (4) Utilities   _____
    2. Facilities and climate
        a. Schools   _____
        b. Churches   _____
        c. Amusement centers   _____
        d. Medical and dental services   _____
        e. Climate   _____

II. *The actual site*
  A. Competition
    1. Number of independent stores of same kind as yours
        a. Same block   _____
        b. Same side of street   _____
        c. Across street   _____
    2. Number of chain stores
        a. Same block   _____
        b. Same side of street   _____
        c. Across street   _____
    3. Kind of stores next door   _____
    4. Number of vacancies
        a. Same side of street   _____
        b. Across street   _____
        c. Next door   _____
    5. Dollar sales of nearest competitor   _____

  B. Traffic flow
    1. Sex of pedestrians   _____
    2. Age of pedestrians   _____
    3. Destination of pedestrians   _____
    4. Number of passers-by   _____
    5. Automobile traffic count   _____
    6. Peak hours of traffic flow   _____
    7. Percent location of site   _____

  C. Transportation
    1. Transfer points   _____
    2. Highway   _____
    3. Kind (bus, streetcar, auto, railway)   _____

  D. Parking facilities
    1. Large and convenient   _____
    2. Large enough but not convenient   _____
    3. Convenient but too small   _____

D. Parking facilities *(cont.)*
    4. Completely inadequate   ____
  E. Side of street   ____
  F. Plant
    1. Frontage — in feet   ____
    2. Depth — in feet   ____
    3. Shape of building   ____
    4. Condition   ____
    5. Heat — type; air conditioning   ____
    6. Light   ____
    7. Display space   ____
    8. Back entrance   ____
    9. Front entrance   ____
    10. Display windows   ____
  G. Corner location — if not, what is it?   ____
  H. Unfavorable characteristics
    1. Fire hazards   ____
    2. Cemetery   ____
    3. Hospital   ____
    4. Industry   ____
    5. Relief office   ____
    6. Undertaker   ____
    7. Vacant lot — no parking possibilities   ____
    8. Garages   ____
    9. Playground   ____
    10. Smoke, dust, odors   ____
    11. Poor sidewalks and pavement   ____
    12. Unsightly neighborhood buildings   ____
  I. Professional men in block
    1. Medical doctors   ____
    2. Dentists   ____
    3. Lawyers   ____
    4. Veterinarians   ____
    5. Others   ____
  J. History of the site   ____

ACCESSIBILITY OF THE LOCATION

Accessibility involves any factors which might impede the flow of vehicular or pedestrian traffic to and from the site in question. For example, the construction of street medians to control the flow of traffic at intersections adversely affects service stations located on the intersection by restricting crossover traffic. Similar restrictions can be imposed by "no left turn" signs or "one-way traffic" streets. Such factors affecting accessibility should be checked out for their impact on business at a particular location. Is the area congested to the point that it would deter customers from coming into the business?

Another aspect of accessibility is the availability of customer transportation via bus, streetcar, or subway connections.

PARKING

Convenient and adequate parking are important requisites to a modern retail location. Downtown merchants were quick to recognize the parking problem. Considerable effort and expense was undertaken in many cities to provide more parking lots and garages to offset this deterrent. Retail merchants have even exerted pressure in some communities for the removal of parking meters as deterrents to downtown shopping. The importance of convenient parking has resulted in provisions for free parking at convenient locations to attract customers.

You must carefully evaluate the site. Is there adequate and convenient customer parking? Parking requirements vary with different types of businesses. As a guide, one study suggested that a supermarket requires twelve parking spaces for each 1,000 square feet of floor space. Small retail and specialty shops require approximately four to five parking spaces per 1,000 square feet of floor space.[6]

TRAFFIC ANALYSIS

One of the useful comparisons which can be made of alternative sites is the volume of traffic passing the particular site. Traffic analysis may include both pedestrian traffic and vehicular traffic. By making an objective traffic count, a factual comparison can be made between sites, revealing what may not be readily apparent on just cursory examination. The important thing is to make the traffic count of different locations on the same day and at approximately the same time, so the conditions are comparable and the comparisons will be realistic.

There is more to taking a pedestrian count than simply totaling the number of passers-by. People running to catch their bus or moving to and

---

[6]Richard G. Thompson, *A Study of Shopping Centers,* Research Report No. 16, Real Estate Research Program, Institute of Business and Economic Research (Berkeley, Calif.: University of California Press, 1961), p. 30.

from their place of work may or may not be potential customers for your particular business. Therefore, it must be determined who is to be counted in the traffic count. It is also important to consider the hour when the count will be made, recognizing that the peak traffic periods are early morning, lunchtime, and afternoon. The peak periods will not reflect as accurate a shopping picture as will mid-morning and mid-afternoon. It has been suggested that the most ideal times to use are 10 a.m. to 12 noon and 1 p.m. to 3 p.m. The pedestrian count may also be differentiated as to male and female, with some considerations as to age variation.

The objective in taking the traffic count is to get a representative indication of the volume of pedestrian traffic. To accomplish this, careful consideration should be given to anything that would distort the normal traffic picture, such as holidays, the day of the week (traffic is usually heavier on the weekend), special events, weather conditions, etc.

The time period of the count should preferably be a half-hour or more. Use the same amount of counting time at each location. Eliminate duplication by avoiding, as much as possible, the double counting of customers entering and leaving a particular store.

VEHICLE TRAFFIC COUNTS

Data on traffic counts along primary streets or highways can often be obtained from city or state government agencies, and may provide useful information for making comparisons between alternative locations. This data may be supplemented by specific traffic counts which would address themselves more particularly to the special needs of the business.

It is sometimes desirable to analyze traffic in terms of the kind of trip involved—a planned shopping trip, a work trip, or a pleasure trip. The essence of a good location is to be in position to serve the kind of customers you are striving to reach.

Figure 7-2 is an example of a form which would facilitate a traffic count, either pedestrian or vehicular, with the arrows showing the direction of traffic. Alongside the arrows the traffic could be classified by sex, by type of vehicle, or on some other basis. Figure 7-3 is a more complex form, which is useful in taking traffic counts at intersections. The various lines show the flow of traffic, the portion making right and left hand turns, and the thru-traffic from all four directions. On either form, note the time period, the date, the weather conditions, and other special factors which may influence the traffic count.

Figure 7–2.
Traffic Worksheet.

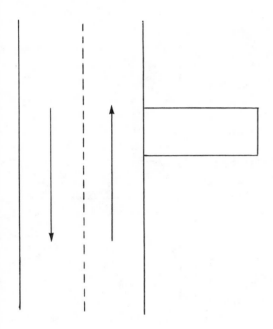

IS THE POTENTIAL INCREASING
OR DECREASING

Check population and business activity in the sector. What is the trend? What factors, if any, are pointing to an increase or decline. Examine critically the businesses adjacent to the site for compatibility. Do they appear to be thriving, progressive, expanding enterprises?

Suburban Trend. The obvious trend in the past two decades has been the movement toward the suburbs. The increasing suburban population, use of automobiles, traffic congestion, and the lack of sufficient parking space downtown have all contributed to the development of suburban business locations. This trend has adversely affected downtown business more acutely in some areas than in others. Determine whether your particular business would be better located in a downtown location than in a

Figure 7-3.
Intersection Traffic Count Form. Note that the numbers preceded by "A" represent count taken in the morning (A.M.) and those preceded by "B" count taken in the afternoon (P.M.).

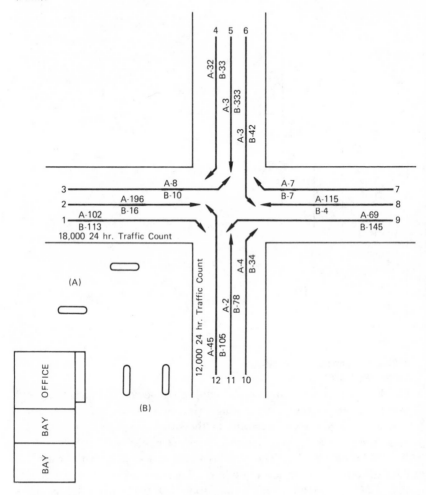

suburban location. Several good locations are now available in the downtown area as a result of the suburban trend. However, availability is not sufficient reason to acquire a location. The specific site should be carefully checked with the needs of the business.

RENT AND ADVERTISING

The relationship between rent and advertising expenses should be clearly understood by the businessman. Obviously, the higher traffic locations usually demand a higher price. In fact, the central business districts are frequently divided in terms of hundred-percent locations—the prime or best locations. Because of the bidding for these locations, the rent is usually very high. In other words, by paying high rent the tenant is assured of high customer traffic past the location.

Many stores desire a location in close proximity to a primary tenant, such as a large department store, to take advantage of the customer shopping traffic generated by the large store. An adjacent location for some businesses would be a distinct advantage even though the rent would be higher. However, when located near a prime tenant it is still necessary to advertise: the central locations make possible the effective use of low-cost-per-reader mass media, newspapers in particular.[7]

The alternative is to consider (as some specialty stores do) locations which are several blocks from the major shopping area, and thereby pay lower rent. However, businesses in secondary locations must depend to a larger extent upon their advertising to generate sufficient customers. This usually requires higher appropriations for advertising. The returns per dollar of advertising expenditure may be less for stores located in the peripheral area; but the combined effect of low rent and modified advertising may produce a profitable operation.

PROXIMITY

A retail store, like an individual, should keep the right company. Studies have indicated that certain kinds of stores do well when located adjacent to other stores that are patronized by the same customers and that seem to fit the same "affinity." Studies of some of these natural clusterings of businesses have disclosed the following:

1. Mens' and womens' apparel and variety stores are commonly located near department stores.
2. Florists are usually grouped with shoe stores and womens' clothing stores.
3. Paint, home furnishings, and furniture stores are generally in close proximity.
4. Restaurants, barber shops, candy, tobacco, and jewelry shops are often found near theaters.
5. Drug stores may be found in any of the above groupings.

---

[7]Baumback, et al., *How to Organize and Operate a Small Business,* p. 153.

There are certain kinds of business neighbors which are undesirable for nearly every kind of retailer. Types of businesses which are normally avoided by shoppers include funeral parlors, garages, hospitals, saloons, and industries with undesirable odors, noises, dust, or smoke.

SITE HISTORY

The most recent history of a particular site being considered should be investigated before making a final decision. If the site has a history of repeated business failures, one would want to approach the site with caution. There must be some logical reasons why the site has not been successful. Also, prospective customers may have formed some unfavorable impressions about the location.[8]

SPECIAL ASSISTANCE

There are specialists who offer assistance in regard to locations and charge a fee for their services. Large companies usually engage experts when making location decisions. Small businessmen motivated by frugality may find special assistance from some of the sources below.

Bankers

In addition to having a very good feel for local business conditions, including business locations, some banks also have a department involving real estate that can give special assistance to customers in regard to business locations.

Trade Associations

In an effort to be of assistance to the members of the association, advice and counseling is provided. They will answer questions on location and provide useful data to assist in making the decision.

---

[8]*Ibid.*, p. 156.

Organized Industrial Districts
(Industrial Parks)

If your business is well suited for occupancy in an industrial district, it would be advantageous to work with a particular industrial park. Many of the required services such as street paving, sewage system, water, power, industrial type buildings, railroad sidings, and other considerations can be provided in an economic manner.

Chambers of Commerce

The tendency of these organizations is to over-sell locations in their particular area, as part of their programs to attract businesses to their community. Nonetheless, they can provide assistance in locating and recommending desirable sites. Certainly, they can make you aware of the sites which are available and about which they are knowledgeable.

Government Agencies

Some assistance in choosing a business location may be available through the Small Business Administration and the field offices of the U.S. Department of Commerce.

Wholesalers and Manufacturers

Good leads are frequently obtained from both wholesalers and manufacturers regarding prospective areas where a new business may be located. Their knowledge of the market enables them to recommend possible leads to investigate.

Miscellaneous Sources

Various transportation companies, utility companies, and state government industrial development agencies provide location assistance to prospective customers or residents. Some of the data which may be helpful from these sources include:

1. Adequacy of water, power and fuel
2. Available transportation and communication facilities
3. Cost and availability of raw materials
4. Size and skill level of the labor force
5. Land cost
6. Market possibilities
7. Existing tax rates, labor laws, and laws and ordinances pertaining to business activities
8. Type, conditions, and costs of buildings located on given sites

SUMMARY

After considering all the factors bearing on the location decision, it should be apparent that locations do not have equal potential. Some locations are definitely superior. If you apply the price-quality rule, you would expect to pay more for the superior location. What you can afford to pay will temper your location decision. By proceeding systematically to analyze the location factors from the general considerations to the specific site considerations, making full use of the special assistance available, the most profitable location for your business can be determined.

8

The Decisions on Facilities and Layout

"When you fail to plan . . . you plan to fail"

Engstrom and MacKenzie[1]

Are you going to adapt your business to the building, or are you going to adapt the building to your business? The purpose of this chapter is to provide some guidelines to help make physical factor decisions which will contribute to the profitability of your business enterprise.

The starting point usually involves a decision on whether to purchase or lease an existing building. An alternative would be the design and construction of a new building; however, because of the greater investment required for construction, a purchase may be more advisable for the new business. Also, the additional time required for construction may adversely affect the initiation of business activity.

---

[1]From Ted W. Engstrom and R. Alec MacKenzie, *Managing Your Time* (Grand Rapids, Mich.: Zondervan Pub. Co., 1967), p. 105. Reprinted with permission of the Zondervan Corporation.

FUNCTIONAL AND SPACE FACTORS

The principal concern here is to match the requirements of the business with the available facilities. A careful analysis of the needs of the business in terms of physical facilities would be prerequisite to initiation of this effort. The value of a particular building is in direct proportion to its suitability for the performance of the activities required by the business. A building which provides excellent facilities for one type of business may be intolerable for another. Factors to be considered include the condition, the shape, the age, and hazards, the heating and air conditioning, and the entrances and exits. The importance of each of these considerations will vary as they pertain to a factory building, a wholesale warehouse, or a retail merchandise business.

The importance of accessibility to the building varies with the kind of business involved. Customer accessibility is of greatest importance in retailing. In manufacturing, receiving raw materials and shipments of finished products are prime considerations. In service-type industries, the accessibilities for customers or clients, as well as the easy access for delivery equipment, are important.

Evaluate the question of accessibility carefully. For example, a retail store building should be examined for unnecessary steps, small entrances, and obstructions, such as pillars or posts, which interfere with customer accessibility. Steps present an accident hazard as well as an obstacle to customers. Perhaps a ramp with non-skid material would be a better solution to differences in elevation. How will goods be received? Are there facilities at the side or rear of the building, or will it be necessary to utilize the front entrance? The front is most undesirable.

Desirable building facilities permit efficient internal transportation. These factors should be considered: adequacy of aisles, traffic lanes, elevators, stairs, and escalators, combined with material-handling equipment for store merchandise or factory raw materials. Consider the availability or possible utilization of chutes, conveyors, hand trucks, dollies, hoists, cranes, and forklift trucks. Will the facilities available meet the requirements for your business?

The building should be large enough to facilitate business operations and allow some space for future growth. The necessity of moves to accomodate growth over the early periods of the business can be minimized by careful analysis of present and projected space needs. Determine the space requirements for your particular business. These may be calculated backwards from the sales forecasts, in terms of square footage required per sales dollar, or in terms of the number of employees to be engaged.[2]

CONSTRUCTION AND APPEARANCE CONSIDERATIONS

Modernizing and Refurbishing

A modern, up-to-date appearance is desirable, not only for retail customers, but also for factory employees. If the building in question is structurally sound but out of date architecturally, it would be desirable to estimate the costs of modernizing or refurbishing to provide suitable facilities. The effective use of color, glass, skylights, and modern lighting will contribute much for an updated appearance.

Interior and Exterior

Appropriate use of color is important in achieving the desired effect in the store or the factory. In recent years a color code has been developed for effective utilization in factories, indicating traffic patterns, hazardous areas, first aid facilities, and fire-fighting equipment.

Rather than guessing the adequacy of load-bearing walls and supporting columns, it would be well to obtain expert opinion from qualified personnel. The use of free-standing walls will add materially to the flexibility in arranging the desired layout. Consideration may also be extended to the matter of noise factors and the advisability of using sound-proofing materials to minimize this problem. Use of sound-proofing materials is not limited to exceptionally noisy areas, but has been found useful in restaurants, banks, and exclusive stores, as well as in noisy factories.

Because of the impact upon customers, the exterior appearance of a building is obviously more strategic to the retailer than to a manufacturer, wholesaler, or repair business. In evaluating the proposed building facilities

---

[2]Clifford M. Baumback, et al., *How to Organize and Operate a Small Business* (Englewood Cliffs, N.J.: Prentice-Hall, Inc., 1973), p. 178.

for your business, consider the costs that may be necessary to modify the exterior to bring it up to your desired standards. There are a number of possibilities to improve the exterior finish of buildings by the use of marble, precast stone, aluminum siding, glass blocks, or two-pane insulating glass walls. It may be desirable to obtain bids on the various materials as well as bids from two or more contractors on the labor to accomplish the project.

Entrances and Exits

Does the building facility in question have adequate entrances and exits to insure a prompt and smooth flow of people in and out of the building? Obstacles and interferences within easy access should be avoided. It has been suggested that in frontages in excess of thirty-five feet should be provided with two doors. Where heavy traffic is anticipated, it may be necessary to have additional exits and entrances. The cost to provide them should be ascertained before making a final decision on the building.

One of the modern trends in entrances and exits is automatic equipment. This will cost more, and the cost may exceed its justification for your particular kind of business. Alternatives include the use of revolving doors or two swinging doors to provide for inbound and outbound customers.

Check if there is a difference in the level between the street and the store floor, as this would constitute an undesirable condition. Steps up or down are considered a customer barrier, and rental prices usually reflect this condition. Should the condition exist, the question as to whether or not it is a sufficient handicap to be modified should be ascertained, and the cost projected. It is important that the delivery entrances be separate from those utilized by customers. Does the proposed facility have convenient access to railroad sidings? Are there access ramps for trucks, and platforms for loading and unloading of merchandise?

Installations and Facilities

LIGHTING

Efficient lighting is essential for both a factory and a store. Whereas the object in the factory is sufficient illumination for safety and efficient work, the object of lighting in the retail store is to provide an atmosphere pleasing to the customers. In either case it is important to determine the adequacy of electric wiring and current to meet the needs of the business. It is costly to add additional electrical facilities, and it would be advisable to ascertain these costs beforehand. Are there sufficient outlets of the proper voltage for the equipment that will be utilized? It may be advisable to have an electrician assess your electrical needs and their cost.

COLOR COORDINATING

Through the proper use of color, desired effects can be produced upon people. To achieve the desired effect, it is necessary to coordinate the colors of walls, ceilings, floors, fixtures, and even merchandise. The general trend has been toward pastel (lighter) colors, which are pleasing and more economical in their light-reflecting abilities. Different effects can be simulated through color. For example, warmth can be simulated by using warm colors of the red and yellow hues. It has been suggested that apparent size can be increased through the use of receding colors such as white, or decreased by the use of advancing colors. Advice on color coordination may be obtained through specialists employed by various paint and decorating companies.

AIR CONDITIONING

Air conditioning is costly, but has become a virtual necessity in retail stores located in warmer climates. Air conditioning is now frequently utilized in factories, particularly where delicately adjusted equipment is involved or where materials require controlled humidity to avoid deterioration.

The concept of air conditioning is advancing to include odor conditioning, so that not only temperature and humidity are being controlled, but pleasant or even sales-stimulating odors are provided.

SANITARY FIXTURES

You should consider providing the following sanitary facilities, located conveniently for the use of workers and customers alike: lounges, washrooms, drinking fountains, and restrooms. Special requirements for sterilization devices may be required for the following kinds of businesses: dairies, hospitals, food-processing plants, cafeterias, laundries, and dry-cleaning shops.

Added emphasis is being directed toward considerations of pollution and waste disposal. Therefore, it is advisable to check for proper plumbing and satisfactory waste-disposal facilities. It may be necessary in certain types of factory operations to provide a vacuum-suction system for removal of sawdust, metal chips, or other waste materials from the processing area. Where chemical processing is involved, the question of decontamination of waste materials presents special problems.

SUMMARY

To minimize costly disruption of potential work sequences, small-business people should provide at least the following facilities:

1. Adequate parking for customers and employees
2. Well-designed interior displays
3. Toilets and other health facilities near work areas
4. Satisfactory housekeeping
5. First-aid kits near work stations
6. Devices to reduce noise and vibrations
7. Eating facilities for employees
8. Aisle space for free flow of materials
9. Transportation facilities to prevent backtracking of materials
10. Private space for key employees

As a final thought, facilities and people in an organization tend to go together like a hand-in-glove. The more that small-businesspeople combine these two assets effectively, the more likely they are to have profitable operations.

PLANNING LAYOUT ARRANGEMENTS

Layout refers to the arranging of machines, fixtures, and other equipment according to a plan. There should be a distinction made between "making" a layout and "planning" a layout. "Making" a layout without a planned layout may be a costly experience. It is important to utilize qualified industrial engineers and competent retail personnel to supervise all major layout revisions. Assistance may be obtained for retailers from their equipment manufacturers, suppliers, wholesalers, or franchisers. Trade associations have also developed model layouts best suited to the needs of particular businesses. For those desiring, consulting firms may also supply helpful advice concerning the layouts for various special kinds of businesses.

The objective is to develop the best layout, and this is defined as the most effective use of space for the particular business. In proceeding with this work, bear in mind that the principal factor is not the area or volume, but the most effective location. Recognize that the same area of volume in one part of the store may in fact be worth many times more than an equal area of volume in another part of the same store. The point is to determine the most effective location.

Planning the layout begins with an analysis of the objectives of the business and of the activities essential to achieving these objectives. To be effective, reference to the specific primary objectives of the business is necessary for establishing an effective layout.

To facilitate layout planning the following factors may prove helpful:

1. Optimum arrangement of equipment (production flow) and merchandise (customer buying habits). Machinery placed in the proper sequence and located conveniently expedites the flow of material and saves factory workers lost motion. Merchandise in the right place at the right time increases sales per customer and reduces steps for sales people.

2. Make use of maximum light, ventilation, and heat, to take full advantage of natural conditions resulting from the building construction. Effectively utilizing windows, doors, vents, and skylights will save eyes, improve work and health, and reduce the cost of lighting, heating, and air conditioning. Customers also appreciate arrangements made for their personal comfort and their ease in selection of proper merchandise.

3. Utilize equipment with maximum efficiency. The improper location of equipment may cause workers to do work by hand when it should be done by existing equipment. For example, if the machine for putting "the finishing touch" on the final processing or packaging of goods requires extra steps, employees may tend to do this work manually or avoid it entirely.

4. Make materials or merchandise readily available to workers or customers. An orderly arrangement will save time for workers in locating materials. Reminding customers of their needs permits them to handle and become familiar with the merchandise.

5. Utilize facilities to maximize clear views of the establishment: management can readily observe all activities of customers and employees; workers can observe customers' presence and movements; and customers can readily see all that the store is offering and the location of particular groups of merchandise.

Now let us direct our attention to the aforementioned principles as they apply to the planning of specific layouts.

Plant Layouts

Manufacturing flow-analysis techniques concentrate on some quantitative measure of movement between departments or activities. Activity analysis is primarily concerned with the non-quantitative factors that influence the location of department or activities. The layout flow patterns can be classified as horizontal (Fig. 8-1) and vertical (Fig. 8-2). Each basic pattern has five varieties. The horizontal patterns include:

   (H1) Straight line, or I flow
   (H2) L flow
   (H3) U flow
   (H4) Circular, or O flow
   (H5) Serpentine, or S flow

Figure 8-1.
Basic Horizontal Flow Pattern: (a) straight, or I flow; (b) L flow; (c) U flow; (d) circular, or O flow; (e) serpentine, or S flow. *Source:* Richard L. Francis, John A. White, *Facility Layout and Location: An Analytical Approach.* © 1974, p. 44. Reprinted by permission of Prentice-Hall, Inc., Englewood Cliffs, New Jersey.

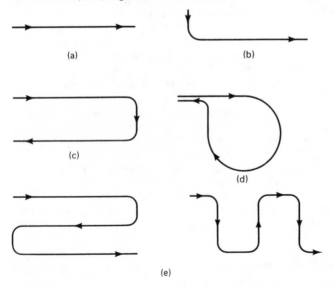

Figure 8–2.
Vertical Flow Pattern. *Source:* Richard L. Francis, John A. White, *Facility Layout and Location: An Analytical Approach.* © 1974, p. 45. Reprinted by permission of Prentice-Hall, Inc., Englewood Cliffs, New Jersey.

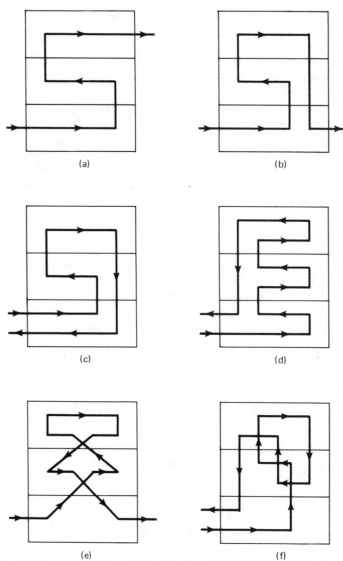

(a)

(b)

(c)

(d)

(e)

(f)

The vertical flow patterns include:

(V1) Useful where there is traffic flow between buildings and their exits, with an elevated connection between the buildings

(V2) Useful where ground-level ingress and egress are required

(V3) Useful where ground-level ingress and egress occur on the same side of the building

> (In V1, V2, and V3 decentralized elevation is present, since travel between floors can occur on either side of the building.)

(V4) Inclined flow — belts, conveyors, and escalators

(V5) Backtracking flow — where the flow returns to the same area (e.g., the top floor as shown in V5)[3]

After developing a tentative departmental arrangement, you should prepare a full diagram. This is accomplished by drawing a flow pattern for each product or product group on the completed departmental arrangement. See Figure 8-3.

Figure 8–3.
Product Flow Diagram.

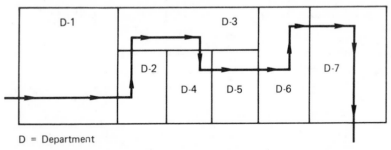

D = Department

Careful examination of the prepared flow diagram will give you some idea of the adequacy of the proposed layout. Straight-line flows, zig-zag flows, and backtracking will be readily apparent.

WORK STATION LAYOUT

A final phase in plant layout calls for the preparation of the work station — where the actual work will be accomplished. A work station refers to the

---

[3]Richard L. Francis and John A. White, *Facility Layout and Location* (Englewood Cliffs, N.J.: Prentice-Hall, Inc., 1974), pp. 31-61.

area occupied by the operator and the equipment he uses. The equipment might include such things as machines, benches, tools, cabinets, materials-handling equipment, or storage containers.

Production departments consist of a collection of work stations, and the detailed layout of a production department is represented by the final arrangement of the work stations. In the process of arranging work stations in some order, it is necessary that you also lay out the individual work stations. You must decide where the various physical objects of the work station are to be located.[4]

Sometimes it may be desirable to move a department from one location to another in order to improve and modernize the plant facilities. Here is a list of points to keep in mind for improving and modernizing facilities:

1. Obtain a complete set of building plans for the authorized area.
2. Determine what must be incorporated into the layout.
3. Check the present service requirements.
4. Secure production data.
5. Prepare good templates.
6. Lay out the templates according to the predetermined flow.
7. Identify where the material comes from.
8. Check the materials-handling possibilities.
9. Ascertain the material control and storage requirements.
10. Determine power usage.
11. Check space requirements for auxiliary operations.
12. Spot the templates on the model.
13. Provide ample space for maintenance.
14. Insure provisions for good housekeeping.
15. Consider growth potential.
16. Have the layout reviewed and criticized by others.
17. Prepare the final drawing of the new layout.

PLANT LAYOUT BOARD

A final step in plant layout is the preparation of a layout board. The plant layout board can be prepared using a piece of wood, metal, fiberboard, or plastic, covered with the floorplan of the building in which the layout is

---

[4]Raymond R. Mayor, *Production and Operations Management* (New York: McGraw-Hill Book Co., 1975), pp. 69–127.

being made. Mark off the floor plan in squares drawn to some scale, and indicate each departmental location that has been decided upon. Show the location of columns, windows, doors, stairwells, walls, and utilities, as these items will have some effect on the final layout.

Next, prepare or obtain templates or models of the facilities to be laid out in each department, constructed to the same scale as the floor plan. A template is a flat piece of material cut to the shape which the facility it represents would assume if it were projected on the floor. Templates can be constructed from cardboard, wood, plastic, etc. In the process of making the detailed layout, you will want to test various locations on the layout board by placing the templates in different positions until the most satisfactory location can be determined. Templates can be fastened to the board by means of tacks, magnets, or tape.[5]

Wholesaling Layouts

The primary function of the wholesale establishment is order filling. It is recommended that optimum use be made of the force of gravity as well of mechanical conveyors and other material-handling equipment, since about 60 percent of the cost of operation is likely to be payroll. Operations may be facilitated by physically separating the major functions such as receiving, "dead" storage, order assembly, breaking packages, packing and shipping, and office work. A possible exception might be to combine receiving, packing, and shipping functions within a smaller plant operation. The layouts of wholesale establishments resemble those of a factory or plant, and many of the good ideas utilized in factory layouts can be applied to the wholesale establishment.

As a rule, most wholesale-warehouse activities adapt themselves to a production-line type of operation (or "order-pick" line pattern), as illustrated in Figure 8-4. The wholesaler's problem is to arrange an order-picking route (layout) and routine that will facilitate the handling of unpredictable assortments without special adjustments for them. Consequently, both the routing and the routine should be flexible in order to meet any reasonable contingency.

One of the objectives in setting up a work-center layout is to minimize

---

[5]Merle C. Nutt, *Functional Plant Planning, Layout and Materials* (Hicksville, N.Y.: Exposition Press, Inc., 1970), pp. 201-206.

Figure 8–4.
A Wholesale Warehouse Layout. *Source:* From Clifford M. Baumback, Kenneth Lawyer, and Pearce C. Kelley, *How to Organize and Operate a Small Business,* 5th ed. Copyright © 1973 by Prentice-Hall, Inc., Englewood Cliffs, N.J. Reprinted with permission of Prentice-Hall, Inc.

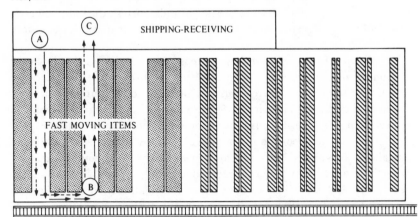

the amount of employee "travel period." Employees in wholesale warehouses frequently walk several miles a day in the routine of filling orders. As illustrated in Figure 8-4, this "mileage" can be effectively lowered by (1) laying out picking aisles so that they are perpendicular to the shipping dock, and (2) storing the fast-moving (large-volume) items on pallet racks nearest the shipping docks. The aisle space between the pallet racks and shelf stock should be approximately four to six feet, depending upon the type of merchandise.

Another suggestion for speeding up order filling is to split orders into "trip routes." To illustrate, the order picker travels up one side of one aisle (A), loading only one side of the trailer; then, traveling down the opposite side of the next aisle (B), he loads the other side of the trailer; and he finishes the trip right back at the shipping dock (C)—with no dead travel time. In the meantime, the other men follow similar picking routes, filling other splits of the order. The process expedites the order-filling activity in the warehouse.

In planning warehouse layouts, wholesalers should determine the feasibility of using mechanical materials-handling equipment and other labor-saving devices. Pallets and gravity chutes frequently offer a means of simplifying materials handling.

Store Layout

Internal design and departmentalization of the store facilitate the service and sales offerings made to the public, and represent the philsophy of the store management. The store layout must furnish the most comfortable setting for triggering purchasing decisions and for maximizing in-store traffic to all sales areas.

Whether free-flow or grid-type areas are used, the basic objective is maximum merchandise exposure consistent with the store image. Store layout and service procedures must facilitate customer purchases and at the same time suggest other items. For example, some supermarket planners believe that the entering customer should be faced immediately with a display of the main portion of the meal. In stores so planned, customers are always confronted with and must pass by the meat counter first. In other supermarkets customers are forced to travel through a maze of milk, vegetables, and canned goods before they can finally arrive at the counter displays featuring main meal selections. Many of the Kroger stores are set up in the "meat counter first" type of layout, while the A & P supermarkets are among those planned in the "meat counter last" type of layout.[6]

Customers are the starting point for sale planning in a retail store. Consequently, the space for some departments must be set up first and sell supporting activities second. The traffic patterns of customers determine the relative worth of various locations on the selling floor, and how displays should be arranged. Space in retail stores has a wide range of economic value. Normally, the higher the turnover rate and the less bulky the item in relation to its cost, the smaller the space allocation and the better the traffic location needed for the department.[7]

Unfortunately, there is no fixed set of rules which will enable you to determine exactly what is the most efficient allocation of space. No two people working separately are likely to recommend the same departmental arrangement: this would be surprising, considering the almost infinite number of different arrangements possible.

Figure 8–5 shows an approximate distribution of the total value (or rent) for space in a small store located on the main floor, when the store has only one entrance. When entrances are possible on two or more sides, such as front and rear or front and one side, the relative amount of traffic

---

[6]Robert D. Entenberg, *Effective Retail and Market Distribution* (Cleveland, Ohio: World Publishing Co., 1966), p. 145.

[7]*Ibid.*, p. 149.

Figure 8–5.
Plot of Sales Floor Values. *Source:* From Clifford M. Baumback, Kenneth Lawyer, and Pearce C. Kelley, *How to Organize and Operate a Small Business,* 5th ed. Copyright © 1973 by Prentice-Hall, Inc., Englewood Cliffs, N.J. Reprinted with permission of Prentice-Hall, Inc.

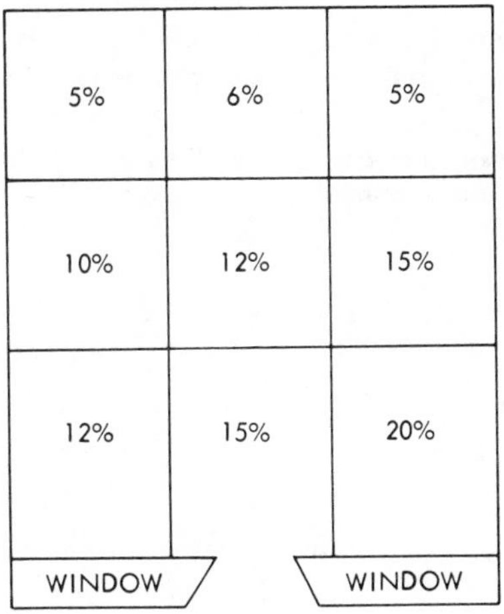

through each door is the important consideration. In those cases the diagram can be used to indicate the relative value of space inward from each entrance, reflecting the differences in the traffic volume. The space which is nearest to the traffic flow offers the greatest exposure to customers and has the greatest sales potential. Consequently, the value of space in a retail store decreases from the front of the store to the rear. There are some authorities who use a straight-line approach, or the "4-3-2-1 rule," in representing the decline in space value. Figure 8-6 illustrates this rule.

A roughly straight-line approach was used in estimating the floor-space values in Figure 8-5. Another assumption was the fact that the space toward the right, as one enters the store, is more valuable than the space to the left. Professor Aspinwall explains his rationale as follows:

> Customers moving in and out of your front door behave just about as do people on the street. Those who know what they want try to go directly to that item. People with no specific items in mind move from place to place as their interest is caught by goods on display. These two types of traffic are known as destination traffic and shopping traffic.
>
> Destination customers tend to move in a logical, thoughtout sequence. Shopping customers, taking a largely random approach, almost always turn to the

Figure 8–6.

The "4–3–2–1 Rule" in Estimating Sales Floor Values. *Source:* From Clifford M. Baumback, Kenneth Lawyer, and Pearce C. Kelley, *How to Organize and Operate a Small Business,* 5th ed. Copyright © 1973 by Prentice-Hall, Inc., Englewood Cliffs, N.J. Reprinted with permission of Prentice-Hall, Inc.

The rent contracted by lease is $2400. per year. Therefore 5000 square feet divided into $2400 = 48¢ per year. This is the average rent per square foot per year for the whole store.

Under the 4-3-2-1 rule, 40% of the total rent is assigned to the front 1/4 of the space; 30% of the total rent is assigned to the second 1/4 of the space; 20% of the total rent is assigned to the third 1/4 of the space, and 10% is assigned to the rear 1/4 of the space.

Typical rent or occupancy cost for a drug store is 5% of sales; so that $2400 = 5% of sales, and 1% = $480, and 100% = $48,000 total sales.

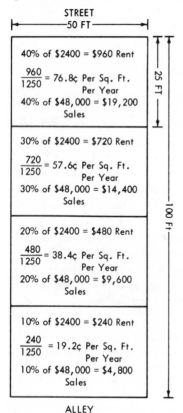

right after they enter your front door. Destination traffic generally will not drift to the right, because of the slower and unpredictable movements of the shoppers. Instead, these customers usually turn left upon entering a store. As a result, shopping traffic tends to circulate through a store in a counter-clockwise direction, while destination traffic moves clockwise. Recognition of this movement provides a key to the layout of goods not only near the door but also within the entire selling space.

Goods with low gross margins and high replacement rates should be located and put . . . to the left of the entrance. This location will afford destination customers immediate access to the staples they buy frequently. It will help them complete their purchases quickly. In contrast, the high gross margin items with low replacement rates should be arranged on the right. When this is done, these goods are seen by the bulk of the shopping traffic; as a result, sales of these items tend to increase.[8]

SUMMARY

Physical factors have a direct bearing on the patronage of a business. As a rule, people like nice surroundings. This applies to employees and customers alike. The remarkable thing is that desirable physical conditions can be had at no additional cost. The choice and use of the right color combination costs no more than buying the wrong color combination. Time taken to carefully plan the physical setting will pay profitable dividends.

The use of planning boards, models, and mockups has proven to be an economical means of effecting desired changes in plant, warehouse or store layouts. It is much easier to modify paper and glue than concrete and steel. "Spend a dime and make a dollar" is an apropos statement when it comes to physical factors.

---

[8]Leo V. Aspinwall, "Are Your Merchandise Lines Paying Their Rent?" *Small Marketers Aids Annual No. 3,* (Washington, D.C.: Small Business Administration, 1961), pp. 8-9.

9

Risk Management

"To be sure . . . insure!"

W. H. Day

Risks are an inseparable condition of running a business. It is imperative, therefore, that they be managed effectively in order to preserve profitable operation.

WHAT ARE THE RISKS?

In order to deal with risks effectively, it is necessary that they be identified. A periodic check of risks is advised as a means of keeping abreast of this important element of profitable management. Each business has a different spectrum of risks and, therefore, assessments should be according to the specific business involved. The small businessperson is confronted with all the risks that face an individual in modern life plus the numerous risks identified and discussed below.

Business Fraud

The small businessperson should be on guard against hoaxes or swindles such as pseudo-charity programs, fake office-repair schemes, misrepresented advertising deals, and fallacious offers. These risks may be avoided by being alert and wary of the suspect cases.

Employment Dishonesty

Various forms of theft are encountered, including the stealing of money, merchandise, tools, postage stamps, stationery, and similar items. Sometimes dishonesty involves embezzlement, forgery, raising checks, or other fraudulent practices. While no businessperson wants to admit employment of dishonest people, there are numerous cases reported annually. The risk must be recognized and dealt with.

Economic Conditions

The various stages of the business cycle describe the process of expansion and contraction within the economy. It would be wise for the small businessperson to utilize the period of expansion to build a strong capital reserve in preparation for periods of contraction, to which small businesses are particularly vulnerable. In periods of acute recession or depression, many small businesses fall.

Another risk associated with economic conditions is price fluctuations. The small businessperson would be advised to follow a careful policy adjusting purchases to inventory needs after careful consideration of the economic forecasts.

Bad-Debt Loss

Whenever a small business extends credit to customers it incurs the possibility of this risk. Recommendations for dealing with this particular problem are discussed in detail in the chapter on credit.

Shoplifting

The losses from this risk have increased in recent years to staggering proportions. It has been reported that such losses amount to 5 or 6 percent of sales revenue, which is about equal to the profit of a department store operation. This risk is uninsurable. However, various attempts have been made to control the risk by means of one-way mirrors, sensitized merchandise tags, and close-circuit television cameras. Some larger stores employ plainclothes detectives to monitor the problem.

Product or Process Obsolescence

The vast amount of research in the industrial sector is producing rapid technological change. This poses a risk for small businesses who fail to keep abreast of current developments and adjust their operations accordingly.

Loss of Key Employees

The success of every business is associated with the key personnel. Loss stems from unexpected death or from leaving the firm for other employment opportunities. It is possible to insure against the loss of key personnel from death. Where a partnership is involved, it is highly recommended that insurance be taken on the partners: in the event of an unexpected death, funds will be available to purchase the partner's share and avoid an untimely dissolution of the business. To meet the risk of losing employees to other businesses, it is recommended that selection and training of replacement personnel be undertaken. This will also facilitate the operation of the business when key personnel are absent.

Property Damage

The assets of a firm (the building, the inventory, etc.) are always subject to damages from fire, theft, floods, hurricanes, and riots. The vehicles owned by the business are also open to loss through theft or damage. Fortunately, these risks can be covered through a planned insurance program.

Public Liability Risks

These risks involve losses to third parties who hold the business responsible. This liability applies to the owners of apartment houses, wholesale establishments, and factories, as well as to retail stores. The risks include not only physical injuries, but also any damage to the property of third persons. The liability extends to the use of products sold by the firm. You're probably aware of cases reported in the newspaper where lawsuits have been filed for the harmful results from consuming canned foods or from faulty cosmetics, and injuries suffered on board airlines, railroads, or buses.

Should these matters go to litigation, the small businessperson may find himself at the mercy of the judge or jury and legal interpretations as to the negligence of his personnel. The need for insurance to cover public liability is apparent. The small-business person should also take steps to minimize losses through better management and good business housekeeping. Safety education programs can also be beneficial where employees are concerned. An ounce of prevention is worth a pound of cure.

LIABILITY TO EMPLOYEES
The health and safety of employees is a responsibility of employers. It is now a general requirement of employers to carry workmen's compensation insurance to provide the necessary protection to employees.

HOW TO DEAL WITH RISKS

Having identified some of the more generally recognized risks confronting small businesses, the various methods for dealing with risks will next be considered. Four basic methods are suggested: avoiding the risk, reducing the risk, assuming the risk, and shifting the risk.

Avoiding Risks

Small businesspersons should be alert to the opportunities to avoid risks by the following means:

SUBSTITUTION

Examine the possibility of replacing high-risk materials used in the processes of a business with materials which have a lesser risk factor. For example, some chemicals used in dry cleaning are more flammable and explosive than others, and the chemicals which are safer may obviate the difference in cost by providing a lower risk factor.

SCREENING

This process is best illustrated in the extension of credit. Not all businesses should extend credit. Those that do extend credit should screen the applicants carefully and eliminate the high-risk customers who may bring bad-debt losses.

ELIMINATION

Some situations provide a means whereby the risk can be eliminated as in the case of reducing personal injury to employees by means of safety equipment. It is the responsibility of the employer to inspect and insure that employees have safety equipment available and are using the equipment — eye goggles, safety shoes, safety clothing, etc.

Reducing Risks

Reducing risks is a matter of good management, and can be enhanced through safety training programs and frequent inspections. By reducing the amount of risks and incident losses, the firm can reduce its cost of its insurance.

Assuming Risks

In certain situations the business has no alternative but to assume the risks, because insurance is either unavailable or too costly. For example, for the firm dealing in fashion merchandise there is an inherent risk in buying merchandise months in advance of sale. The consequences of assuming this risk can be minimized by being cognizant of the customers' tastes and trends in the marketplace.

Shifting Risks

There are three means open to the small businessperson to shift the risk to others. They are insurance, subcontracting, and hedging.

INSURANCE

Purchasing insurance is the most common method of shifting risks. Insurance companies are willing to insure a business against a wide spectrum of risks, for the payment of specified premiums.

SUBCONTRACTING

When there is a reservation about the capability of a business performing certain functions of a particular project, the business may elect to engage a subcontractor who assumes this responsibility and the risks inherent.

HEDGING

Whereas hedging was initially confined to the trading of grains and other agricultural commodities, it has been expanded to include many other products in recent years. It is suggested that the businessperson determine if the commodities involved in the business are eligible for hedging practices. Hedging is really designed to protect the businessperson's normal trade profit from price fluctuations in the marketplace. While hedging may be thought to apply to large businesses only, it is an available and recommended practice for the small businessperson. Information assistance can be obtained through a local stock trading or brokerage firm.

INSURANCE

Select a Good Insurance Agent

A knowledgeable, licensed insurance agent or broker can offer valuable assistance in recommending the right insurance companies, discussing various kinds of insurance coverage, giving explanation of policy terms, calculating insurance costs, and comparing different company costs.

The insurance agent wants to sell insurance. To best assure the most appropriate insurance program for your company, you should be up on the subject of insurance. You need to be in a position to tell the agent what you want and then let him suggest the best way to obtain it.

To be more effective in matters pertaining to insurance, understanding insurance terminology will prove helpful.

Insurance Terminology

Indemnity. The term indemnity is derived from the principle of insurable interest. It means that if a loss occurs, the insured can only collect for the actual cash loss, rather than for the amount stated in the policy. Assume that you carried $20,000 of tornado insurance on a building worth $10,000, and that a total loss was incurred to the building. The actual cash that would be paid to you would be determined by applying an allowance for depreciation against a current replacement cost of the building. If your building was depreciated 50 percent of its original value, the building would only be worth 50 percent of the replacement cost. As the owner, you would receive $5,000.

Coinsurance. If you owned a $50,000 building insured against a fire loss for $25,000, would you collect in full for a $10,000 fire loss? The answer is negative. With coinsurance, the principle involves pooling the risks of many business organizations and paying those who actually incur losses. Obviously, the premiums must be adequate to provide an income sufficient to meet the losses as well as the operating expenses, and still provide a profit for the insurance companies.

Experience has shown that not all buildings are completely destroyed by fire. Therefore, to obviate the necessity of the client paying insurance on the total cost of a building only partially destroyed, a coinsurance clause is used to facilitate paying only a partial rate. In other words, the use of coinsurance enables the businessperson who is the owner of a building to share the potential loss with the insurance company by also insuring the premium cost.

Assuming that the owner of a building wanted to insure 60 percent of its market value, the savings on the annual insurance premium costs may be considered as an offset against the potential losses incurred. However, this does not mean that any losses incurred up to 60 percent of the building value would be paid in full by the insurance company. The building owner would be subject to the coinsurance clause of the policy. The common percentage of market value used in coinsurance is 80 percent. Therefore, if the building was insured at 60 percent of its value, and 80 percent was the coinsurance percentage, the building owner would recover 60 over 80 (60/80) times the loss incurred. If he had a $10,000 loss, he would recover $7,500. Thus coinsurance really means a shared risk.

A more detailed illustration of coinsurance will amplify this concept. The XYZ Company has a small building valued at $20,000. Under the coinsurance policy, it is insured at 80 percent of the market value, or $16,000. This amount is the face value of the owner's policy ($16,000). The liability of the insurance company will be for the full amount of the losses up to $16,000. Should there be a complete loss on the building, or $20,000 loss, the result would be the owner bearing a $4,000 loss and the insurance company paying $16,000 — the face amount of the policy as maximum liability.

A formula for computing insurance company liability under the coinsurance principle is given below:

$$\text{Insurance Company Liability} = \frac{\text{Face Value of Policy}}{\text{80\% of Property Value}} \times \frac{\text{Amount of Loss}}{\text{Incurred}}$$

Applying the formula, it can be seen that if the XYZ Company had insured the building for only $8,000 (less than 80% of the market value) and then incurred an $8,000 loss, the company could only collect $4,000 (8/16, or 1/2, times $8,000). This would be true even though the face value of the policy was $16,000. If the owner of the building desired more coverage, the face value of the policy could be increased.

Subrogation. Subrogation is a right that the insured gives the insurer to recover loss from third parties to the extent that the insurer indemnifies the insured for a loss. This is an important feature of property and liability insurance. To illustrate, assume somebody drives his car into a business building. The insurance company would pay damages of $5,000 to the business owner according to the building policy. If the owner has subrogation rights, the insurer could proceed against the car owner for his negligence. Assuming this action was successful, the insurer could recover the entire $5,000 from the car owner's insurance company.

Insurable Interest. This implies that the insured party must have an interest in the insured item at the time of loss. To be effective, the insured must stand a chance of loss of something that he possesses. To illustrate, suppose you owned a building and later sold it, but you did not change the insurance policy. Subsequently a fire occurred, but the insurer would not pay damages because of the change of ownership.

Misrepresentation. Should the insured misrepresent facts on the insurance application, and there is a subsequent loss, the insurer can refuse to pay for the loss suffered. However, the false statement must be material in order for the insurer to refuse payment for a loss. To illustrate, let us assume you obtained a policy from an insurer, and stated that you had no serious losses within the previous five-year period (when, in reality, you had two serious losses). A policy was issued, and there was another loss. Upon investigation by the insurer, a discovery was made of the previous losses. The insurer could refuse payment for your current loss on the basis that the misrepresentation was material, and the court would undoubtedly uphold the denial of payment.

Deductibles. Deductibles are usually expressed as a specified dollar amount or a percentage of loss which the insured pays in the case of a loss. A desirable feature of deductibles is that they discourage over-insurance. They permit the insured to bear part of the loss for a predetermined reduction in premiums. An alert insurance agent will use this advantage for selling automobile insurance. Assume the premium for $50 deductible collision insurance on the company delivery truck is $90 per year. The premium for $100 deductible might be only $50. By having the $100 deductible policy, $40 is saved, but the insured gives up $50 in collision coverage for each accident. In other words, if the $50 deductible collision is purchased instead of the $100 deductible, the added coverage is purchased at a high rate: $40 is being paid for $50 additional coverage.

Warrant. This is a statement made by an insured and incorporated in the written terms of an insurance policy. Whereas a misrepresentation is considered material, a warranty need not be material in order to void an insurance contract. The insurer can void a contract by virtue of the fact that a statement made by the insured is not carried out. To illustrate, should the insured make a statement that all doors and windows will be locked at the close of business each day, and this is not done, the policy can be voided by the insurer.[1]

---

[1]V. A. Grieco, *Management of Small Business* (Columbus, Ohio: Charles E. Merrill Pub. Co., 1975), pp. 127–29.

Types of Insurance

LIFE INSURANCE
By means of life insurance, protection can be provided for the business against the death of the entrepreneur or of key personnel in the firm. Serious loss can result when the services or the capital of a key individual are lost to the firm. If the firm pays the premium as a regular business expense, it would have at least a measure of protection against such losses. As noted earlier, the use of life insurance in the case of a partnership is highly advisable.

FIRE INSURANCE
The businessperson may elect to insure all or part of the potential loss of assets due to fire. Coverage may be obtained for both the building and its contents. Should the businessperson desire to expand the coverage, additional riders may be purchased with the fire insurance policy to provide coverage against explosion, windstorm, hail, riot, aircraft, vehicle-caused damage, and smoke damage.

LIABILITY INSURANCE
Liability to the owners of small business firms may arise from 1) their actions, 2) actions of employees during employment, or 3) conditions within the business.

It is important to carry adequate liability insurance, because the damages awarded to individuals injured on company premises often reach large sums. For example, if a customer was injured through conditions on the premises due to the negligence of the store, the damages could reach upwards of $100,000. Few small businesses could sustain this type of loss. In determining the amount of liability insurance coverage, bear in mind that a judgement could be obtained against your business by a court. If the liability insurance is not adequate to cover the judgement, the difference must be paid by the business.

MARINE INSURANCE
This type of insurance may be obtained to protect goods during shipment. There are two types. One applies to ocean marine shipments and the other applies to inland shipments by rail or motor freight. In one instance,

marine insurance may involve a commercial floater which insures business property against various hazards wherever located.

FIDELITY AND SURETY BONDS

To protect against dishonesty of employees who are handling company funds and/or to insure the fulfillment of contractual obligations entered into, use fidelity and surety companies that provide bonds for these purposes. The premiums are well worth the protection provided in both instances.

AUTOMOBILE INSURANCE

This constitutes another form of property and liability insurance. There are several types of insurance available for covering vehicles: collision, theft, fire, damages from malicious mischief, and glass breakage. The automobile liability coverage includes other people's property, other automobiles, persons in other vehicles, and persons in the insured automobile.

Automobile insurance involving property damage usually has a deductible clause, wherein the owner pays the amount specified as deductible and the insurance company pays all amounts above that. For example, in the case of a $50 deductible policy, the owner would pay the first $50 and the insurance would pay damages above the $50 deductible. It is well to compare the difference in premium rates with the different deductible amounts, to ascertain the best insurance for the least cost.

CREDIT AND TITLE INSURANCE

Credit insurance is usually limited to non-financial firms, such as manufacturers and wholesalers who sell to other businesses. Credit insurance applies primarily to trade credit.

Title insurance is utilized in connection with real estate transactions: the buyer insures the acquisition of a clear title.

BUSINESS INTERRUPTION INSURANCE

This can be provided to protect a business in case it is interrupted by power or water failure, windstorm, tornado, flood, fire, or other disasters. This insurance normally covers loss of profits as well as fixed expenses including interest payments, taxes due, utility charges, salaries to key employees, and depreciation. The purpose is to provide money to hasten the reopening of the business.

The payments by the insurance company are made if the following conditions prevail:

1. A business must be a going concern at the time of loss.
2. The damage must occur when the policy is in force.
3. The business shutdown must occur because of the loss.
4. The property loss must occur from an insured hazard.
5. The business must have been profitable enough to be able to pay all fixed expense charges.
6. The policy must contain a coinsurance clause ranging from 60 to 90 percent of insurable value of the business.

WORKMEN'S COMPENSATION AND EMPLOYER'S LIABILITY INSURANCE

Without this insurance, the owner-manager will be liable under both common law and worker's compensation laws to indemnify employees of any losses incurred. It is possible, by maintaining a good accident record below the average, to obtain a lower premium cost for this type of insurance. This may provide an incentive for the businessperson and employees to minimize the occurrence of accidents in the business.

Insurance Coverage

While there are many types of insurance, those deemed essential for the business are fire insurance, automobile insurance, workmen's compensation insurance, and liability insurance. Those insurance types which are considered desirable include group life and health insurances and business interruption insurance.

The objective with insurance is to be adequately covered, avoiding both over-insurance and under-insurance. When businesspeople become knowledgeable about insurance matters they can more effectively deal with insurance companies in obtaining the necessary coverage at minimum cost. The policy issued by an insurance company should be clearly understood. It contains these three important elements: 1) the meaning of the terms essential to understanding the insurance policy, 2) the legal requirements of the insurance contract, and 3) the rights of the insured and the obligations of other parties.

As a businessperson proceeds to acquire insurance coverage, the following logical steps will be helpful:

1. Endeavor to cover the largest possible loss exposure first. Relate this to the costs of premium payments which are available for protection. Consider adequate property evaluations, as well as high liability costs because of expensive court awards.
2. Utilize deductible where applicable.
3. If your loss experience record is low, negotiate for lower premiums with the insurance company.
4. Shop around for comparable insurance rates.
5. Risk exposures change over time and should be constantly reviewed in terms of policy coverage.
6. As a standard procedure, review insurance coverage annually for possible changes that have transpired within the company.
7. As you prepare to negotiate, take various bids from different insurance companies. In no case accept an insurance package from an insurer simply because it was submitted with a bill.[2]

Because the cost of insurance may be significant to the small business, it is suggested that various ways be adopted to minimize insurance costs. A reduction in insurance may be accomplished by leasing some of the assets required in the business, instead of purchasing them. Another suggestion is that you negotiate with suppliers for shipments to customers to be made on a drop ship basis, which reduces insurance requirements.

THE FAIR PLAN

"FAIR" is an acronym for Fair Access to Insurance Requirements. Under this plan, the insurance companies operating in a particular state enter into a pooling arrangement whereby they share risks in high-risk areas and agree to pay their proportionate share toward the full sum of an approved claim. FAIR plans have been introduced in twenty-six states and in Puerto Rico and the District of Columbia. The plan works as follows:

A businessperson (or homeowner) unable to get property insurance in ordinary channels obtains an application from the FAIR plan headquarters or from an insurance agent, broker, or company. He fills out the form and returns it. An inspection of his property is made. If the property meets minimum insurance requirements, a policy is issued upon payment of a premium.

Even if certain dangerous conditions do exist, the property may be declared eligible for coverage — but at an increased rate until these hazards are eliminated. If the property is found to be uninsurable because of

---

[2]*Ibid.*, p. 135.

excessive hazards, the inspector points out these deficiencies, and the owner may have them repaired and request another inspection. The principal deficiencies are faulty wiring, faulty heating units, generally dilapidated conditions that make property subject to trespass by derelicts, and poor housekeeping—such as accumulations of rubbish. Protection offered through FAIR plans include fire and extended coverage—riots, civil disorders, and other perils.

In only one of the FAIR plan states, however, does the FAIR plan include protection against crime losses—one of the most important problems of small businesses located in deteriorated urban core areas. To fill this void, the Federal Crime Insurance Program was launched by the U.S. Department of Housing and the Urban Development on August 1, 1971.

FEDERAL CRIME INSURANCE PROGRAM

In some urban core areas, privately underwritten crime insurance is totally unavailable, or available only at prohibitive premium rates. As long as crime and civil disorder continue to flourish in these areas, the responsibility for providing insurance coverage against these hazards would seem to rest with the government. The private-insurance sector does not have the resources to provide protection against hazards stemming from social revolution—at prices that homeowners and businesspeople can afford to pay. That the federal government was ready and willing to assume this responsibility was evidenced by the recent enactment in Congress of an amendment to Title XII of the National Housing Act. Under the provisions of this amendment, the Department of Housing and Urban Development (HUD) is directed to review the types of crime insurance available in each of the states, either through the normal insurance market or through a state FAIR plan. Crime insurance as defined in the amendment means insurance against burglary and robbery, and includes broad-form business and personal theft insurance, but not automobile insurance.

In any state where such instance was not provided at "affordable" rates by August 1, 1971, HUD was authorized to make it available through the facilities of the federal government. The conditions of such insurance, including the setting of rates and determination of insurability, are at the discretion of HUD and may vary from state to state or from locality to locality within a state. HUD is also empowered to utilize insurance companies as fiscal agents—to market the coverage and service the insured business (or homeowner), thus making available to this program the expertise and experience of the private carriers. By 1972, Federal Crime

Insurance was available in the urban core areas of nine states and the District of Columbia, and three insurance companies were writing policies under this program. All licensed agents in each of these states are eligible to take applications for insurance.

It is interesting to note that one of the conditions required for this insurance is that the businessperson install adequate safeguards and security measures.[3]

RULES OF RISK MANAGEMENT

Professors Robert L. Mehr and Bob A. Hedges have developed the following rules of risk management which will be helpful in developing a satisfactory program of risk management for your business.[4]

1. *Don't risk more than you can afford to lose.* No firm can possibly eliminate or transfer all of the risk which it faces; it obviously must assume some of the risks. The most important factor in determining whether a particular risk should be transferred (to an insurance company) or assumed (by the firm) is the maximum potential loss which might result from the risk; if the loss would be likely to force the firm into bankruptcy, or cause it serious financial impairment, then the risks should not be assumed.

2. *Don't risk a lot for a little.* There should be a reasonable relationship between the cost of transferring the risk (the cost of insurance) and the value that accrues to the insured firm. For example, the additional premiums required to eliminate or reduce "deductibles" in many types of insurance is quite high in relation to the added protection. This rule also reinforces the first rule: The firm that neglects to purchse insurance against severe losses is risking a lot (a possible loss) for little (the premiums paid).

3. *Consider the odds.* Contrary to popular opinion, a high probability that a loss will occur does not indicate that the risk should be insured. In fact, the contrary is true: the greater the probability of occurrence, the less appropriate is the purchase of insurance for dealing with the risk. In the first place, losses that occur with relative frequency are *predictable* and

---

[3]Clifford M. Baumback, et al., *How to Organize and Operate a Small Business* (Englewood Cliffs, N.J.: Prentice-Hall, Inc., 1973), pp. 282-83.

[4]Robert I. Mehr and Bob A. Hedges, *Risk Management in the Business Enterprise* (Homewood, Ill.: Richard D. Irwin, Inc., 1963c.), pp. 16-19. Adapted by permission of the publisher. *See also* Emmett J. Vaughan, "A Mini-Course in Risk Management, Part I," *Underwriters Review* (January 1971), pp. 9 and 14.

are typically *small* losses that can be assumed by the business without too much financial difficulty; they are often budgeted as "normal" costs of doing business and thus are included in the prices paid by customers. Some common examples are shoplifting and bad-debt losses. Secondly, where the probability of loss is high a more effective method of managing or controlling the risk is to *reduce* it by adopting appropriate precautionary measures.

As a final note, the reader is reminded of the overriding importance of the first rule of risk management, as discussed above: *Do not risk more than you can afford to lose.* Clearly, the probability of fire, theft, or casualty loss is less important than the possible size of a loss should the casualty occur.

To summarize planning for risk management, the following steps are suggested: 1) recognize major risks, 2) develop a program of safety, 3) select key personnel and delegate specific responsibilities and authority, 4) periodically review the insurance program carefully, and 5) adapt your insurance program to changing business conditions.

SUMMARY

Risk is an inevitable fact of doing business. When risk is not properly handled the projected profits will be adversely affected, and sometimes the business becomes a casualty. Hence, the recognition of the risks and proper handling of them is of paramount importance. Because of the extensive nature of risks in business and the various means of insuring them, the selection of competent insurance counsel is a decision with "profit" connotations.

Carefully identify all of the known risks with which you are confronted. Consider the alternatives for dealing with each risk. Develop your plan and put it into action. As conditions change, remember to modify or amend the "risk plans."

Avoid *negligence* as a plague. Remember "risks" are a threat to managing a small business profitably.

10

Personal Parameters

*"What e'er thou art
act well thy part."*

Inscribed on a stone arch in Scotland

Your business profit depends on who? YOU! Regardless of the factors affecting profit, it is you who must make the decisions. How well you make those decisions relates directly to your personal capabilities.

PERSONAL FACTORS

Whether directly or indirectly, you are largely responsible for making the business profitable. While it is possible to make a longer list of desired personal ingredients, seven strategic qualifications will be considered here: Peopleability, Createability, Communicability, Timeability, Manageability, Problemability, and Decisionability.

Peopleability

Someone said management is directing people, not directing things. Put in other words, success is people. Your profits will be affected by your ability to successfully handle your personnel. Typically, there are two ways of using people. One is to keep them in the dark so they cannot learn your job. The other is to train them well so you can delegate more responsibility. The failure of a company to grow is often linked to a lack of developed personnel. To be effective, your people must be informed of your plans and the progress of these plans, to enable them to make a maximum contribution. Teach them the habit of giving you frequent progress reports. Give them exercise in thinking for themselves. Teach them to *save your time*. Place responsibility gradually, and build feelings of responsibility. Give complete responsibility for certain parts of the work. Make them accountable for responsibilities, and evaluate them frequently. Encourage the assignment of new responsibilities as fast as they are able to take them on. Teach them to confess mistakes promptly and to accept criticism constructively. A good rule: praise in public, criticize in private.

HOW TO MAKE CRITICISM WORK FOR YOU

In your relations with people, one of the key factors is how matters of criticism are handled. Make criticism work for you. Choose the right time and place, and make clear that your interest is in the employee, in his succeeding on the job, and in his becoming more valuable to the firm and to himself.

Explain the importance of the error. Criticize the act rather than the person. Lay the error on the line: vagueness cannot produce improvement. Be specific about the remedy. Even better, have your employee be specific about what he would suggest in retrospect as a correct way to handle the situation. Remember that the only people who avoid mistakes are those who do nothing at all. Be ready to listen. Give the employee the opportunity to speak and ask questions. Make his job meaningful, and show him his importance to the organization and how his success adds to the overall operation. Follow up to be sure the agreed action actually took place and that your employee learned from experience. Remember, too, that you can frequently accomplish more by indirection than by frontal assault. Your employees can be a divine *forta* in multiplying profits.

Createability

Have you ever thought of yourself as a creative person? How creative are you? Createability relates to profitability. You can become a more creative thinker. You can develop more ideas—profitable ideas. Here are some tips to practice to increase your createability. Listed below are suggestions compiled by the U.S. Army Management School, Fort Belvoir, Virginia, in its *Workbook for Military Creative Problem Solving:*

1. *Be optimistic in your approach.* Remember that for most things, somehow, somewhere, there is a better way.
2. *Consider* yourself a thinker as well as a learner and a doer—an idea man or woman as well as a man or woman of action.
3. *Develop a honeybee mind.* Gather your ideas everywhere. Don't be afraid to associate ideas fully. Let your mind buzz freely from one idea or source to another. Be "open to experience" and stimuli of all sorts—both from within and in the world around you.
4. *Sharpen your nose for problems.* Be curious about things that seem wrong or inadequate. Listen to the complaints of others. Jot down your own dissatisfactions with things and situations. Develop an attitude of constructive discontent—welcome problems as opportunities not only to accomplish something but to sharpen your creative abilities.
5. *Learn to play with ideas.* At times you must "regress"—back off from the problem and try to think about it with the naivete and freshness of a child.
6. *Learn to recognize the inhibiting factors of blocks to the free play of the imagination*—whether they be perceptive, cultural, emotional or otherwise.
7. *Look for the "elegant" answer.* Don't be satisfied with just any solution to a problem.
8. *Be alert for the welcome "hunches."* When you get them, do something about them.
9. *Be courageous and independent* in your thinking and persistent in the face of frustration and difficulty—but employ an alternating type of persistence so as to invite incubation and insight.
10. *Continue to acquire a growing body of knowledge* about your field—but don't hesitate to challenge "sacred cows"—long-standing but possibly outmoded or erroneous concepts.
11. *Be alert for the unexpected.* Serendipity or the "happy discovery" happens only when you are actually seeking something. As Pasteur said, "Inspiration is the impact of a fact on a prepared mind."
12. *Organize your approach.* Find or devise a methodology that fits your problem and your personality. Break the process up into small step-by-step pieces ("divide and conquer"). If you don't do it in an organized way, you probably won't do it at all.

13. *State your problem carefully.* Don't let the statement suggest the answer. For instance, if you ask a man to think up a new way to toast bread, you've already suggested a toaster. What you really want is a new way to dehydrate and brown the surface of the bread. State it this way, and you open up new idea opportunities.

14. *Schedule practice sessions* with yourself, that is, conduct your own private brainstorming sessions each day. Come up with ideas—good, bad, and mediocre. Never mind the duds. Accept all ideas from yourself; don't reject any. Write them down. Unless you drill your mind regularly to produce a bag full of ideas, you haven't really decided to be creative.

15. *Carry your idea trap around.* A pad and pencil, that is. Keep them with you all the time. Why? Because ideas are elusive. They will drift out of your grasp as readily as they drift in. Better trap them on paper—in black and white.

16. *Incubate.* Relax your mind. After a hard day's work, let it wander. (Daydream while you walk home from work. Try a hot bath or shower, restful music.) After a good night's sleep, get up an hour early, take a long walk, meditate. Take an airplane ride, play golf, or go fishing. Use the two-day formula: set your problem aside for a day, then hit it hard after a day's rest.

17. *Use idea banks and idea museums.* Ideas don't fall out of the blue. Keep a dream file of clippings, notes from your idea trap, pamphlets, etc., even if you can't work on them right now. Idea museum? This is your reference library. Keep scanning it for ideas. Store them up to solve future as well as present problems.

18. *Be enthusiastic, confident.* Your willpower controls your imagination and is affected by your emotions. So build faith in yourself by scoring successes on little problems before you tackle big ones.

19. *Find the right time of day*—the time of day when you're most creative. You know the time when you're full of drive. That's the time to build up a stockpile of ideas. The time for "red light" thinking comes when your mind isn't running creatively.

20. *Set a quota; and a deadline, too.* Force yourself to do a little better each time. Strive for a set number of workable solutions to every problem. A deadline keeps you from putting things off from day to day.

21. *Don't kid yourself with vague ideas.* Force yourself to reduce them to specific propositions, thus firming up the problems your mind must solve.

Communicability

As you increase your createability new ideas will be forthcoming to enhance the profits of your business. One of the essentials to successfully implementing new ideas is communication. To be fully communicative requires expertise in listening, reading, speaking, and writing. Our purpose here is to highlight the important aspects of these subjects and demonstrate their relevance to profitable business operations. Do you realize that an average person is exposed to 2,000 messages in each twenty-four hour period? But the surprising thing is that the average person only catches about 500. Furthermore, 70 percent of our conscious day is spent in various forms of communication.

LISTENING

If your listening skill is average, 75 percent of the messages you send are not effectively received. How many of these messages are vital to your business profits? By increasing your listening ability 50 percent or even 75 percent, you should be a more effective operator — a more profitable operator. To help you improve your listening ability, consider these ten guides developed by Ralph Nichols:[1]

1. Find areas of interest.
2. Judge content, not delivery.
3. Hold your fire — over-stimulation is almost as bad as under-stimulation, with the two together constituting the twin evils of inefficient listening.
4. Listen for ideas. Focus on central ideas and try to recognize the characteristic language in which these ideas are usually stated.
5. Be flexible. Note-taking may help or it may be distracting.
6. Work at listening, for listening is hard work!
7. Resist distractions.
8. Exercise your mind.
9. Keep your mind open.
10. Capitalize on thought speed.

One of the ways you can tap ideas from customers, employees, competitors, and others is by sympathetic listening in the day-to-day informal contacts. How much is a profitable idea worth? Is it worth the time to listen?

READING

Our schools teach reading through the eighth grade. The average eighth grader reads fewer than 300 words per minute with less than 70 percent comprehension. If you read better than that, chances are the further gains

[1]Ralph G. Nichols and Leonard A. Stevens, *Are You Listening?* (New York: McGraw-Hill Book Co., 1957).

can be attributed to individual effort. It is possible to increase reading ability to 1,200 words or even 2,500 words per minute through improvement programs such as Evelyn Wood's Reading Dynamics. Improved reading would enable you to read more in the same time or would give you more time to spend on other profit-making activities. Successful businesspeople are well informed, and much of their information was obtained by reading.

SPEAKING

Because of the limited availability of courses in speaking, you probably have not had any special training in this subject. Unless you attended an exceptional high school and participated in the annual play or possibly with the debate team, your experience is limited. There is the possibility you have invested a couple of hundred dollars plus a few nights a week and derived some benefits from one of the Dale Carnegie, or similar, courses. Regardless of your past training, the importance of being able to speak effectively makes it necessary that you "up" your expertise in speaking.

By becoming a good speaker—and you can—you will be a better, more complete executive. As you learn to think and talk on your feet— and you can—you will do a more constructive organizing and selling job for yourself and for your firm. You will be more effective in negotiations and secure more profits. In addition, you may avail yourself of the frequent calls to give informal talks and formal addresses. If you can accept these invitations with confidence, you can bring your firm considerable credit, favorable publicity, and material benefit.

The average speaker's task is almost identical to that of a good salesman: he must attract his audience, interest them, convince them, and then sell them. Your speaking ability could add to the profit of your business.

WRITING

Frances Bacon said that "Reading maketh a full man, but writing maketh an exact man." A businessman in this modern world must be capable in the art of written communication. Whether the medium is an interoffice memo or an important letter to a customer or supplier, expertise in the use of language is an essential asset. There are a variety of courses offered in evening schools to help you improve your writing ability. Good communications will contribute to increasing your profit.

Timeability

Have you ever wondered why some people accomplish more than others do? The answer is, they make better use of their time; they plan to accomplish more. They develop timeability. You cannot delay the clock or hasten it. You cannot buy time or give it away. But you can manage your activities so that time works for you. Time is money. Effective use of time means more time for increasing profits.

> *Lost, yesterday, somewhere between sunrise and sunset,*
> *Two golden hours, each set with sixty diamond minutes,*
> *No reward is offered, for they are gone forever.*
>
> Horace Mann, *Aphorism*

Perhaps a succinct way to focus on considerations of timeability is to present two summaries prepared by twenty-five heads of Christian organizations who met in Chicago at a management seminar. The first summary listed the greatest time robbers (not listed in order of importance):[2]

Misplaced items
Visitors
Unanticipated interruptions
Commuting
Long letters
Waiting for people
Failure to delegate
Mediocre personnel (instructions required)
Lack of preparation (conferences, etc.)
Correspondence delays (shuffling papers)
Reading material not relevant to job
Unnecessary correspondence (outgoing)
Telephone interruptions
Poor organization
Coffee breaks
Procrastination
Routine details

---

[2]From *Managing Your Time* by Ted W. Engstrom and Alec MacKenzie. Copyright © 1967 by Zondervan Publishing House. Used by permission.

In contrast, the second summary prepared by the group listed *the greatest timesavers:*[3]

> The Committee of Two — avoid involving any unnecessary persons in the decision-making process.
>
> Correspondence — fast answers. Scribble response on letter or memo. Xerox copy for your file, and return original.
>
> Correspondence — handle only once — can't put it back in the pile! Answer it or get it where it can be answered.
>
> Correspondence follow-up — if you must wait for information before answering, mark for F/U file (i.e., one week). Secretary pulls out in one week and returns to you with information necessary for answer.
>
> Insure understanding when delegating — extra time invested to insure complete understanding pays big dividends in time saved ultimately!
>
> Appointments by secretary — time taken to develop good system of handling appointments pays off.
>
> Delegate reading — why not? Benefits others besides yourself. Also gives you picture of other talents of your team, while enormously broadening your coverage of important materials.
>
> Conference phone call with pre-arranged agenda — can accomplish amazing results at a fraction of cost in time and travel money. From three to perhaps six persons in as many cities on the same hookup.
>
> Have secretary answer correspondence — aim to delegate as much of the correspondence as she can handle well. One organization aims for seventy-five percent to eighty percent of all correspondence by secretaries, who sign the boss's name and present complete file to him with letter for signature.
>
> Shorter memos and letters — conscious effort here can bring amazing results.
>
> Wastebasketry — master the "quick toss" technique!
>
> Form letters — where personal touch is not essential.
>
> Planning and organizing time — a look ahead may be worth two behind!
>
> A good secretary — worth her weight in gold, excellent seminars offered for executive secretaries.
>
> Management training — careful selection of an occasional seminar provides needed bread . . . objective view . . . solutions others have found to same problems . . . current thinking in profession of management.
>
> Trained staff — all of the foregoing applies to staff . . . set example . . . expect them to follow (let them know your expectations) . . . follow-up.

As John J. Corson puts it, success is in many (maybe most) cases a direct result of the way time is used. Successful people have learned how

---

[3]*Ibid.*

to make time. Others can learn. He suggests six rules for getting the most out of the working day, whether it be seven hours or fourteen hours.[4]

First, decide what you want from your time. Whatever your decision in using time, you still need to get the most out of your working hours.

Second, plan your time. Victor Hugo wrote: "When the disposal of time is surrendered to the chance of incidents, chaos will reign." Unfortunately, many businessmen allow their day to operate at the pace of chance incidents. Without a plan for the day, you take what the day gives you. The consequence of failing to discipline oneself in the use of time and by failing to accomplish what is required is time wasted on matters that do not contribute to desired ends.

The best-spent time is that used to plan the use of time! The statement, "When you fail to plan you plan to fail" is most relevant with regard to the effective utilization of time.

Third, put time where it counts. This point is aptly described by the story of the farmer who told his wife he would plow the "south forty." He started early to oil the tractor. He needed more oil so he went to the shop to get it. On the way he noticed the pigs weren't fed. He went to the corn crib, where he found some sacks. That reminded him that the potatoes were sprouting. He started for the potato pit. As he passed the woodpile, he remembered his wife wanted wood in the house. As he picked up a few sticks an ailing chicken passed. He dropped the wood and reached for the chicken. When evening arrived, he still had not gotten the tractor to the field — and so time goes. Do you find yourself having difficulties like the farmer getting to the "south forty"?

Fourth, delegate well. A businessman with more than eight people reporting directly to him loses time by seeing people whose activities should be supervised by subordinates. Another way a businessman loses time is in long conferences with his staff trying to reach decisions instead of forcing his aides to accept their responsibilities.

For example, Benjamin Fairless, former chairman of U.S. Steel, was quoted as saying, "I pick out people whom I can trust to do things right and to whom I can delegate authority." Make it clear to your staff that you want them to spend time on their problems to be sure the problem is clearly defined and a solution has been thought out before bringing the matter to you. Use delegation as one means of making the time you need.

Fifth, concentrate intently. You can avoid having to reconsider problems by concentrating your efforts intently and allowing sufficient time to

---

[4]John J. Corson, "Make the Time You Need," *Nation's Business*, no. 44, 90-3 (October 1956).

resolve the problem. In writing on this subject, John Corson described a sales manager coming to a vice-president's office to report criticisms in handling new trainees. The two men agreed that "something must be done." Ten minutes were consumed as the two men exchanged opinions on sales training. They separated with a vague feeling of agreement but with no specific understanding as to who was to do what. They dismissed the problem, only to have to consider it again and again until they finally put a sufficient amount of concentrated executive brain power on it to hammer out a program, a schedule, and a budget. You can save a bundle of minutes by disposing of problems through concentrated effort.

Sixth, respect time. It is reported that on the death of Douglas Southall Freeman — long-time editor of the Richmond *News Leader*, radio commentator, lecturer, director of a foundation and three corporations, and author of eleven volumes of distinguished biography — *The New York Times* commented that the genuis of the man lay in almost inhuman self-discipline. A sign over the clock that faced the visitor who came to his office read: "Time alone is irreplaceable; don't waste it." The genius of Mr. Freeman's accomplishment was that his conscience would not allow him to waste time.

Manageability

Have you seriously considered your capabilities in managerial functions — planning, organizing, and controlling?

PLANNING

Do you know how to plan for profits? What is your plan? Do you know how to implement your plan?

Planning appears easy, and much conversation is made about the subject. But Henry Ford is reported to have said that planning is the most difficult work in all the world, and that is why so few people engage in it. How much time do you spend in planning your operations? How much time do you spend planning for profit?

You will find detailed information in other chapters on the vital aspects of planning for increased profit.

ORGANIZING

A well-known management consultant, R. C. Davis, stumped a class in management with the question, "Why do small businesses remain small?" The typical answers were: insufficient capital, lack of specialization, noncompetitive, etc. But R. C. Davis continued to nod his head in negative reply. The class exhausted their ideas and still failed to produce the answer to the question. Finally, Davis supplied the answer: small businesses remain small because they are limited to what one man can do in twenty-four hours. He made his point, not to be forgotten soon by the members of his class. The inability to organize and delegate will mitigate the growth of profit.

A positive example of the foregoing is J. C. Penney. He opened his first store in Kemmerer, Wyoming. Instead of stopping with the organization of the original store, he hired a manager to run it and started a second store. In this way he organized and delegated continually, multiplying profits along the way, becoming one of the largest merchandizing industries. A simple formula for organizing can be written with three words.

$$\text{ORGANIZING} = \frac{\text{WORK}}{\text{PEOPLE}}$$

Yes, organizing is simply dividing work by people. How well have you organized the work in your business? When starting a business it may be necessary for one person to do a variety of tasks; but as growth evolves, efficiency would require reassignment and the use of the principle of specialization. Do you make full use of temporary employees during seasonal peaks in business? What about part-time help as a way to delegate responsibility at a minimal cost? For example, find a part-time accountant, a part-time window trimmer, even part-time sales help. Does your business have organizational balance, organizational stability, and organizational flexibility?

Someone had a sign on his desk which read, "Are you helping us seek a solution or are you part of the problem?" The sign certainly raises a vital question. Have you so organized and delegated your business so you spend your time maximizing profits, or are you bogged down with a multiplicity of tasks which preclude your efficient performance? Are you using "delegation" or are you a one-man band?

Don't Be a One-Man Band

DON'T

    —do jobs your employees are paid to do. It isn't fair to them, yourself, or the company.

—save time by doing the work rather than explaining how to do it. The few minutes spent explaining a job to an employee will pay off in hours saved later when he does it properly.

—keep all the knowledge to yourself in fear someone below you will pass you up when he learns your job. Keep learning yourself and keep teaching your workers.

—be a "hustling Harry." Plan your day and the day of your employees. Set time schedules to get jobs done and avoid making every project a super-rush priority.

—try to direct and play the instruments, too. You're the leader and your employees are the music makers in your band.

DO

—give employees authority when you give responsibility. Don't keep hovering over them waiting to catch them in an error or doing the job improperly.

—be part of the team and set the example for team players rather than "one-man bands."[5]

Do you really know how to organize resources to make a profit? Read on. There are more answers in the subsequent chapters.

CONTROLLING

Before you can have control, you need to know what you are controlling. The purpose of control is to insure the accomplishment of the objective. In this book the objective is more profits; therefore, to have control one must first set the profit objective and schedule the time frame for accomplishment. The parameters involved, such as budgeted expenditures for production and marketing, must be stipulated in the operation plan so that the basis for control is established. It is simply a matter of plotting results against the projected performance and making the necessary adjustments which provide control. The control process necessitates the proper utilization of planning and organization.

It is the failure to provide adequate control which so frequently explains why a business is not more profitable. Without proper controls, a plan to make a profit fails to be implemented effectively.

Make full use of forecasting, budgeting, reports, control charts, analysis, and evaluation to maximize profits in your business. These matters need not be complicated, and the "how to do" explanations are provided in subsequent chapters.

---

[5]"The One-Man Show," *Bulletin for Supervisors,* Dartnell Corporation.

Problemability

To be a good problem solver, you need to know how to recognize and define problems. All too frequently, businessmen waste their time on the symptoms of the problem instead of coming to grips with the problem itself. The profitability of your business will correlate well with your problem-solving ability.[6]

IDENTIFY THE PROBLEM

A problem is an obstacle, an impediment to be overcome. It precludes the accomplishment of objectives and goals. Someone said the difference between getting somewhere and nowhere is the ability to make a start. The starting place in problem solving is the definition of the problem. The executive who tries to solve problems by depending on abstract reasoning, experience, general information, memory, or superficial survey of the problem situation is headed for ultimate disaster.

Kipling said, "I have six faithful serving men; they taught me all I know, their names are: What, Where, and When, and How, and Why, and Who . . ." Use these six when you try to fix the problem; and when you can write a clear statement of the problem itself, you are halfway to a solution.

Difficulty arises in distinguishing between a bad result and the basic problem. As in the case of sickness, symptoms are more apparent than the disease. The rather common headache is the symptom to many related diseases. For example, a headache can be symptomatic of eye strain, sinusitis, hayfever, common cold, high blood pressure, or a brain tumor. Obviously, to treat the symptom with aspirin will not necessarily cure the disease.

Some years ago a colleague of mine admitted his only son, age sixteen, to a hospital. The doctor diagnosed the headache as symptomatic of a chronic allergy. While being treated for an allergy, the boy passed away from the consequences of a brain tumor at the base of his brain. Had the problem been defined, the proper solution could have been administered to save his life.

The proverbial problem alleged by most small businessmen is "declining sales volume." However, declining sales is symptomatic of the problem which could be caused by a number of conditions, such as poor product,

---

[6]T. F. Staton, "How to Simplify a Problem," *Nation's Business* (June 1957), p. 721.

improper pricing, inadequate promotion, insufficient selling effort, and others. As in the case of medicine, the symptoms in business are more apparent than the disease. The important thing is to narrow down and get below the surface, analyzing from the general to the particular and from the obvious effect to the not-so-obvious cause.

GATHER DATA

Collect all the information that might have a bearing on the problem. Assume nothing where it is reasonably possible to obtain facts and figures. The amount of data gathered depends on the nature of the problem and the amount of time. Rarely does a man make a mistake because he knows too much; therefore, do not shortcut the information gathering phase. Also, avoid stacking the evidence by confining the search to data and facts that tend to support any preconceived ideas. To do so is to camouflage the fact that you have already jumped to a conclusion.

Next, organize the facts into usable form. For example, plot the cost-per-unit figures on a graph, which will be more meaningful than a long column of numbers. A good sales map will convey more at a glance than will an hour of reading reports.

Evaluate each item of information. Is it absolutely reliable, probably reliable, or not to be trusted too far? Is this an established fact, an expert opinion, or just an opinion? One of the best ways to gather reliable data is to get out of the office and go look for yourself. Ask the man who is running the machine or the salesman making the rounds.

LIST POSSIBLE SOLUTIONS

This is the creative thinking phase of the problem-solving process. It is a good place to utilize whatever group dynamic techniques you may have developed for joint attacks on problems by members of your company. Keep an open mind—let imagination roam freely over the facts collected. As you proceed, jot down every solution that seems possible to you or anyone else working on the problem. Resist the temptation to evaluate the proposals as you go along. Rather, list plausible and seemingly absurd ideas as well, remembering that the more possibilities you list during this phase the less risk you will run of settling for a merely workable, rather than the best, solution. Continue studying the data as long as there seems any possibility of deriving additional ideas, solutions, explanations, or patterns from it. Try working on the problem awhile, and then stop and do other things. Let it jell in your subconscious mind. Later, return with a fresh insight and continue your efforts.

TEST POSSIBLE SOLUTIONS

Evaluate the possible solutions. Be objective. Test each solution separately by using a common yardstick. It will be necessary to develop some criteria for the test. Perhaps criteria are best raised as questions which you ask of each possible solution. It has been suggested that they may be drawn from three general categories:[7]

1. *Suitability.* Will this solution do the job? Will it remedy the problem situation completely, or partially? Is it a permanent or stop-gap solution?
2. *Feasibility.* Will this plan work in actual practice? Can we afford this approach? How much will it cost?
3. *Acceptability.* Will the company president (or board, or union, or customers) go along with the changes required by this plan? Are you trying to drive a tack with a sledge hammer?

Rank the criteria as you formulate it on the basis of relative importance. For example, is this test one that a possible solution absolutely must pass, or is it merely something that would be nice to accomplish?

You may proceed by rating all possible solutions on the same chart, listing the solutions down the left side of the chart and the criteria across the top. It is possible to have different grading methods—alphabetical, such as A through F, or numerical, such as 0 through 100—as possible scales for rating the various criteria.

SELECT THE BEST SOLUTION

Now you must make a decision. Sometimes one clearly superior solution will stand out; but this is not often the case. Sometimes the best solution is a combination of two or more of the better solutions tested. Your aim should be to arrive at the best solution, not just a workable one.

PUT THE SOLUTION INTO ACTION

Solutions on paper do not always work well in practice. Scientific problem solving does not stop with the solution that appears best in theory. Consequently, the solution should be applied and the result observed. In the process, some modifications may be suggested. If success is not achieved, perhaps you defined the problem incorrectly in the first place: you got the wrong solution because you tackled the wrong problem.

Problem solving is not easy, but these six steps should help you

---

[7]*Ibid.*

improve your skill and thus enhance the profits of your business. In the words of Thomas Robert Gaines, "Desiring is helpful, but work and desire are invincible."

Decisionability

Improving your decision-making capabilities can enhance profitability. Considerable sophistication has been added to the decision-making process by incorporating the use of complex forecasting formulas and analytical procedures. However, with or without the use of these aids, the decision will have to be made by you. There are some basic considerations which will help you make better decisions. First, analyze the alternatives. Second, balance the benefits. Third, consider the consequences involved in each decision.

Each alternative should be analyzed in terms of five resource factors of acceptability: the money, the people, the materials, the time, and the space to effect the alternative. For each alternative, ask whether you have the five resources. If not, move to the next alternative. Of the alternatives remaining, balance the benefits in terms of costs, tangible and intangible difficulties, and risks. Next, consider the alternatives in terms of consequences, should things go wrong. What would be the cost of each alternative? Is there a plausible way out in case of failure? The alternatives which do not offer a reasonable contingency plan should be rejected. Now, of the remaining alternatives consider potential benefits: the one with the most significant benefits is your decision.

Remember, facts are needed to insure sound decisions. Because decisions are made by human beings, emotions, feelings, and attitudes strongly affect how facts will be analyzed, interpreted, and used. Certainly, a manager's intuition based on experience and knowledge of employees and conditions is vital to the decision process, but without facts a manager's intuition becomes guesswork.

Elbert Hubbard observed:[8]

> *It does not take much strength to do things,*
> *but it does require great strength to decide what to do.*

---

[8]Hubbard's quote appears in Jerrald F. Young, *Decision Making for Small Business* (New York: John Wiley and Sons, 1977), p. 40.

SUMMARY

Yes, your business can be profitable. You are one of the major factors affecting profits. Your business profits relate to your personal abilities, and profits will increase as you improve these abilities: how fast and how much depends on you.

Managing a small business profitably requires the following steps:

1. Begin with a profitable opportunity.
2. Establish business goals and objectives.
3. Secure professional assistance and information when needed.
4. Obtain adequate funds.
5. Select the best location.
6. Purchase physical factors wisely.
7. Protect against risks.
8. Meet all legal obligations.
9. Use recommended management functions.
10. Make salable products.
11. Satisfy customer demand.
12. Generate sufficient sales income.
13. Establish appropriate credit policies.
14. Effectively handle the human equation.
15. Promote good customer relations.
16. Develop dependable suppliers.
17. Conduct a periodic profit audit.
18. Maintain profitability.

You will find a practical approach to the above requirements presented in the chapters of the book. Read well: profits are elusive, but you can manage a small business profitably by strict adherence to the requirements.

THE
OPERATING
PHASE

11

Managerial Functions

*"The foremost managerial capability
is organizing and operating a management team."*

Gardiner G. Greene[1]

Success or failure of a small business depends upon management. What is meant by management? There are several definitions depending upon the orientation of the writer. Samuel Feinberg, Fairchild Publications columnist, defines the subject in his preface to "How Do You Manage?" as follows: "Management or leadership—take your choice—is the art of getting things done through people."[2] Management boils down to leadership, and the various functions of leadership will be the material emphasized.

The first essential in leadership is self-management. Feinberg pointed out that over 65 percent of family or individually owned department or specialty stores existing in 1929 have disappeared or have been sold to chains. Reasons identified by him are an indictment of business managers who failed to manage themselves.

---

[1]From Gardiner G. Greene, *How to Start and Manage Your Own Business* (New York: Mentor Books, 1975), p. 141. Reprinted with permission.

[2]*Ibid.*, p. 140.

Handmaidens of this virtual suicide complex: greed, vanity, stubbornness, smugness, lethargy, and ignorance. Some manifestations of such sins of commission or omission as nepotism, hazy lines of jurisdiction, ineffective top management, wrangling among principal owners, poor communications up and down the line of command, disregard of human values, apathetic executives, and rank-and-file employees, playing the game of "follow the leader," unhealthy balance between (product) lines, deterioration of property, fixtures and equipment, and backwardness in expansion.[3]

In their publication "The Failure Record Through 1965," Dun and Bradstreet confirm that poor management is the overwhelming cause of business failure, accounting for 91.4 percent of failures. The breakdown is as follows:

    9.9% — Lack of experience in the line
  18.8% — Lack of managerial experience
  21.4% — Unbalanced experience
  41.3% — Incompetence

Such lack of management relates to the following pitfalls, according to Dun and Bradstreet. "Inability to avoid conditions which result in inadequate sales, heavy operating expenses, receivable difficulties, inventory difficulties, excessive fixed assets, poor location, competitive weakness."

The essence of developing an effective management team is captured in these words inscribed on the tombstone of Andrew Carnegie:

Here lies a man
Who knew how to enlist
In his service
Better men than himself.

Developing a management team is the key to growth, a means whereby a small business may be expanded to additional outlets just as fast as a competent team can operate outlet number one. What are the functions of executive leadership? What activity characterizes a successful manager? Three words effectively encompass the essentials of managerial leadership. It is the execution of the activities involved in these three terms which provide the accomplishment of successful management. A successful manager *initiates, delegates,* and *evaluates* his business activities.

---

[3]*Ibid.*

WHAT DOES IT MEAN TO INITIATE?

To initiate means to get things started. Starting a business requires establishing goals and objectives, then mapping out a program through planning that will insure the successful accomplishment of the stipulated goals and objectives. Planning is looking ahead. It includes not only objectives and guidelines for achieving objectives, but also an orderly, carefully considered strategy for operating the business.

Basically, effective planning involves the following steps:

1. Establish objectives.
2. Formulate basic assumptions, in terms of noncontrollable factors.
3. Semi-controllable factors (firm share of market, company price policy, and employee productivity).
4. Controllable conditions: selection of new products, expansion into new markets, a relocation of business site, and major remodeling of facilities.
5. Search for alternative courses of action.
6. Evaluate alternative courses of action.
7. Put the plan into action.

HOW CAN YOU PUT A PLAN IN MOTION?

Use an Idea File

How can you initiate through planning activity? A simple way to facilitate planning is to utilize file folders with a tab—"objectives and plans." As objectives are established for the company, write them down on the top of a piece of paper; then, as ideas and thoughts occur, simply add them on the list prepared for that particular objective sheet. Priorities as to plans which require scheduling and timing will be ordered in terms of their importance.

Make a Planning Form

Someone has suggested that a planning form be designed to facilitate this important function. In so doing, a planning form should have the following characteristics:

1. Space for objective statement, details of planning, time interval, responsible persons, cross-referencing to other objectives and files.

2. Sufficient size to accommodate the written statements of objectives.

3. Specific areas for which the planning is imperative, such as the standard list of management areas: financial, sales, building and equipment, personnel, purchasing, production, administration, and office. A list of planning suggested by Peter Drucker includes: marketing standing, innovation, productivity, physical resources, financial resources, profitability, manager performance, manager development, worker performance, worker attitude, and social responsibility.[4]

Use the PERT Method

Program Evaluation and Review Technique (PERT), while normally used as a technique of control, offers a method of planning the accomplishment of nonrepetitive objectives. The businessman can use PERT to plan in great detail. PERT can be helpful in identifying trouble spots and time delays and facilitates resolving these difficulties. Someone has compared PERT to a planning map—the step-by-step procedure shown over time.

The diagram, Figure 11-1, illustrates a PERT method, the result of a planning effort. There are basically two elements to be considered. The first are the "activities," identified by the lines connecting the numbered circles (events). Numbers appearing on the lines signify the time in days required to complete the activity. Therefore, those using the PERT network can see the relationship of the various activities and events including the total time required for the project. The second elements are called "events" and are identified by the numbered circles indicating separate phases of the project, or the beginning of one activity and the completion of another.

After preparing the network based on the necessary activities and events, the next concern is the estimate of time required. The object is to determine the earliest possible time to complete the project. To do this, the times in days of each activity are added from the preceding event to secure the time to complete the next event, e.g., from event 1 to event 2 takes 4 days. The number 4 is placed on the top of circle 2. The time required to complete activities to event 4 is 10 days. The number 10 is added to the previous number 4 and the total 14 is placed on top of circle 4.

[4]Peter F. Drucker, *The Practice of Management* (New York: Harper & Brothers, 1954), p. 53.

Figure 11-1.
PERT Network. Cross-hatched lines signify a critical path.

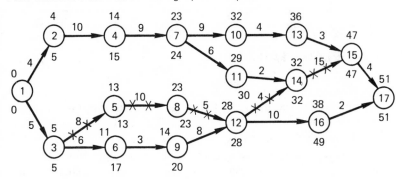

The process is continued moving to the right. However, when two lines converge (events 11 and 12 at 14) the highest number (32) is used.

The numbers appearing below the numbered circles, events, are calculated by reversing the first procedure. Thus, beginning at event 17 with 51 days, the 51 is placed under circle 17 and the days required for each activity are subtracted. When two activities converge the lowest number is used, e.g. 14 and 16 converge at event 12 and 28; the lowest number is used instead of 39. Upon reaching event 1 the bottom number should be 0.

Those using the PERT network can see the relationship of the various activities and events including the total time required for the project. As will be noted in Figure 11-1, the earliest possible time to complete the project is 51 days reached by two pathways, 40 days and 51 days. The largest figure, 51, is the "critical path," because any increase in time required on this pathway would increase the time required to complete the entire project. To identify the critical path the connecting lines are cross-hatched. Another indication of the critical path is the fact that the numbers above and below the events along the path will be identical. In Figure 11-1 the critical path runs along events: 1, 3, 5, 8, 12, 14, 15, and finishes at 17. The numbers above and below these events are the same. In other words, there would be no time to maneuver along the critical path. There would be no slack time, but along the other paths the difference in the numbers above and below the events show the amount of slack time.

The control of operations can be facilitated by checking the actual progress in terms of time provided for in the PERT plan. Corrective action should be taken on any deviations noted. Major changes affecting the project may necessitate a revision in the PERT network.[5]

WHY DO PLANS FAIL?

Success is not guaranteed by simply planning. Situations sometimes produce failure of the best laid plans. Sometimes failure is due to the fact that necessary knowledge to formulate an accurate plan was not available. For example, an advertising person might originate some appealing television commercials aimed at selling industrial materials, overlooking the fact that machine tools are sold primarily on the basis of personal contact and documented evidence of productivity and durability: thus an expensive campaign of television commercials might produce no sales whatsoever.

A second reason for the failure of a plan may be unrealistic goals. A buyer of high-fashion ladies' apparel who purchases an entire spring line of clothing because of personal appeal is courting disaster if the personal feeling is not compared to the tastes of customers. The proper guideline is to buy what the customer wants, even if the styles are ridiculous in the opinion of the buyer.

Third, plans sometimes fail for lack of a sufficient time frame. A businessman may blunder through the program, going from one extreme to another, adjusting to every short-term variation. It is necessary to observe the plan from an overall standpoint, with due allowance for minor variations from time to time.

Scapegoating is another cause of failure. It occurs when the owner, sensing a discrepancy between anticipated results and what has been produced, concentrates on finding the person to blame for the shortcoming. Someone said, "I've been able to stay in this job for eighteen years because of my ability to delegate blame." Where might he be now if he had a more positive attitude?[6]

Another common reason why plans fail is simply because those

---

[5]Additional information on PERT method of planning and control can be found in Henry L. Sisk, *Management and Organization* (Cincinnati, Ohio: South-Western Publishing Co., 1977), pp. 484–89, and George R. Terry, *Principles of Management* (Homewood, Ill.: Richard D. Irwin, Inc., 1977), pp. 254–56.

[6]David E. Shepard, *From Personal to Professional Management* (Boston: Holbrook Press, Inc., 1976), p. 86.

persons responsible for carrying them out do not understand the plans; they do not know what they are supposed to be doing. This is simply a case of poor communications, which will be dealt with later.

Failure may also stem from the fact that a businessman over- or underestimated the strengths and weaknesses of the business and its employees. Such an error may put the company in a competitive situation where it is unable to compete, or it may cause the company to avoid an opportunity where it might succeed with relative ease.[7]

WHY DELEGATE?

Whether or not to delegate is often considered a personal choice on the part of the individual manager. In reality there is no choice. If one is to be a true manager, delegation is a must.

The organization is formed by allocating the responsibility and authority to subordinates. To have an effective organization, it becomes essential that the right persons be assigned the right things to do. To put it another way, employees be assigned the work they are capable of doing. In some instances it will be necessary to train employees so that they can be prepared to accomplish the work which has been assigned to them.

The Organization Formula

In contemporary business operations there are numerous formulas utilized in accomplishing various facets of business operations. The following formula is unique in that no numbers are used, but it portrays a fundamental concept with regard to organizing a business. In fact, it becomes operative through the delegation process.

Remember:

$$O = \frac{W}{P}$$

The formula is translated: organization equals Work divided by People. The work of the organization divided by people through the

---

[7]*Ibid.*

process of delegation will result in the organizational structure for the firm. This process should not be carried out in a random manner, but by a careful meticulous effort to match up the individual capabilities with the work requirements.

Authority and Responsibility

One of the basic axioms of organization is: in the delegation of responsibility there shall be a commensurate delegation of authority to act. This is one of the most frequently violated principles of organization, particularly in small business. The essence of the principle is that when an employee receives an assignment he should also be given the authority or power to carry out the assignment. Sometimes the reverse procedure produces another error by the small businessman; that is, reversing the delegation process. After making the delegation, some businesspeople have the habit of taking back what has been delegated, which becomes most frustrating to the employee. After telling the employee what he is supposed to do in terms of his responsibilities, the boss jumps in and interferes with the employee's assigned job.

Span of Control

The number of subordinates reporting to an assigned leader is the span of control. There has been much controversy about the number of people who should report to a superior. However, it is commonly accepted that a reasonable span of control is between five and seven. This number can perhaps be increased where the work of the subordinates is homogenous. The number should perhaps be held down in cases where the subordinates have heterogenous assignments.

Unity of Command

To have an effective process of delegation it is important that the employee have only one boss giving directions or delegating. The employee should be given a direct explanation of who he is responsible to and who he takes orders from. Chaos usually results when more than one boss begins giving instructions, which are sometimes conflicting. This situation is not at all uncommon, especially in a family business.

On one occasion a new secretary had been employed for a small business with the assignment to work for the office manager. However, instructions were soon being given to the new secretary by the secretary to the president as well as by the credit manager. After the situation became impossibly confused, the new secretary reported to the personnel manager, "They are all giving me orders, telling me that their work must be done first, and it is impossible to please all three." After reviewing the matter with the three bosses, it was determined that she was employed to work for the office manager. It was decided that if either the secretary to the president or the credit manager had work that needed to be done by personnel in the office, it would be filtered through the office manager and thereby accomplished in an orderly manner.

Chain of Command

The designation for this principle is probably derived from the military. It simply means that there is a line of authority which runs through the organization from the top to the bottom. It is important that this chain of command be explained to the employees so that they know the authority relationship between the various individuals in the organization. Employees should be instructed to respect this chain of command and to avoid bypassing their boss in going to a higher authority in the organization.

WHAT IS DEPARTMENTATION?

This is the process of gathering together the activities that are related under one unit of organization. As the volume of work increases beyond the point where the businessman may do all of it himself, it becomes necessary to divide the work, managerial as well as operative activities, with employees that are added to the firm. There are a number of ways to allocate activities. Some of them are as follows:

Function

The different kinds of work in the business are the functions. The basic functional areas include finance, production, and sales. Other areas, sometimes regarded as secondary, include personnel, engineering, accounting, research, and traffic management. Regardless of the size of the company, a functional system can be understood and implemented to advantage. Businesspeople should consider that when only one man is doing production work, he is a production department; one salesman is a sales department. Thus, new employees can be readily classified according to their functional work. After categorizing these various functional areas of the business, the organization chart can be developed and utilized.

Customers

The products of a firm are usually sold to a range of customers through different channels of distribution. Customer breakdown may include original-equipment-manufacturer's department, the service-station department, the catalogue department, the wholesale and retail departments, the men's, women's and children's departments, and any other departments through which customers are served.

Products

Where only one product is involved in a company, there will be other means of departmentation utilized. In those cases where a wide variety of products are offered departmentation may be the means of improving the effectiveness of the organization. An example of product departmentation would be a supermarket which has a grocery department, produce department, meat department, and a frozen food department.

Time

Time departmentation is related more to production workers and departments than to administrative or sales departments. The latter two usually work the regular work day of normal business hours. In the case of the production workers there is frequently a differentiation by time — the first, second, third, or swing shift. Consequently, a department in a plant may be divided according to personnel assigned to the different work shifts.

Letters and Numbers

As the company grows new departments may be added and designated alphabetically or by number. An example is the practice of the labor unions to identify locals, such as "Local 307."

Geography

This involves a departmentation on the basis of areas within the operational scope of the company. It usually has more importance with those companies dealing on a regional or national basis. Nevertheless, some small companies do operate on a rather broad market basis and will find it useful to departmentize according to a geographical area or division, such as Intermountain area, Pacific Northwest division, Western region, etc .

Machinery

The use of particular machinery may be appropriate in departmentizing a production department — for example, stamping room, grinding room, polishing room, and paint room.

Job

Sometimes it becomes helpful to departmentize organization groups to do a special project for a particular job assignment. On the basis of such departmentation, the project may be assigned a number or even the name of the customer for which the project is being accomplished.

The work of departmentation is continuous as the company grows — additional work is added, new products are developed, new processes are initiated, etc. As changes take place in the organization, the relationships between individuals and groups must be redefined, new organizational charts drawn, and job descriptions revised.[8]

Formal Versus Informal Organization

The organization chart depicts the formal organization of the business. It portrays the established relationships between people in the company, demonstrates the basis of organization, depicts the chain of command, and shows the relationships between the various functions performed.

However, there is also present in every organization what has become known as the informal organization. In a sense it is the invisible organization, because charts are not usually drawn to indicate the informal relationships. If charts were attempted, there would be many of them, due to the many kinds of relationships which are in fact the informal organization of the business.

Businesspeople do not create informal groups. They are formed by the members of the organization at all levels to satisfy human needs. The informal group seems to evolve from the gregarious nature of people wanting to join together on the basis of common interests or similar backgrounds. Informal organization exists and should be recognized, but it is not necessarily bad. It may be good, particularly if you learn how to utilize it. For example, you may want to have a successful recreational event for the employees of the company. The one employee who is most regarded as influential on recreational activities may well be the one to promote the event successfully.

Sometimes the results of the informal group can be negative, as when informal groups restrict output by putting pressure on their members, or terminate production entirely, or they reject a new foreman, supervisor, or even new employees. The company would then find it necessary to take steps to counteract such actions.

WHO SHOULD EVALUATE?

An effective businessman plans what he wants to accomplish by setting objectives and establishing a program to reach those objectives. After he has assigned the work to be done by delegating it to the various employees in his organization, the next important function is evaluation.

---

[8]*Ibid.*, pp. 161–164.

Performance must be compared with what was originally desired. The process of evaluation (comparison) is a continuing process of identifying activities that are not in keeping with the desired performance standards, so corrective measures can be taken for improvement. The process of evaluation is futile without the inclusion of corrective action when needed.

WHAT SHOULD BE EVALUATED?

Sales

A sales forecast broken down into monthly or weekly quotas becomes a basis for evaluation with the actual sales performance. Increased sales is the usual standard for most companies, and provides a goal which is utilized for motivating the personnel in the sales department. A budget is usually established to insure the accomplishment of the forecast of sales, and this becomes a basis of evaluation. The evaluation of sales results should include both the results from the personal efforts of salesmen and the effect of the nonpersonal selling effort — advertising and sales promotion. A combination of the two represents the total company sales effort. When the sales results do not measure up to the projected sales, some revision should be made. Evaluation is useless unless measures are taken to bring the actual performance in line with desired performance.

Cost

Sales cost money — for the materials used, the direct labor, the allocation of overhead, administrative expense, utilities, transportation, and depreciation, just to mention a few factors. The summation of costs deducted from sales income are used to determine the profits. When the costs exceed amounts projected in relation to the sales target, then profits will be less than desired. Some action should be taken either to increase sales or to reduce costs to projected levels. Sometimes costs cannot be controlled, such as with increasing prices commonly associated with inflation. It may be necessary, therefore, to raise the price per unit in order to compensate for increasing costs and thereby maintain the desired profit percentage.

Profit

Rather than wait until the end of the operating period to determine profits, continuing evaluation should be made to avoid disappointment. As indicated earlier, profits can and should be budgeted. You may set profits as a percentage of sales or a return on investment, or profits may be compared as a goal with some other index, from which periodic statements of progress can be derived. Normally, the income statement and balance sheet are distributed monthly so that responsible people can evaluate the status of progress. Budgeted statements are helpful in making comparisons and locating areas where remedial steps are necessary to insure profitability. Corrective action may possibly point to increasing sales, reducing costs, changing or reducing sales efforts, lowering or eliminating minimum standards of quality, or taking any number of other steps to improve the bottom line figure.

Cash

It is imperative that adequate cash be available to meet the ongoing obligations of the business. A business may show a profit and still not have cash available to pay debts, compensate employees, or pay accounts payable. It is of utmost importance that cash flow be under control at all times. A budget statement, sometimes referred to as a cash-flow statement, can help facilitate control. Pertinent information on the statement includes the amount of cash on hand at the beginning of a period, the end of flow from sales, accounts receivable, sales of securities, and cash from any other source. Also included are the reductions of cash during the same period (as a result of paying salaries, accounts payable, taxes, dividends, interest, etc.) and the closing cash balance. When the cash-flow statement indicates a period in which the company will be out of cash, it becomes necessary to provide the cash or remove the need for it. To illustrate, a retail business usually requires additional cash to build its inventory in anticipating the Christmas season. In some instances, the company can do without the increased inventory buildup, but this would result in a reduction of sales and thus would not be a viable alternative. Other possibilities include borrowing money from the bank, writing creditors to delay paying bills until after the December holidays, obtaining merchandise on consignment, or taking some other measures to provide the necessary funds and prevent the possibility of bankruptcy.

Capital Expenditures

It is well to anticipate those items of equipment that will be required in the business, such as typewriters, automobiles, delivery trucks, office furniture, fixtures, and warehouse equipment. By anticipating these needs, a budget can be prepared for the acquisitions. Sometimes, however, there are non-materializations of sales or unforeseen costs which preclude making the capital outlay for the items desired. In this case certain action may be required. The company may have planned for the acquisition of a new delivery truck. If sales are down, though, it may be decided that the present delivery truck can be utilized longer in the hope that maintenance costs may be lower than the cost of buying a new truck. Still another possibility, should the old truck be too worn out, is to sell the truck outright and arrange for a delivery truck on a contract lease basis. This would provide deliveries without necessitating undue strain on cash.

SUMMARY

Certain nomenclature has been used here to designate the managerial functions. The number of functions expressed in the management literature varies between authors. It seems meaningful from the personal standpoint of the manager to summarize these functions as *initiate, delegate,* and *evaluate.* These are the essentials. The managing process is continuous: as one program is initiated, another is delegated and still another is being evaluated—which results in another initiation and so on.

Effective implementation of the managing process is facilitated by use of the accepted principles discussed in this chapter, namely: authority, responsibility, span of control, unity of command, and chain of command.

Small-business operators should understand the proper use of formal and informal organization. Use departmentation as an effective means of delegation. Determine what you need evaluated and who should do it. Utilize the results by incorporating the information toward a more profitable enterprise.

12

Materials
Management

*"There Is As Much Profit
In A 1.5% Purchasing Saving
As In A 10% Sales Increase"*[1]

The average manufacturing company spends 53.7 percent of its sales dollar on goods and services. *This fact poses a tremendous possibility for savings that will lead to added profit.* For example, take the XYZ Company, with a sales volume of $6,000,000. Its cost to purchase material, supplies, and services would run $3,222,000. With an average profit margin of 8.2 percent (before taxes) it would take $600,000 in sales to make a $49,200 profit. But a reduction of only 1.5 percent in purchasing costs would mean an identical $49,200 in additional profit. No wonder progressive managements consider purchasing so important in maximizing profitable operations.

Materials management has been defined as planning, organizing, and controlling of all phases of the acquisition, storage, and transportation of all materials, supplies, parts, etc. up to the point of use. Efficient materials management can result in the following advantages:

---

[1]Reprinted with permission of *Purchasing* Magazine, Boston, Massachusetts.

1. A lower unit cost of product, accomplished by efficient buying, lower transportation costs, minimum storage costs, fewer interruptions from lack of materials, and the benefit of the psychological factor stemming from more competence in the production schedule

2. Shorter production time achieved through better supply conditions

3. By means of an adequate supply of materials, fewer funds tied up in capital equipment

4. Better morale as a result of fewer work stoppages

5. Company growth promoted

6. Less capital tied up in inventories

7. Minimized waste and obsolescence

THE SEVEN PHASES OF MATERIALS MANAGEMENT

Participation and Setting of Material Standards

In a large firm this function is normally carried out by a committee. This is even recommended for the small firm, so that the various viewpoints of the management team — manufacturing, marketing, finance, and purchasing — may be coordinated to maximize the company effort. A coordination of these various viewpoints will enhance the effectiveness of the materials management function.

Procurement

This activity concerns acquiring materials and supplies by one of several common processes, namely, by manufacture, by purchase, by borrowing, or by rent (lease).

Reasons to Make	*Reasons to Buy*
1. To retain the secret of a process or material.	1. To cut the unit costs by buying — predicated on the principle of specialization, it is sometimes possible to buy cheaper than it can be made.

Reasons to Make	*Reasons to Buy*
2. To more effectively utilize otherwise idle machinery or manpower.	2. To engage in reciprocity. The only true justification, as will be explained later, is in cases where *certeris paribus* conditions exist.
3. To obtain proper quality requirements.	3. To avoid the higher cost of machinery and equipment to make certain parts and materials.
4. To be more certain of deliveries.	4. To avoid spreading management too thin. The more activities engaged in, the more management must know, but may not know.
5. To keep highly skilled personnel who might otherwise leave during temporary layoff, etc.	5. To increase community goodwill. This may be a good practice in terms of public relations to patronize local suppliers.
6. To reduce the unit costs of product by cutting the unit costs of parts or materials, particularly if you suspect collusion on price by suppliers.	6. To avoid the cost of product research.
	7. To avoid antitrust action. Even small firms may be suspect where integration raises suspicion before the FTC.

HOW CAN YOU DECIDE WHETHER TO MAKE OR BUY?

List the cost elements — equipment, labor, material, administration, and overhead — and compare costs of making versus buying.

THE PRINCIPLE OF TAPERED INTEGRATION

Tapered integration is the tendency of manufacturers to make more of their needs (parts, supplies, etc.) in periods of depression than in periods of prosperity. Figure 12-1 is a graphic presentation of the principle of tapered integration.

Receiving and Inspection

A system should be established to insure the proper procedure in receiving and inspecting incoming materials. Some of the forms that you might want to include are the purchase contract, a receiving report, an

Figure 12–1.
Principle of Tapered Integration.

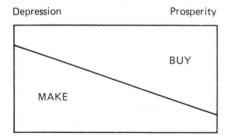

Depression   Prosperity

BUY

MAKE

inspection report, a rejected materials report, and references to standard specifications. This is an important responsibility, and should be assigned to a specified person.

Some points to consider in executing the function of receiving and inspection are listed below. From a legal standpoint, rejection must be made within a "reasonable" time, or the order may be deemed accepted.

1. Receiving inspects for quantity.
2. Inspection inspects for quality.
3. Should quantity expected be given to receiving?
4. Should boxes be broken for detailed count?
5. Routing of receiving and inspection reports, stores, traffic department.
6. Should receiving clerks sign the bill of lading before counting contents?
7. Prompt forwarding of paperwork is needed before invoices are matched.
8. Should receiving be given a copy of the purchase order?
9. Should samples be used, or a complete quality check made?
10. Should coverage for destructive inspection be in the quantity ordered?
11. Should inspection be on own premises, or on vendor's?
12. The fault of vendor or carrier should be determined, when possible.
13. Notification should be given to the using department.
14. Specify the routing for the bill of lading.

Storage and Issue

The object here is to provide suitable facilities for storing materials until they are requisitioned for production. This would include raw materials, manufactured parts, and also semi-manufactured or work-in-process goods. The problem of space is two fold. First, determine how much space to set aside, which depends upon the type of storeroom arrangement used. Consideration must be given to the amount of space required for average inventory as well as for maximum inventory requirements. Secondly, the location of the storeroom which must be integrated into the production picture. The location should be strategic with regard to the areas of use.

It is recommended that the responsibility for company storerooms be fixed on one person and that storerooms be under lock and key at all times. Most companies are very particular about protecting cash and the responsibility for it, but very careless in the matter of controlling and protecting supplies in stockrooms.

It is frequently more economic to rent or lease storage space for temporary requirements than to invest capital for construction and ownership. Storage innovations (pallets, forklift trucks, apron conveyors, etc.) may be helpful in reducing costs and thereby contributing to more profits.

Some basic principles of good storage would be the following: (1) efficient utilization of space — e.g., tiering of pallets, steel banding of pallet load; (2) accessibility of materials — it is possible to receive false reports of shortages when materials are not readily accessible; (3) flexibility of arrangement — it is desirable to have bins and other storage fixtures constructed so that they can be modified, moved, and varied to suit the changing storage requirements; (4) provisions should be made for actual physical turnover of material regardless of the method of evaluation of inventory practice — by utilizing a storage unit with two approaches (front and back), it is possible to have the new stock move in from the rear and issue from the front, and maintain a turnover based on First-in-First-out, or "FiFo"; (5) provide for ease of physical counting — this can be facilitated when material is stored in a standard unit, or palletized load; (6) reduce the need for physical handling — in planning the storeroom layout, consider that for material handling the ideal setup would be "all mechanized"; (7) provide ready inspection of materials — the storage arrangement should permit sampling of items at any time to check their conditions.

Inventory Control

PHYSICAL INVENTORY

The legal requirement is that a physical inventory be taken each year to establish an accurate accounting statement for tax purposes. Most physical inventories are poorly done, with quite a latitude of error. Some of the reasons for the difficulties are: the fact that most people who take the inventory are not acquainted with the merchandise or materials involved; misstatement of quantity due to incorrect counting, especially where physical effort is required to make the count; and frequent omission of items where several teams are engaged in the inventory—unless the duties are specified carefully and the work supervised closely.

One advantage of the physical inventory is that you have a count of the inventory. It also provides an opportunity to cull out those items taking up space and not likely to be used. A better valuation can be ascertained for the inventory if the accountant will take the time to determine value of items in the market.

THE BIN TAG

This simple record is widely used and frequently located on the side of the receptacle in which the material is being stored. Usually, the bin tag gives a description of the item (part number), the quantity received, and the balance of items after each issue. In other words, at any point in time it should show the exact number in the receptacle. Businesspeople usually have a problem of knowing the usage rate (how much they use over a given period of time). This could be overcome by putting the date on the bin tag along with the quantity; then, by reference to the bin tag when the salesman comes by to take an order, it would be possible to know how much should be ordered. Simply figure out how much is sold over how long a period of time, and how much time will be required to have the order filled. The same information can be maintained on a file card and posted from sales records. By checking the cards, those with low quantities can be pulled for use in the next order list. Stubs are sometimes prepared with perforated tabs that can be used by smaller merchants for ordering purposes. Another important information item on the bin tag is the order point.

HOW TO DETERMINE THE ORDER POINT?

First determine the usage rate by calendar day. Second, ascertain the delivery period by calendar day. Multiply the daily usage rate by the number of days in the delivery period, which will equal the absolute minimum point. Next, determine the amount of safety margin in terms of calendar days and add that to the absolute minimum, which should equal the desired order point. The safety margin should be based on past experience (showing the longest possible delay as a usual occurrence) and governed also by the location of the supplier. As an illustration, assume that the usage rate is seven units per calendar day and the delivery period is four days: the absolute minimum would be twenty-eight units; this plus a safety margin of one day, or seven additional units, would make the order point thirty-five units.

Balance of Store's Ledger is a record which is usually prepared one sheet per item in the inventory. Column headings usually include memorandum, on order, on hand, reserved, and available. The balance of the "on hand" or "available" column can be used to indicate the order point. When the specified quantity is reached, the reorder should be initiated. You should never have a minus quantity in the "on hand" column, though you might have a minus quantity in the "available" column if you schedule production requirements beyond the quantity on hand. The "available" column equals the amount on order plus the amount on hand, minus the reserve. It is best to put the order point figure in the "available" column if scheduling period is longer than the normal purchase period. However, put the order point figure in the "on hand" column when the purchase period is longer than the scheduling period.

Some systems should be devised in the business for indicating the need for an order to be placed. Usually, a purchase requisition form is used for this purpose; however, a specification card may also be used.

The list of factors below should be taken into consideration in determining the quantities of materials and merchandise to be purchased.

How Much to Buy?	*Buy Less*
1. Quantity discounts	1. Storage costs (space costs, handling, interest on investment, insurance)
2. Transportation charges	2. Style changes
3. Purchasing costs	3. Deterioration
4. Scarcity buying	4. Availability of working capital

On an anticipated rising market, the policy of quantity buying may be useful to minimize the impact of increasing prices on the cost of doing business. The savings on the cost of goods sold will have to be balanced against storage costs and interest charges for the period of time involved. Where the market is affected by falling prices, the buying policy would be switched to a hand-to-mouth operation to avoid excessive inventory costs.

HOW DO YOU DISPOSE OF SLOW-MOVING MERCHANDISE?

Accepting the desirability of selling slow-moving merchandise at less than normal markup or less than cost is a difficult lesson for a businessperson to learn. Style merchandise is particularly vulnerable to this risk. Other products are affected by fading, deterioration, etc. by being kept in stock too long. Slow-moving merchandise should be disposed of promptly.

The Small Business Administration and the Department of Commerce have prepared suggestions and ideas for assisting small-business people in resolving the problem of slow-moving merchandise: (1) make traffic obstacles of large displays of the items; (2) offer special discounts for quantity purchases; (3) put specially colored lights on displays; (4) offer one-cent sales; (5) place slow-moving goods next to best sellers; (6) have grab-bag sales; (7) use specially colored price tags; (8) offer "Special of the Day" items.[2]

HOW TO DETERMINE THE ECONOMIC ORDERING QUANTITY

A formula has been developed by industrial buyers for determining desired quantities for their type of buying. The factors in the formula include the dollar amount used in the previous year, the cost of issuing a purchase order, and the costs of storing, insuring, protecting, and maintaining inventory on hand. When these are known, the formula illustrated on the next page can be utilized.

Salvage

It is necessary to determine the scope of salvage operations for the particular company. In this regard it is helpful to classify the different items involved: (1) Re-work—something that is damaged in the production process, but can be made serviceable through re-work operations. (2) Scrap—items which have an economic value and can be disposed of for a monetary sum. No special operations are required except bail or packing for shipment. (3) Waste—those materials which have no economic value and therefore must be disposed of without remuneration.

---

[2]Dan Steinhoff, *Small Business Management Fundamentals* (New York: McGraw-Hill Book Co., 1974), p. 172.

Economic ordering quantity $= \dfrac{2AB}{i}$

Where A = annual usage in dollars
$\quad\quad\ B$ = cost of issuing a purchase order, in dollars
$\quad\quad\ i$ = cost of carrying inventory,
$\quad\quad\quad\quad$ expressed as a percentage of the inventory value

To illustrate the use of this formula, let us consider a firm which used $10,000 of product P last year; it costs $1 to issue a purchase order; and it costs 5 percent of the inventory value to store, insure, and protect it (0.05 percent). When we insert these figures into the formula, it becomes:

Economic ordering quantity $=$

$$\sqrt{\dfrac{2\,(\$10,000)\,1}{.05}} = \sqrt{\dfrac{\$20,000}{.05}} = \$400,000$$

The square root of $400,000 is $633, as follows:

```
       6  3 3
   √ 400,000
      36
       400
       369
       3100
```

123

1263

Proof   633
             633
            1899
            1899
           3798
         $400,689

The most economic ordering quantity is, therefore, $633 each time an order is placed.

This formula uses a square root, but the time spent calculating it is worthwhile. It takes the guesswork out of the buying process.[3]

---

[3]Adapted from *Small Business Management Fundamentals* by Dan Steinhoff. Copyright © 1974 by McGraw-Hill, Inc. Used by permission of McGraw-Hill Book Company.

Efficient management of salvage operations, usually assigned to those connected with materials management, can be a factor toward increasing profits.

Transportation

If transportation is an important factor in terms of the volume of materials moved into the company and also the volume shipped out of the company, it may pay to utilize the services of a professional transportation consultant. Many companies have contributed substantially to their profits from the use of such specialists. Expertise in the many ramifications pertaining to transportation could result in worthwhile savings to the company.

From an internal standpoint, the transportation from storage areas to operational areas and manufacturing processes, as well as that from one productive operation to another, bears careful analysis from the standpoint of minimizing costs while providing efficient movement of materials. Where the internal transportation function warrants, a special internal transportation department may be formed and provided with equipment to accomplish the work on definite schedule.

PURCHASING PROCEDURE

Ascertaining the Need

The need for purchase of material may originate from the use of the bin tag, the balance of store's ledger, production control, product design, office units in the company, or almost any supervisor who has a need to be filled. The purchasing system is usually activated by the issuance of a purchase requisition to the purchasing department or to the individual with the responsibility to activate purchasing.

Accurate Description of the Commodities Desired

Commodity specifications may be communicated in terms of brand name, physical or chemical properties, a blueprint, market grades, performance requirements, or by supplying a sample of the desired item.

Selection of Sources of Supply

SURVEY PHASE

Possible sources of supply may be obtained through the Thomas Registry of American Manufacturers, the MacRae Bluebook, the classified section of the telephone book, trade journals, catalogs, salespeople, industrial advertising, and publications of research organizations. This phase of activity will culminate with a list of those who could supply the needed items.

INQUIRY STAGE

The object here is to find out the relative qualifications of suppliers. This evaluation will extend beyond the simple terms of sale to include financial condition (possibly, verification through Dun & Bradstreet). It is advisable to send several requests for quotations.

ANALYSIS STAGE

On the basis of analyzing all possible suppliers, a conclusion should be reached as to the best source of supply.

EXPERIENCE STAGE

With satisfaction obtained from existing suppliers on the basis of experience, patronage would be continued. Should it be desirable, however, new sources would be selected and evaluated for future decisions.

Placing the Order

Negotiations would be conducted with the source of supply to obtain satisfaction with regard to price, quality, and service, with assurances that the quantity could be supplied at the desired time for delivery.

Legal Aspects of Purchasing

The details for legal requisites in business have been presented in Chapter 5. With regard to purchasing, the law of contracts, agencies, and sales are of particular concern. Specific questions regarding the legality of actions to be taken should be cleared with the lawyer representing the company.

Follow-Up

The object of this activity is to insure that the materials purchased arrive on time so that there will be no delays in manufacturing operations, or even shutdowns in the case of shortages of critical items. Various means of communication are used in this function, including postcards, (form) letters, telegrams, telephones, personal visitations, and (in special instances) the assignment of a person to the supplier's plant to insure continuous supervision of follow-up activities.

Completion of the Record

In this final activity in the purchasing procedure, the necessary entries on appropriate records will be made so that files can be kept up to date on strategic information about suppliers.

PURCHASING POLICIES

Commercial Bribery

It is alleged that the buyer always pays for the gifts—nothing is for nothing—and the seller usually puts the cost of the gift in the selling price. If you find it is customary in the community to accept gifts, and you desire to prohibit this, you should be prepared to pay a higher level of compensation and then bargain with suppliers to give a better deal in terms of service, delivery, etc. However, if purchasing personnel want gifts, it is practically impossible to stop them: they are usually delivered through indirect routes. If your company has a policy of not accepting gifts, and gifts are received, the policy should provide a disposition of the gifts (given to charity or issued as a part of regular materials in the company) or return the gifts to the senders at their expense.

There is always the fine line between advertising and gifts. Sometimes the effect is the same whether it is advertising or a gift. If you want to be strict in this policy, you may desire to remove all items with the names of suppliers on them from company premises.

Reciprocity

Generally speaking, this idea is unsound from a business standpoint. By its very nature, it ties your hands regardless of product quality, delivery, or price. Whenever you are confronted by a salesman who claims that his company purchases a considerable quantity from your company, it may be advisable to check to determine exactly how much. If you want to keep your initiative in purchasing, do not engage in a policy of reciprocity. There is one exception: when *ceteris paribus* conditions (all things equal) apply, those customers should be favored.

Suppliers' Salesmen

Some system should be devised so that all the salesmen have an opportunity to show their line or to leave advertising materials to be examined. Some means of screening should be established so that salesmen with products not used by the company may have the option of leaving materials without taking time for an interview.

Local Buying

This is similar to reciprocity, but here the supplier is being favored because he lives in the same community. A blanket policy of buying from suppliers in the neighborhood is not necessarily good business. Some of the advantages may be a greater assurance of delivery and the possibility of operating on a smaller inventory. However, costs should be compared with outside sources. If they compare favorably in service and cost, by all means patronize the local sources. Certainly, this patronage would have a positive effect upon public relations and on employee relations.

Loyalty to Suppliers

First and foremost, give fair treatment to all suppliers. This may be insured by the use of public bids or requests for quotations from all qualified bidders. Pay a reasonable price. Be willing to reject prices which would bring financial distress to the supplier. Some companies even estimate what a reasonable cost should be, as an indication of what is fair with regard to price.

TESTS OF PURCHASING EFFICIENCY

Budgetary Control

With a materials budget or a budget for the purchasing department, a means of control is established; and the ability to operate within the budget specified is some measure of efficiency.

Other Criteria

Comparative analysis and evaluation of the following items may also help to indicate a measure of purchasing efficiency for the company: (1) number of orders placed; (2) number of invoices passed; (3) dollar value of invoices passed; (4) cost of purchase orders; (5) percentage of cash discount; (6) percentage of orders less than five dollars; (7) percentage of rush orders; (8) percentage of overdue orders; (9) number of changes in purchase time; (10) number of notifications held; and (11) number of people.

Finally, these questions would further add to evaluating efficiency: (1) Is the organization of the department based on sound principles? (2) Is the physical layout of the department well planned? (3) Is there a reasonably well-defined procurement policy? (4) Are the procedures reasonable?

SUMMARY

The potential savings through efficient materials management presents another avenue for increasing the profitability of your business. Remember that there is as much profit in a 1.5 percent purchasing saving as in a 10% sales increase.

Review the seven phases of materials management. Consider methods for creating additional savings.

Examine the suggested steps in the purchasing procedure. Can you suggest ways and means for improvement? What are the critical areas? How can control be maintained?

Are the principle purchasing policies sufficient? What additional activities should be included under policies?

Serious intent to manage a small business profitably is shown by the effort expended in evaluating purchasing efficiency. The advances made in this endeavor should have a positive impact on company profits.

13

Managing
Human
Resources

*". . . teach people correct principles
and they govern themselves."*

Joseph Smith[1]

Ralph Davis said that a small business remains small because it is limited to what one man can do in twenty-four hours. Successful men, in terms of expanding businesses and profits, learn how to multiply their capabilities through other people. Certainly, the growth of a business is dependent upon developing capable people who can assume important responsibilities.

The story of J. C. Penney is a classic example of managing human resources profitably. J. C. Penney began his first store in the small town of Kemmerer, Wyoming. After launching his first store successfully, J. C. Penney employed a manager and went on to organize a second store; and the process was repeated over and over again. By selecting and training competent personnel, the J. C. Penney Company grew to become one of the largest chain store organizations in the world.

Your goals may not include such a scope of operations. However, the profits of your enterprise correlate with the caliber and type of person-

[1]From sermon by John Taylor, 18 May 1862, *Journal of Discourses,* 26 vols. (London: Latter-Day Saints' Book Depot, 1854–1886; Reprint ed. 1967), 10:57–58.

nel you select and how you utilize them in the operation of your business. The purpose of this chapter is to consider the ways and means of assisting you to be effective in managing human resources.

EMPLOYING PERSONNEL

Recruiting

What are your immediate personnel needs? In terms of your objectives, what will be your long-range personnel requirements? Consider the next job you want to fill in your business: what are the job requirements? In the process of recruiting you will find it very helpful to have a *job description* outlining the various duties of the particular job you want performed. The job description becomes a helpful guide in matching the job requirements with the qualifications of applicants being considered. Based on the nature of the applicant desired, recruiting may be accomplished from the following sources:

OPEN DOOR
A "help wanted" sign in the window may attract the attention of possible applicants. Sometimes people drop in, without any announcement, and apply for a job. Even though the particular job they apply for may not be open, it may be worthwhile to have them fill out an application form for future reference.

PRESENT EMPLOYEES
One of the most fruitful leads to applicants for small firms is a present employee. The recommendations of good workers may supply excellent applicants.

FORMER EMPLOYEES
The opening that needs to be filled may fit the qualifications of a former employee. Should they not be available, they may provide good leads.

EMPLOYMENT AGENCIES
There are federal, state, private, and personnel-search agencies. The governmental type agencies provide their services free, and may prove adequate. Private and search agencies usually charge for the special services rendered.

FIRMS DISCHARGING PERSONNEL

Firms releasing personnel because of cut-backs or other reasons may be able to offer good leads. However, remember that the best employees are not the first to be let go.

SCHOOLS

The placement offices of trade schools, business schools, and universities are often helpful in placing students and alumni.

TRADE AND PROFESSIONAL ASSOCIATIONS

Various local organizations may have placement services to assist in the placement of their membership. A low-cost notice in the society journal or newsletter, or possibly a notice on the bulletin board, may be productive of good prospective employees.

MILITARY

Many persons who have completed their military career have skills and knowledge that can significantly aid the small business firm's manpower requirements.

LABOR UNIONS

Certain types of personnel, such as electricians, plumbers, and carpenters may be secured through the local labor unions.

PART-TIME EMPLOYEES

Because of the fluctuation in business caused by peak periods, it may serve the personnel needs of the small-business person to utilize part-time personnel. In fact, it may be a very practical means of minimizing labor cost to utilize part-time personnel during daily peak periods, obviating the necessity of having excess personnel at slack periods of the normal working day. Possible sources would include students, both high school and college, retired persons who desire only a few hours of employment per day or per week, and perhaps individuals whose health only permits a limited amount of work.

Selection

Recruiting a job applicant is only the first step in the process of obtaining qualified personnel. From among the applicants, the small-business person must make a choice. The following tools are recommended to assist in this endeavor: the application, interviewing, tests, and references.

APPLICATION

The application should be designed to the particular needs of a company. It should contain basic information such as age, sex, marital status, military service status, previous employment, social security number, education, and personal references. For preliminary selection, the only physical data required is the height, weight, and any physical defects of the applicant.

The application is also useful in providing factual information about the employee, and it can be used as a permanent record to which additional experience and training may be added. A typical application blank is illustrated in Figure 13-1.

INTERVIEWING

Interviewing applicants is helpful in ascertaining appearance, speech, poise, and other characteristics. In preparation for an effective interview, the interviewer should carefully study the information on the application, the job description, and the specifications needed in connection with the job to be filled. The object of the process is to hire an individual qualified to fill the requirements of a particular position.

The physical setting and location of the interview is important. Select a suitable place where interruptions will be at a minimum. First off, put the applicant at ease. Begin with general questions designed to elicit conversation from the applicant, to "break the ice." If possible, it may be desirable to have more than one member of the firm interview the candidate.

The interview is also useful in pointing out information to the applicant concerning the company, employment conditions, compensation, company policies, and similar data. Questions of the applicant may also be answered. The applicant receiving favorable consideration for employment should receive specific instructions and encouragement as a part of the interview. The rejected applicants should part with a feeling of good will: they may even be considered at a later date.

TESTS

There are three general types of tests which may be used during the selection process: performance tests, psychological tests, and the physical examination. It should be kept in mind that a test is used to make the

Figure 13–1a & b.
Application for Employment. *Source:* Ernest L. Loen, *Personnel Management Guides for Small Business,* Small Business Management Series, no. 26 (Washington, D.C.: Small Business Administration, 1961).

APPLICATION FOR EMPLOYMENT

Date _____

Print Name _____

Address _____

City-State _____ Phone No. _____

In case of injury notify:
Name _____
Address _____

Marital Status _____
No. of Dependent Children _____
Other Dependents _____

Physical Defects (explain) _____

Position Desired _____

Earnings Expected _____

Date Available _____

Soc. Sec. No. _____

Height _____ Weight _____

Sex _____ Birth Date _____

Citizen of U. S.: Yes _____ No _____

Have You Ever Been Discharged from a Position _____

EDUCATION

School	Name and Location	Dates From	To	Years Completed	Dipl./Degree Yes	No	Major Course (Subject/Degree)
Grade							
High School							
College							
Graduate School							
Business or Trade							
Other							

Extracurricular School Activities _____

Current Hobbies _____

ARMED SERVICES RECORD: Have you served in the U. S. Armed Forces? Yes _____ No _____

Dates: From _____ To _____ Branch _____ Final Rank _____

Type of Discharge _____ Current Draft Status _____

PERSONAL REFERENCES

Name	Address	Occupation

EXPERIENCE (in chronological order)

Present Employer		Address	Kind of Business	
Starting Date	Starting	Salaries Present	Reason for Leaving	
Job Title	Supervisor's Name			May we Contact?

Description of Work _____

207

Figure 13-1b.

EXPERIENCE (continued in chronological order)

Next to last Employer		Address			Kind of Business	
Starting Date	Leaving Date		Salaries		Reason for Leaving	
			Starting	Leaving		
Job Title		Supervisor's Name				May We Contact?

Description of Work _____

_____

Employer		Address			Kind of Business	
Starting Date	Leaving Date		Salaries		Reason for Leaving	
			Starting	Leaving		
Job Title		Supervisor's Name				May We Contact?

Description of Work _____

_____

Employer		Address			Kind of Business	
Starting Date	Leaving Date		Salaries		Reason for Leaving	
			Starting	Leaving		
Job Title		Supervisor's Name				May We Contact?

Description of Work _____

_____

Employer		Address			Kind of Business	
Starting Date	Leaving Date		Salaries		Reason for Leaving	
			Starting	Leaving		
Job Title		Supervisor's Name				May We Contact?

Description of Work _____

_____

ADDITIONAL EXPERIENCE AND INFORMATION (licenses, special machines, etc.)_____

_____

_____

_____

_____

_____

_____

INTERVIEWER'S COMMENTS _____

_____

_____

Date of Interview _____   Interviewed By _____

selection process more effective. A test should be utilized to measure the intended purpose, but should not be the sole basis for selection. Under the provisions of the Civil Rights Act, tests must not discriminate against any specific group on the basis of sex, race, religion, color, or national origin. Because of some of the technical aspects of testing, it is recommended that tests be administered and interpreted by those with expertise. The small-business person may receive assistance in this regard from educational institutions, practicing psychologists, personnel institutes, or even from public employment agencies. The following is a list of kinds of tests and related jobs.[2]

Test	*Related Jobs*
Clerical Aptitude	
Minnesota Clerical Test	Office jobs
SRA Typing Skills	Typists
The Short Employment Tests	Office jobs
Creativity and Judgment	
AC Test of Creative Ability	Engineers
Owens Creativity Test for Machine Design	Engineers
Watson-Glaser Critical Thinking Appraisal	Executives
Dexterity	
Stromberg Dexterity Test	Foundry moulders, punch press operators, assemblers
Purdue Pegboard	Radio tube mounters, production jobs
O'Connor Finger and Tweezer Dexterity Tests	Instrument assembly
Intelligence	
Wonderlic Personnel Test Adaptability Test	Clerical, factory, maintenance, and sales jobs
Wesman Personnel Classification Test	
Concept Mastery Test	Managerial or executive job candidates

[2]Herbert J. Chruden and Arthur W. Sherman, Jr., *Personnel Management* (Cincinnati, Ohio: South-Western Pub. Co., 1976), p. 150.

Test	Related Jobs
General Aptitude Test Battery	United States Employment Service programs
Nonreading Aptitude Test Battery	
Employee Aptitude Survey	All types of jobs from executive to unskilled
Flanagan Industrial Kit	
	Wide variety of jobs — battery includes 18 short tests covering 18 different job elements

Interest

Strong Vocational Interest Blank	Administrative and sales jobs
Minnesota Vocational Interest Inventory	Various skilled jobs

Mechanical Aptitude

Test of Mechanical Comprehension	Variety of engineering and mechanical jobs
Revised Minnesota Paper Form Board Test	Mechanical shop work, drafting, design

Personality

Gordon Personal Profile and Inventory	Office workers, computer programmers, others
Edwards Personal Preference Schedule	
Guilford-Zimmerman Temperament Survey	Salespersons, supervisors
	Insurance salespersons, office workers
Thematic Apperception Test	Executives
California Personality Inventory	Managers and supervisors

Supervisory and Managerial Abilities

How Supervise?	Managerial and supervisory jobs
Supervisory Practices Test	
Management Aptitude Inventory	
Leadership Opinion Questionnaire	

REFERENCES

References can be checked when the applicant has met the preliminary requirements. This provides a means of verifying the truthfulness of the applicant's statements made on the application form and during the interview, as well as an opportunity for gaining additional information. Some companies find it desirable to obtain financial and personal data by paying a small fee to a local credit bureau. This provides a very helpful supplement to the usual statements given by past employers or personal friends about the applicant.

When making a reference check be alert to the accuracy of dates of employment, claims for responsibility, actual salary figures, or any information which may have been falsified concerning experience or education. The small-business person must carefully evaluate the information received from rererences. While confirming the data given by the applicant, be careful in accepting former employers' excessive criticism or praise.

An example of the credit bureau report is given in Figure 13-2. It is different from the ordinary credit report in that it provides educational background, employment history, and presumptive information concerning the character of the individual as obtained from public records. Under the terms of the Fair Credit Reporting Act of 1971, when an employer requests such a report from the local credit bureau there must be a notification to the job applicant within three days after ordering the report, stating: (1) that the report was requested; (2) that it might contain information about his character, personal characteristics, and mode of living; and (3) that the applicant has the right to request additional information concerning the nature and scope of the investigation—in which case the employer is obligated to comply with this request, in writing, within a period of five days. Such notifications are required whether or not the applicant is employed. However, in the case of an individual who has not specifically applied for the job, and who the employer may simply be screening because he might offer the job, such notifications are not required.

Orientation

The first few days on the job are important. The task of employee orientation may be summed up in these words: "Make the employee feel at home on the job." Try to understand the apprehension, even fear, that may be felt by a new employee. Take time to introduce the newcomer to other employees, to company facilities, to company operations, and to the particulars of the job. Explain the policies of the company so that the new employee knows what is expected. It may even be advisable to assign an employee to act as a "sponsor," to help the new employee become successfully orientated.

Figure 13–2.
Personnel Employment, Credit, and Character Form. *Source:* From Clifford M. Baumback, Kenneth Lawyer, and Pearce C. Kelley, *How to Organize and Operate a Small Business,* 5th ed. Copyright © 1973 by Prentice-Hall, Inc., Englewood Cliffs, N.J. Reprinted with permission of Prentice-Hall, Inc.

NAME AND ADDRESS OF CREDIT BUREAU MAKING REPORT

S P E C I M E N

PERSONNEL REPORT

Credit Bureau of Anytown
1234 Main Street
Anytown, Anystate 77036

DATE RECEIVED	DATE MAILED
8/3/72	8/6/72

CONFIDENTIAL *Factbilt* ® **REPORT**   FOR   XYZ Corporation

IN FILE SINCE: 6/65

This information is furnished in response to an inquiry for evaluating credit risks. It has been obtained from reliable sources, the accuracy of which is not guaranteed. The inquirer agrees to indemnify the reporting bureau for any damage arising from misuse of this information, and this report is furnished in reliance upon that indemnity. It must be held in strict confidence, and must not be revealed to the subject reported upon. If adverse action is taken based on this report, the subject reported on must be so advised and the reporting agency identified.

REPORT ON (SURNAME):	MR , MRS , MISS	GIVEN NAME	SOCIAL SECURITY NUMBER	SPOUSE'S NAME
DOE	Mr	Albert Frank	562-24-2716	Evelyn

ADDRESS	CITY	STATE	ZIP CODE	FROM	TO
8888 Oak Circle	Anytown	Anystate	77000	6/67	8/72

FORMER ADDRESS	CITY	STATE	ZIP CODE	FROM	TO
2036 Irving Drive	Thattown	Anystate	78000	10/65	6/67

DATE OF BIRTH: (IF NEAR 21, CONFIRM)	MARITAL STATUS	NUMBER OF DEPENDENTS INCLUDING SPOUSE
10/25/32	married	4

[ ] OWNS RESIDENCE   [ ] RENTING   [X] BUYING   [ ] BOARDING   [ ] LIVING WITH PARENTS   [ ] LIVING IN MOBILE HOME

EMPLOYMENT HISTORY

PRESENT EMPLOYER AND KIND OF BUSINESS	POSITION HELD	SINCE	MONTHLY INCOME
ABC Equipment Sales	Sales Manager	3/70	$ 1000

ESTIMATED INCOME FROM OTHER SOURCES
EXPLAIN: Wife employed part-time as receptionist; average $300 mo.

MOST RECENT FORMER EMPLOYER AND KIND OF BUSINESS:	POSITION HELD	FROM	TO	MONTHLY INCOME
DEF Corporation	Asst Manager	1/68	3/70	$ 900

ADDRESS OF MOST RECENT FORMER EMPLOYER:	REASON FOR LEAVING:	WOULD THEY RE-HIRE?
6006 Main Drive Thattown	Opportunity with ABC Co.	[X] YES [ ] NO

PREVIOUS FORMER EMPLOYER AND KIND OF BUSINESS	POSITION HELD	FROM	TO	MONTHLY INCOME
GHI Sales & Service	Route Salesman	1965	1/68	$ 800

ADDRESS OF PREVIOUS FORMER EMPLOYER	REASON FOR LEAVING	WOULD THEY RE-HIRE?
2 Interstate Street	moved to Anytown from Thattown	[X] YES [ ] NO

EDUCATION:

		NO. OF YEARS COMPLETED	WHEN GRADUATED	GRADE AVERAGE	COLLEGE MAJORS AND DEGREES EARNED
HIGH SCHOOL	Washington High, Thattown, Anystate	12	1950		
COLLEGE	State University at East Bend	4	1954	3.2	BS in Business Admin.

PUBLIC RECORD:

RELATING TO ANNULMENT OR DIVORCE. SHOW DISPOSITION OF CASE.	none
RELATING TO CRIMINAL CONVICTION. SHOW DISPOSITION OF ANY CASE.	none
RELATING TO CIVIL SUITS, JUDGMENTS OR BANKRUPTCY. SHOW DISPOSITION	none
RELATING TO PROPERTY OWNERSHIP.	Property Deed filed Apr. 1967 Recorder Office for purchase of lot at 8888 Oak Circle

CREDIT HISTORY AND REMARKS WHERE SPACE IS INSUFFICIENT ABOVE:

KIND OF BUSINESS	DATE ACCOUNT OPENED	DATE OF LAST SALE	HIGHEST CREDIT	AMOUNT OWING	AMOUNT PAST DUE	TERMS OF SALE AND USUAL MANNER OF PAYMENT
B 601	1965	1967	$20,000	$16,500	00	I-1
B 500	1970	12/70	3,500	1,500	00	I-$79-1
D 608	8/65	9/69	342	00	00	0-1
H 302	4/68	1/72	1,342	450	00	I-$45-1

FORM 17

Member Associated Credit Bureaus, Inc.

PRINTED IN U.S.A. 6/70

Training

A small-business person may spend much time and money in obtaining new employees; but unless the effort is backed with an effective training program, considerable losses may result. It is quite common for a small-business person to disregard training because he feels there is no time. The attitude that an employee can "pick up" the knowledge and skill required for the job may not only be inadequate, but very costly to the business. A small-business person would do well to consider these questions: What job openings are expected? Which employees need to be trained? What kind of training is needed by each employee? Regardless of the specialized or generalized knowledge an employee has, additional training is necessary in the specific techniques and activities required to satisfy the new employer.

There are several methods of training suitable for small businesses.

ON-THE-JOB TRAINING

This method allows for two different approaches: turn the man loose on the job and let him ask questions if he encounters problems; or assist the man in learning the job by providing a well-planned program. The latter may be accomplished by the four-step approach known as JIT (job instruction training):

1. *Prepare* the trainee by explaining to him the nature and importance of the job, as well as how it fits into the overall process.
2. *Present* the operation to the trainee, being careful to patiently explain and demonstrate each task involved in the job. Be sure to stress key points and welcome the trainee's questions.
3. *Tryout* the operation to see whether the trainee understands key points of the job. Have him explain key steps as he goes along, and comment if necessary; criticize diplomatically.
4. *Follow-up,* review and evaluate the performance to see how effectively the instructions have succeeded and what improvements are desirable.

GROUP TRAINING

In this method, a number of employees may be involved. Conferences, lectures, informal discussions, and role playing are useful methods for presenting information about new processes or new machines. Group training may also be used for developing future foremen or managers, for instruction on special techniques ("how to make a sale"), or for providing general information about business operations or some method of solving common problems. It may be possible to obtain training films to present to a group of employees. These are available through trade associations, audio-visual centers at major universities, film renting agencies, or governmental agencies.

SPECIALIZED TRAINING

Vocational training sponsored by state and federal organizations, covering a wide range of jobs, may be available at little or no cost in most communities. The United States Department of Labor and the United States Office of Education administer programs for adult training. There are also a number of other specialized programs available through school systems that provide coordinators for the purpose of administering specialized training programs.

OTHER TRAINING POSSIBILITIES

For certain types of trades, it may be desirable to utilize apprenticeship training. Within the small business there may be an opportunity to provide training through job rotation. This not only provides a means of combating the problem of monotony, but it enhances the value of the employees by giving them additional training.

Another possible training resource would be the suppliers of the business. They can often provide useful instruction with regard to the equipment or materials they provide.

The small-business person should recognize that training should not be confined to employees only; be quick to sense the importance of developing personal capabilities and skills as the head of the organization as well. Suggestions for doing so are outlined in Chapter 10 covering Personal Parameters.

Compensation

Compensation becomes a strategic factor in obtaining qualified applicants, retaining them in the business, and motivating them to maximum performance. Small-business people should understand fully how to compensate employees on a fair and equitable basis. It is also important to know how to "mix" the monetary remuneration paid to employees with the "fringe" benefits paid. The compensation policy of the firm will be modified by the presence or absence of "union scale," the impact of competitive compensation, and the cost of living in a particular area.

It is important to make equitable differentiation between the relative worth of jobs. This may be accomplished through "job evaluation." This is a process of comparing jobs on the basis of factors such as skill, education, responsibility, working conditions, effort, and similar factors. Assistance in establishing a job evaluation program for your company may be obtained from the faculty of nearby universities.

The options which are commonly considered for the purpose of payment to employees include straight salary, hourly payment, piece rate, and bonus or commission.

Employee Benefits

Commonly referred to as "fringe benefits," these items have had a substantial increase both in number and in cost in recent years. It has been estimated by the United States Chamber of Commerce that the cost of fringe benefits as a percentage of wages and salaries paid has increased from 3 percent in 1929 to over 26 percent. In the survey conducted by the Chamber of Commerce, employee benefits average 30.8 percent of the payroll of all companies included. While frings benefits are more common ion larger firms, many small businesses have had added some benefits to retain employees.

To illustrate the types of items covered under fringe benefits, the following list is provided.

Paid vacations
Paid holidays
Paid rest periods, lunch periods, wash-up time, travel time, etc.
Profit-sharing payment
Employee meals furnished by the company
Insurance plan (life insurance, health insurance, accident insurance)
Payment for jury duty, National Guard, or Military Reserve duty
Bonuses (Christmas, year-end)
Discounts on goods and services purchased by employees from the company
Pension plan
Employee education
Unemployment compensation
Workmen's compensation
Legally required insurance payments (old age, survivors', disability, and health insurance)

As a matter of company policy, it would be well to indicate which specific holidays will be taken and paid for by the company, such as Christmas Day, Thanksgiving Day, Independence Day, etc. The vacation policy should also be indicated. In some companies one week may be given after one year of employment. The number of days or weeks of vacation is increased over time: for those employees with greater longevity, more extended vacations are provided.

Sick-leave benefits are also important to employees of small firms. A common practice is to allow an employee to earn one day of allowance of sick leave per month of employment. The small-business person should consider (as with wages) the prevailing standards within the community as guidelines. A good employee-benefit program should be productive in generating high morale among the employees.

Transfers and Promotions

Changes in the occupation of workers, which are not properly considered as promotions, are normally called transfers. The following four conditions suggest needs for transfers:

The elimination of a particular job
A request for a change by an employee
The feeling by management that the worker has been misplaced
Fluctuations in the requirements for certain types of jobs

A promotion is a new assignment with greater difficulty, requiring more skill or some increased measure of responsibility, and is consequently a better-paying job. In the selection of personnel for promotion, merit and seniority are important factors. Seniority should only be used in those cases where employees are equal in qualifications. The use of data from performance appraisal (which will be discussed later) can be most helpful in ascertaining who should be promoted and to what position. Some companies have found it very useful to make an assignment on a trial basis before deciding on a promotion.

Employee Records

To have a more effective personnel program, it is recommended that some records appropriate to the needs of the business be developed and utilized, rather than trusting to memory those important items of information which should become a part of the employee's file. An efficient and easy managed records system can be set up for the individual employee by using a nine-by-twelve inch envelope. Place the name of the employee on the tab, which includes his employment application, birth and citizenship certificates, etc. A personnel report form can be designed for use by supervisors in reporting outstanding work performance, progress on the job, change in work attitude, tardiness, absence, and breach of discipline. Such information is recorded on the personnel report form, dated, signed by the supervisor, and given to the individual in charge of personnel — who files it in the employee's envelope. Having a simple system of employee records will keep the personnel authority informed about the employee. Through minimum record keeping, a permanent file on the employee will be available for use in promotions, counseling, transfers, discipline, and in union negotiations of grievances, if necessary.

MAINTAINING PERSONNEL

Personnel Problems

ABSENTEEISM

One of the most common problems of management is the worker who does not come to work. Absenteeism results in temporary unavailability and is characteristic of lower-paid occupations. It is usually dealt with by threats of dismissal. The effect of absenteeism on productivity is usually under-estimated.

Perhaps the best remedy for absenteeism can be better determined after understanding the specific causes. Five of the most common types of absenteeism are listed below.

Chronic absentees are those who have developed a habit of staying away from work because of relatively minor discomforts or inconveniences that most people would take in stride. They simply have a bad habit. Chronic absentees can usually be distinguished by one or a combination of signs: (1) they consistantly account for more days lost than other people in the department; (2) they have very little tolerance for frustration or pressure; and (3) this pattern has continued for a long time.

Escapist absentees are those whose interest in the job is so low that other interests — especially hobbies and enjoyable pursuits — compete effectively with the job. Escapist absentees are usually engaged in some favorite endeavor (such as hunting, fishing, or some sport activity) when they are absent from work. They are best described as persons who are trying to extricate themselves, at least temporarily, from a situation which they dislike but cannot afford to leave permanently. Escapist absenteeism may be identified by these distinguishing marks: (1) it occurs sporatically, a day here and a day there, rather than several consecutive days; (2) it tends to fall just before or just after a weekend or a holiday; and (3) the absentees almost always feel underutilized in their jobs.

Immature absentees are not necessarily young, although this is the leading kind of absenteeism among younger workers. "Immaturity" refers to ideas and attitudes, not to age.

Abusive absentees are comparatively rare, but difficult — and so memorable that it sometimes seems there are more of such people than there are. Abusive absentees are less interested in time off than in proving a point, such as the fact that they will not tolerate what they regard as favoritism or unfair treatment. The reasons for their absences are not usually disguised.

Legitimate absentees are those employees who are unable to work because of illness, or who must be absent for a reason which the company rules recognize. Sooner or later, almost every employee falls into this category. Identification is easy; absences are rare and they are probably legitimate.

Absenteeism may be a problem in your business. If it is, it should be dealt with by an appropriate policy and procedure.

Turnover

Turnover results in a permanent unavailability of employees. It is more characteristic of higher-paid occupations and is typically dealt with on financial premises. Its effect on productivity is usually overestimated. There are two definable demographic groups that seem to be more susceptible to voluntary turnover than do other groups: young people of all kinds under the age of twenty-five, and better-educated men in the age thirty-five to forty-five range. Some of the factors affecting the younger group include impatience, limited tolerance for frustration, curiosity, lack of binding commitments, uncertainty as to what one really wants to do, and the fact that young people are given the least desirable assignments.

If turnover manifests itself in serious proportions, the following standard prescription may offer possible solution: (1) Find out why people are leaving. Rather than using the "exit interview," contact the persons four to six weeks after they have terminated — when they are both more objective and more voluble. Be on the lookout for general patterns rather than individual problems, and make whatever corrections are necessary. (2) Be sure wages and salaries are competitive. (3) Endeavor to increase nonfinancial satisfactions, especially by decreasing unnecessary controls on personal initiative, and also by adding planning and decision functions to those jobs most afflicted by turnovers.[3]

Grievances

Grievances involve complaints of all varieties, such as psychological or financial injuries, failure to keep promises, or simply unfairness. Considering human nature and organizational life for what they are, practically everyone is likely to be aggrieved at some time or other.

In writing about grievances, Saul Gellerman says they have characteristics of a fluid: when channels are not provided for them, they cut their own. If they are dammed, they will exert great pressures against the weakest point, and the dam will always be in danger of giving way. Grievances can be condemned, ignored, or debated; but none of these tactics will make them go away. The best formula for handling grievances is to "nip them in the bud."

HOW DO YOU UNCOVER GRIEVANCES?

1. Recognize the signs of a grievance.
2. Investigate tardiness and absenteeism with the idea of uncovering a grievance.
3. When quantity and quality of output are off, look for a grievance.
4. Listen to workers expressing their grievances.

HOW DO YOU RESOLVE GRIEVANCES?

This outline of procedure may be helpful:

1. Define the problem.
2. Gather the facts from as many sources as possible.

---

[3]Saul Gellerman, *The Management of Human Resources* (Hinsdale, Ill.: The Dryden Press, 1976), pp. 121–146.

3. Formulate solutions in terms of policies and principles.
4. Back up your best possible solution with strong arguments.
5. Make sure the solution is applied.
6. Follow up on the effectiveness of the solution.
7. Evaluate the procedure to determine if the settlement of grievances is bringing management and workers closer together.

Union Relations

A lot of small business people run scared when the subject of a union is raised in connection with their employees. This is pure foolishness. It is legal for the employees to be represented by a union, and the righs of the employees are specified according to law. The rights of management are also specified by law, and the mere presence of a union need not be regarded as a tragedy. There are many firms both large and small who have enjoyed a cooperative relationship with unions representing the employees.

The greatest difficulty arises when the small business person endeavors to negotiate union relations without the benefit of special assistance or legal counsel. Most small employers have little or no knowledge of the federal and state labor laws, and have no time to acquire this knowledge. If the question of a union arises, consult with your lawyer. If necessary, obtain special legal counsel for guidance and direction in establishing a proper labor contract. The details of a labor contract appear in the appendix of this chapter.

Discipline

Discipline means training to act in accordance with rules or instructions designed to train for proper conduct or action. It also implies punishment for violation of rules or for behavior that is unbecoming. Wisdom would dictate not too many rules; but the rules that are established, should be upheld. The following guidelines should prove helpful in maintaining the proper discipline among company personnel:

1. Everyone should understand why these rules and regulations exist.
2. Employees should be informed about discipline policies.
3. Avoid taking action while you are angry.
4. Be sure discipline is in order before administering it (get the facts).
5. Get the offender's side of the story.

6. Reprimand in private.
7. Avoid sarcasm and ridicule.
8. Consider extenuating circumstances.
9. Avoid rules that are too rigid.

Terminating Employees

Terminating employees is not a pleasant experience. It may become necessary to terminate people because they have failed to measure up to expectations or because there is a company cutback. The usual tendency is to procrastinate as long as possible, with the attitude of "give George just one more chance." Usually, this process is a form of rationalization — when in reality you are almost certain that the person will not make it. Make a decision. Take the proper action, and avoid repeated warnings, probationary periods, etc., which merely prolong the agony. When you permit a low performer to stay around, you damage the morale of the entire group. Worse than that, you handicap the functional area for which the person is responsible. Give the employee notice (usually two weeks) and tell him to use the two weeks to get another job. Don't keep him around the business after he has been terminated.

When you are confronted with a cut-back the situation is more difficult. It becomes necessary not only to release the marginal employees but some of those you would like to retain if it were not for the economic problems. The important thing is to make the necessary cutbacks without demolishing the morale of the remaining employees. It is recommended that you make the cuts at one time, if possible, and avoid the weekly terminations every Friday. While the effect of one cut may be shocking, it will challenge the remaining employees to close ranks and try to get the job done without the people who have left. By "dropping off" a few each week, the effect would be to destroy the morale of the remaining employees, who wonder if their names will be next.

Of course, assisting employees who are terminated for either reason, is recommended.

Performance Appraisal

Recognizing that a prime factor for profitability is effective personnel, it is a wise policy to have a periodic evaluation of the performance of employees. Employee rating may be conducted as often as necessary.

Figure 13-3.
Employee Rating Scale. *Source: Personnel Management,* Administrative Management Course Program, Topic 6 (Washington, D.C.: Small Business Administration, U.S. Government Printing Office).

Employee Rating Scale

Name _____ Date _____
Dept. _____ Job _____
Rated by _____

Instructions

This Rating Scale is an aid to measuring—with a reasonable degree of accuracy and uniformity—the abilities of one of your employees and his skill in his present job. It will help you to appraise his present performance as compared with previous performance in the same job; and it may indicate promotion possibilities. Because the rating requires your appraisal of the employee's actual performance, snap judgment must be replaced by careful analysis. The following instructions may be helpful.

1. Disregard your general impression and concentrate on a single factor at a time.
2. Read all four specifications for each factor before determining which one most nearly fits the employee.
3. In rating an employee, make your judgment on instances occuring frequently in his daily routine. Don't be swayed by isolated incidents that aren't typical of his work.
4. Don't let personal feelings govern your rating. Make it carefully so that it represents your fair, objective opinion.

Factor	1	2	3	4
a. Quality of work	Poor; often does unacceptable work; is careless, requires constant supervision.	Fair; needs supervision and frequent checking.	Generally good; makes only occasional mistakes; requires little supervision.	Excellent; work is A-1 most of time; makes very few mistakes; needs supervision only very occasionally.
b. Quantity of work	Very slow; almost never does complete job in time assigned for it.	Erratic; sometimes fast and efficient, othertimes slow and unskillful.	Steady worker; does job consistently, and occasionally does more.	Exceptionally fast; does work quickly and well; does extra work to stay busy.

c. Flexibility	Very adaptable; fast learner, quickly meeting needs of new situation or assignment.	Quick; learns new assignment in short time if given some instruction.	Adequate; requires thorough, complete instruction before taking on new duties or new	Does not adapt readily to new situations; most of the time, instructions must be repeated.
d. Job knowledge	Full knowledge of job; able to proceed alone on almost all work.	Well informed about job; rarely needs instruction or assistance.	Passable knowledge of job; needs frequent instruction and continuing supervision.	Limited knowledge of job; shows little desire to improve.
e. Responsibility	Excellent Attendance record; most reliable in doing work assigned; can always be depended on.	Attendance record good; reliable in work.	Some absences; occasionally needs reminder to do work assigned.	Irresponsible in attendance; seldom carries out orders without being prodded.
f. Housekeeping and safety	Keeps work area spotless; is unusually careful about safety.	Keeps work area clean; is careful about safety.	From time to time, cleans work area; is occasionally negligent about safety.	Never cleans working area; is reckless in behavior.
g. Attitude	Exceptionally cooperative; very interested in work; always helpful to others and considerate of them.	Usually cooperative; attentive to work; gets along well with others.	Some cooperation, but is often indifferent both to fellow workers and to quality of own work.	Uncooperative; often complains; is a disruptive influence among other employees.

However, semiannually would be a most appropriate time frame. To enhance such a program it is suggested that the ratings be conducted by at least two people in the organization. One would be the manager of the small business and the other would be the immediate supervisor or a member of the management team.

There are a number of factors for which an employee may be evaluated, depending upon the type of work assignment. The more common items would include skill, effort, attitude, and responsibility. Comparing ratings over a period of time enables the small-business person to note progress of the individual and recommend areas for improvement.

One of the most essential parts of the evaluation program is the counseling after the appraisal has been made. This phase is often neglected. To minimize the apprehensiveness of employees, emphasis should be placed on positive accomplishments, not just negative factors. After all, the purpose of the employee evaluation program is to help the employees improve their performance. The form in Figure 13-3 may be helpful in inaugurating your personnel evaluation program.

Improving Performance— Motivation and Morale

Morale has to do with employee attitudes toward the work situation. Morale is not the same in all companies; nor does it remain the same over a period of time in a particular company. The particular degree of morale at a given time has a direct impact on the profitability of the enterprise. Low morale can contribute to low profits and high morale can contribute to high profits.

There may be various ways of ascertaining the degree of morale in an organization. A common method is the use of a morale survey. A questionnaire is prepared with various questions to be answered, indicating the range of satisfaction by the personnel. The importance of morale would indicate that it should be measured periodically so that appropriate steps may be taken to maintain high morale or to improve morale.

A number of symptoms may point to low morale: declining productivity, high employee turnover, increasing numbers of grievances, higher incidence of absenteeism and tardiness, increasing number of defective products, higher number of accidents, or a higher level of waste materials and scrap. The small-business person should analyze these symptoms and ascertain the cause—the problem. It is only by defining the underlying problem that the small-business person will be able to determine a proper solution.

By paying attention to employee behavior you may be able to ascertain which of the following situations characterizes your company: Do you receive healthy complaints, unhealthy complaints, or no complaints at all? A healthy complaint may not lead to a deterioration of morale, but that is no reason for ignoring it. Unhealthy complaints may lead to a deterioration of morale, or even to undesirable behavior. The third case—no complaints—is the most difficult situation to deal with. Rather than assuming all is well, investigate. A morale survey may be helpful to reveal the true situation.

One of the most important factors affecting morale is the style of leadership. Sometimes unconsciously, the owner-manager does things that are damaging to the morale. By using an anonymous survey, some of the conditions—leadership patterns—may be surfaced for consideration. The important question remains: are you willing to improve morale when the improvement depends on you?

Some guidelines have been offered which may prove helpful:

1. Tell and show your employees that you are interested in them and that you would be glad to have their ideas on how conditions might be improved.
2. Treat your employees as individuals; never deal with them as impersonal variables in a working unit.
3. Improve your general understanding of human behavior.
4. Accept the fact that others may not see things as you do.
5. Respect differences of opinion.
6. Insofar as possible, give explanations for management actions.
7. Provide information and guidance on matters affecting employees' security.
8. Make reasonable efforts to keep jobs interesting.
9. Encourage promotion from within.
10. Express appreciation publicly for jobs well done. Offer criticism privately in the form of constructive suggestions for improvement.
11. Train supervisors to think about the people involved, insofar as practicable, rather than just the work.
12. Keep your people up-to-date on all business matters affecting them, and squelch rumors with correct information.
13. Be fair.[4]

---

[4]Martin M. Bruce, "Managing for Better Morale," *Small Marketers Aids Annual No. 4* (Washington, D.C.: Small Business Administration, 1962), pp. 59–60.

MOTIVATION

Whether you subscribe to Abraham Maslow's Hierarchy of Needs, Frederic Herzberg's Two-Factor System, Douglas McGregor's Theory X and Theory Y, Peter F. Drucker's Management by Objectives (MBO), or the theory of Management and Motivation called the "Managerial Grid" advanced by Robert R. Blake and Jane S. Mouton, the significance of all these contributions from research indicate that people do not necessarily work harder when they are promised more money; nor do they slack off when deprived of the monetary rewards. The essence of it all is that people are motivated by different things. It is imperative for you to understand employees individually. Know their true motives, needs, and desires so that you can properly address yourself accordingly and motivate the employee.

One of the objectives of managing human resources is to achieve a high degree of motivation. This is a great challenge. Progress in achieving this object should result in positive inputs toward increasing the profitability of the firm. Someone said that the only true motivation is self-motivation. In this sense, a small-business person cannot motivate a subordinate, but a small-business person can provide opportunities for subordinates to do things or provide incentives that would lead to the satisfying of the subordinate's need. The small-business manager can motivate personnel by providing chances for the subordinates to fulfill their needs.

SUMMARY

In the final analysis, business is transacted with people, for people, and by people. In still another sense, it is your people who can make your business or break your business; and to a large extent the answer depends on you. Which will it be?

Looking at the broad strokes in the human resource picture, there is the employment system, the personnel maintenance function, and the performance question. Your employees deserve to know what their job is and who their boss is. Too frequently these two basic items are completely overlooked with regrettable consequences.

If you maximize the contribution of each employee, you will provide a worthwhile development program. In supporting the cost of a training program, bear in mind that you will "pay" for training one way or the other. Well-trained personnel are more productive. Untrained personnel can be destructive.

Take time to know the human resources—the human equation—in your business. Successful small-business people have expanded businesses and profits by learning how to multiply their capabilities through people.

As an appendix to this chapter, some information about union contracts has been included.

The Union Contract

The signing of a union contract is an important occasion. It signifies that all the stresses and strains of the bargaining sessions are over and that the two parties have finally reached an agreement. The signing ceremony is an important symbol to many workers and it is a good idea to publicize it accordingly. Whether or not each worker gets a copy of the contract, the entrepreneur would do well to call a management meeting after the signing to make sure his employees understand each clause thoroughly. The managers can then clarify any point for employees under their supervision.

Smooth union—management relations are greatly enhanced if the contract is clear and concise on every point. In drawing up an agreement, it is therefore well worthwhile to include all of the following points:

Preamble. Since the union contract is in part a public-relations tool, it is not out of place to begin by briefly mentioning its purpose and the desire of management and union to reach a harmonious working agreement.

Conditions of recognition. Controversy sometimes develops because contracts were left vague on this point. Thus, it pays the manager to mention the kind of union security his company is offering: for example, union shop, maintenance-of-membership, sole bargaining, and/or check-off (in which union dues are deducted before paying union employees).

Management clause. Immediately following the union-recognition clause, there should be a statement of management's rights, responsibilities, and the areas of action in which it remains free from questioning by the union. This clause can be quite controversial. Thus, the employer needs as much contract protection as he can get. He should also make sure that he gets this clause in where it belongs, rather than tucked away somewhere at the end. The smaller employer cannot afford to have his rights merely implied.

Working conditions. Because this area of collective bargaining affects employees directly, the union contract should cover all these points and any others that may apply to the company because of environmental circumstances: right to hire and fire; hours of work, including clauses to explain when overtime begins, when Sunday begins and ends, and when holidays begin and end; seniority, including provision for all situations—plant-wide, departmental, job, ability, and family status.

Wages. It is wiser to cover wages in a supplementary agreement, or in an appendix, because the contract may provide for annual or semiannual review that will result in changes in wage rates.

Health and welfare clauses. The contract may provide that the employer make a deduction from the employee's salary for the union health and welfare fund. However, according to the Taft-Hartley Act, sums so deducted may be used only for deaths, sickness, accident, retirement, medical, and unemployment benefits. Employees are permitted to contribute only if the fund is established under a written agreement and is administered jointly by employer and employees. These points should be mentioned in the contract.

Grievance-handling procedure. No union contract should be without a clause specifying what a grievance is (wages usually are not included) and how to file a grievance, step by step. The employee should know exactly to whom he should present his grievance, what to expect after that, and what his next steps are if the first one brings no results.

Continuation clause. Every contract should provide an expiration clause. In the case of a blanket contract with several craft unions involved, it is wise to state the wages separately but use the same basic contract with identical expiration dates.[4]

[5]Ernest L. Loen, *Personnel Management Guides for Small Business* (Washington, D.C.: Small Business Administration, 1961).

14

Manufacturing

*"That carpenter is not the best
Who makes more chips than all the rest"*

A. Guiterman

The importance of manufacturing in the United States is attested to by the fact that there are over 300,000 manufacturing establishments. A great majority (95.7 percent) of manufacturing establishments have fewer than 250 employees.

TABLE 14-1

Employment Size	Percentage
1 – 4	38.4%
5 – 9	12.9%
10 – 19	13.6%
20 – 49	16.0%
50 – 99	8.2%
100 – 249	6.5%
250 – 499	2.5%
500 – 999	1.1%
1000 – 2499	0.5%
2500 – Over	0.2%

Source: U.S. Bureau of the Census, Census of Manufacturers. Subjects, The Statistics: *Size of Establishments.* (Washington, D.C.: U.S. Government Printing Office, 1972).

Recognizing the importance of manufacturing as small business, the purpose of this chapter will be to consider the essential elements for managing a manufacturing operation profitably.

PLANNING AND CONTROLLING MANUFACTURING

The objective of planning and controlling manufacturing is to secure an orderly processing rate of products sufficient to meet the delivery schedule for customers. This objective may be achieved by: the elimination of production bottlenecks, the efficient utilization of manpower and machines, and the avoidance of stoppages. Planning and controlling activities should facilitate the flow of work through the plant with minimum production delays. Some of the major causes for work stoppages are listed below:

1. Planning errors
2. Material shortages
3. Bad parts or materials
4. Machine breakdowns
5. Lack of proper tools, dies, jigs, fixtures, or gauges
6. Absent personnel

There may be additional reasons for work stoppages. However, minimizing the above prime reasons will contribute considerably toward profitable manufacturing operations.

To establish an effective control system for manufacturing involves the performance of five essential functions: three involve planning and two involve control.

PLANNING

The object of this function is to determine in advance the necessary raw materials and parts along with the number of workers, the number and type of machines, and the completion times for each of the different operations involved.

Routing

The object of this function is to establish the operations to be performed, to determine the proper sequence, and to designate the flow of materials through the production process. This work is facilitated by route sheets, or operation sheets, which are used to prescribe what is to be done and how it is to be done.

Scheduling

The object of this function is to assign a time frame to the production activities. The preparation of a master schedule will show the dates when delivery is promised to customers, with a breakdown showing detailed schedules for the semi-finished parts — necessary so that all components will be available at the proper time and place to facilitate completion of all operations necessary.

Dispatching

The object of this function is to insure that the three previous planning functions are executed as planned. Dispatching involves issuing work orders and progress reports for the purpose of controlling manufacturing.

Expediting

The object of this function is to ascertain the progress of the production plans and to eliminate bottlenecks to insure the completion of the manufacturing plan.

To facilitate planning and controlling manufacturing operations, a variety of charts have been developed to implement the control process, such as the Gantt chart illustrated in Figure 14-1. A chart is a graphic representation of the manufacturing situation. A Gantt chart provides a listing of the shop operations and machines in sequence on the verticle axis, and the horizontal axis provides a time scale which can be regulated by days and hours. It is suggested that the appropriate type of charts be developed and utilized to facilitate the productive process for the particular company. (See Figure 14-1 for details.)

Figure 14–1.
Gantt Chart (Scheduling Chart for Manufacturing). *Source:* George R. Terry, *Principles of Management,* seventh ed. (Homewood, Ill.: Richard D. Irwin, Inc., 1977c.). Reprinted with permission of the publisher.

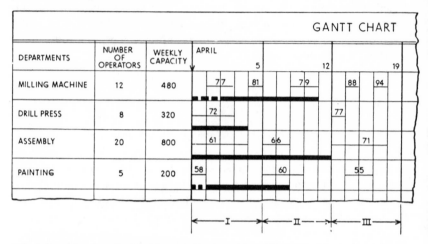

Scheduling gives practical implementation to a plan. The above illustration is known as a Gantt Chart, originally developed by Henry L. Gantt, a management practitioner prominent at the beginning of the twentieth century. The manufacturing departments are listed down the left side. The time frame, divided into weeks, is designated along the bottom as I, II, and III. You will note that week I ends on April 5th. Opposite each department there are two lines, one heavy and one light. These lines represent starting and ending times for work in each department. For example, in the painting department, during the week ending April 5th, order No. 58 is scheduled to be initiated and completed on Monday. The heavy line opposite each department represents the cumulative time scheduled for the respective department. Hence the painting department is scheduled for six days involving order numbers 58, 60, and 55. This chart is illustrative of the control charts that can be developed to facilitate control of manufacturing operations.*

Two factors directly affect the production control system, the nature of the product and the type of manufacturing involved. The control functions required for making color television sets are quite different from those required for making bread. Also, production control functions vary from the intermittent to the continuous type of manufacturing processes. Producing custom furniture presents a different control matrix than do the continuous operations of a fruit-processing plant.

---

*George R. Terry, *Principles of Management,* 7th ed. (Homewood, Ill.: Richard D. Irwin Co., 1977), pp. 175–76.

IMPROVING WORK METHODS

The object of this effort is to control waste, reduce worker fatigue, and enhance efficient productivity—all of which should contribute to the maximization of profit from the manufacturing function in the business.

Waste Control

Our prime concern is the elimination of waste as it relates to time, materials, and machinery in the performance of various jobs. In order to control waste it is necessary to identify the sources and to institute appropriate control measures. Some areas to check include waste from poor buying, stock pilferage from storerooms, poor material-cutting methods, using inefficient or obsolete equipment and tooling, failing to return surplus materials to the stockrooms, loafing of personnel, and idleness of expensive equipment and machinery.

Effective salvage operations and utilization of unavoidable waste materials can also contribute to profitable operations—for example, in the sale of sawdust, scrap metal, packing cartons, and materials.

Another dimension of waste control is the establishment of consumption standards. It is essential to determine the amounts of materials required for the production of each unit. Comparisons can then be made between the standard amount established and the actual usage in operations. Corrective action can be initiated in those cases where usage is excessive. This data is also useful in the evaluation of worker performance.

Work Simplification

Work simplification is a vital part of improving work methods. Simplification includes the elimination of unnecessary or superfluous items. An analysis should be made of the entire operation, as well as of specific motions of individuals involved in performing repetitive work. Areas to be investigated include time, space, weight, distance, and factors related to the manufacturing process, for the purpose of determining the movement sequence with the aim of reducing the physical effort and achieving the shortest completion time. Familiarity with the principles of motion economy (as they relate with the layout of the work area, the designing and use of tools, and the use of the hands and body movements) will be helpful in making progress with regard to work simplification. Some of the most widely used principles are listed in the following paragraphs.

Principles of Motion Economy—
A Check Sheet
for Motion Economy and Fatigue Reduction[1]

These twenty-two rules or principles of motion economy may be profitably applied to shop and office work alike. Although not all are applicable to every operation, they do form a basis or a code for improving efficiency and reducing fatigue in manual work.

Use of the Human Body

1. The two hands should begin as well as complete their motions at the same time.

2. The two hands should not be idle at the same time except during rest periods.

3. Motions of the arms should be made in opposite and symmetrical directions and should be made simultaneously.

4. Hand motions should be confined to the lowest classification with which it is possible to perform the work satisfactorily.

5. Momentum should be employed to assist the worker wherever possible, and it should be reduced to a minimum if it must be overcome by muscular effort.

6. Smooth continuous motions of the hands are preferable to zigzag motions or straight-line motions involving sudden and sharp changes in direction.

7. Ballistic movements are faster, easier, and more accurate than restricted (fixation) or "controlled" movements.

8. Rhythm is essential to the smooth and automatic performance of an operation, and the work should be arranged to permit easy and natural rhythm wherever possible.

Arrangement of the Workplace

9. There should be a definite and fixed place for all tools and materials.

10. Tools, materials, and controls should be located close in and directly in front of the operator.

11. Gravity feedbins and containers should be used to deliver materials close to the point of use.

12. Drop deliveries should be used wherever possible.

13. Materials and tools should be located to permit the best sequence of motions.

---

[1]R. M. Barnes, *Motion and Time Study: Design and Measurement of Work.* Copyright © 1968 by John Wiley and Sons, Inc. Reprinted by permission of John Wiley and Sons, Inc.

14. Provisions should be made for adequate conditions for seeing. Good illumination is the first requirement for satisfactory visual perception.

15. The height of the workplace and the chair should preferably be arranged so that alternate sitting and standing at work are easily possible.

16. A chair of the type and height to permit good posture should be provided for every worker.

Design of Tools and Equipment

17. The hands should be relieved of all work that can be done more advantageously by a jig, a fixture, or a foot-operated device.

18. Two or more tools should be combined whenever possible.

19. Tools and materials should be prepositioned whenever possible.

20. Where each finger performs some specific movement such as in typewriting, the load should be distributed in accordance with the inherent capacities of the fingers.

21. Handles, such as those used on cranks and large screwdrivers, should be designed to permit as much of the surface of the hand to come in contact with the handle as possible. This is particularly true when considerable force is exerted in using the handle. For light assembly work the screwdriver handle should be so shaped that it is smaller at the bottom than at the top.

22. Levers, crossbars, and handwheels should be located in such positions that the operator can manipulate them with the least change in body position and with the greatest mechanical advantage.

Work Standards

When the improved or "best" method has been determined, it should be established as a work standard so that all workers can be trained in it. Standardization implies conforming to preferred or established ways of doing things. A standard becomes the basis of measuring performance — a basis for comparing the actual with the desired results. Some areas for which standards may be established include: product standards indicating tolerances and quality desired; design standards indicating tolerances of components parts, which will insure interchangeability; materials standards which specify form, composition, and similar characteristics of raw materials; performance standards which specify output rates, motion sequences, and material usage; process standards which deal with plant operating methods and workplace layout; equipment standards which specify appropriate size and capability for particular manufacturing operations; and working-condition standards, which involve light, temperature, and layout considerations.

Time Study

After completing an analysis of work operations, attention may be directed to the analysis of individual jobs, by applying the principles of motion study previously mentioned. With the proper attitude toward improving performance, the activities may be advanced from motion study to actual time studies. Most small firms may not have personnel with the expertise to perform accurate time studies. However, the advantages of having time studies as a means of developing useful work standards should be carefully investigated. The establishment of time standards facilitates such activities as scheduling and controlling production as well as incentive wage plans based upon output.

Some corrollary benefits to the time study include: improving layout, mechanizing materials handling, proper locating of machine controls, installing safety devices, and improving product design. A time-study engineer may be employed to achieve these advantages.

Quality refers to those characteristics which suit a product to a particular need. There are various degrees of quality possible in some products. However, only the desired quality is important: quality of a lesser degree may preclude the sale of the product; quality of a higher degree may preclude profitability from operations because of the higher cost to achieve it. The desired quality, in terms of demand for the product, must be ascertained with care. The supply of the particular quality will be the means to profitable operations.

Inspection

Inspection presupposes that there are known standards by which the products may be judged. In some operations the "eye method" is used, and quality is dependent upon the training and capability of the inspectors. Some inspections can be accomplished with the use of equipment, such as measuring devices and gauges, and the inspector should receive training in the use of these items of inspection. In addition to being honest and objective, the inspector must be capable of withstanding the pressure which shop personnel may generate to pass questionable items.

Inspection standards used in manufacturing are established by means of design tolerances. These tolerances are usually set for each important quality variable, and provide the limits of variation permitted above and below the desired measurement. Obviously, the tolerances established by the manufacturer should meet the requirements of the customer. The inspector must reject those items which fail to meet the tolerance limits.

It is important to determine where and when to inspect. The insurance of proper quality in raw materials demands that there be inspection at the receiving room. Subsequent inspections should be made at critical points—before those operations which would conceal existing defects and/or after operations which may produce excessive amounts of defects. Inspection may also precede the transfer of lots from one department to another—to avoid passing on any defective materials to further processing that would add to the cost of items which may ultimately be rejected. Such inspection may be referred to as a *clearance inspection.* Perhaps the most important inspection of all is the *final inspection,* which clears the product for transfer to the customer. In addition to inspection of materials and products in process, it is imperative that the inspection equipment be checked for suitability and that the plant facilities are checked periodically—including the electrical equipment, boilers, furnaces, and other machinery.

Some items may require "100 percent inspection," which may prove to be expensive. Because of the cost of inspection, efforts should be made to minimize it. One of the ways to do this purpose is to convert to inspection by automatic machines. In such instances the automatic machine setting and consequent check of operations is tantamount to insurance of satisfactory quality control.

Statistical Quality Control (SQC)

The use of statistical methods may be warranted for some manufacturing operations. While these control methods are more sophisticated, the process is not unreasonably complicated. Examples of the type of control charts used in SQC are shown in Figure 14-2 and Figure 14-3. Statistical procedures for preparing similar charts will be found in the bibliography material at the end of the text.

Control charts are developed and used to indicate the operation of a process within the prescribed limits of tolerance. Once the control limits are determined, the use of the charts is a matter of posting sample values and reporting exceptional results. Corrective action should be promptly

Figure 14–2.
Sample X Chart (Average Length in Each Sample). *Source:* Adapted from Broom and Longenecker, *Small Business Management* (Cincinnati, Ohio: South-Western Publishing Company, 1975), p. 508. Reprinted by permission of the publisher.

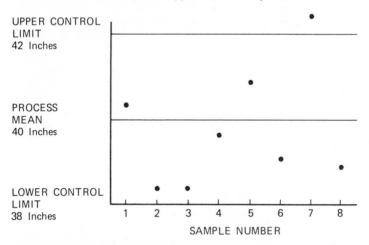

The variable being controlled in the above chart is the average length of pieces of lumber. Each of the eight samples taken consecutively contains twelve items. It is the average length of the twelve items in each sample which is plotted on the control chart. That the above operation was out of control is indicated by the two consecutive identical measurements at samples 2 and 3. This is a case of difficulty being indicated even though the values fall inside the control limits. An out-of-control condition is also indicated in the case of sample value 7, which falls outside of the upper control limit.

instituted as needed to maintain satisfactory manufacturing operations. In cases of stable manufacturing operations, the advisability of using statistical quality-control methods should be investigated as a possible means for effective quality control at minimum cost.

MAINTAINING PLANT FACILITIES

Because work stoppages can be costly and machine breakdowns are the major cause, maintenance is a vitally important function in small manufacturing establishments. A number of activities are included under plant

Figure 14–3.
Sample R Chart (Range of Lenghts in Each Sample). *Source:* Adapted from Broom and Longenecker, *Small Business Management* (Cincinnati, Ohio: South-Western Publishing Company, 1975), p. 509. Reprinted by permission of the publisher.

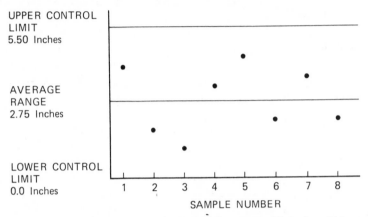

The above chart reflects the plotting of the range of lengths within each of the eight consecutive samples. The range value is the difference in length between the longest and the shortest of the items in each sample. The plottings of the samples indicate that the process is within the control limits set: thus no remedial action is required.

maintenance, such as repairing broken or malfunctioning equipment, lubricating and inspecting equipment, and replacing worn parts. Janitorial services and routine maintenance activities also come under the purview of plant maintenance operations. The object is to maintain effective production.

The activities of plant maintenance may be viewed as: (a) corrective activities which involve both major and minor repairs or restoring the condition to a satisfactory level; or (b) preventive activities involving inspections of activities intended to prevent breakdowns. Careful attention to the preventive activities will minimize costly, wasteful emergency repairs. The frequency of maintenance activities should be gauged in terms of the critical or strategic importance of machinery and equipment. These maintenance activities may be accomplished by utilizing a machinist (with special assignments) or production personnel, as occasion demands. Those requirements beyond their capabilities may be contracted to outside sources. The important elements with regard to maintaining plant facilities are: specific assignment of responsibility; and follow-up to insure that the activities are being carried forward—particularly the preventive maintenance activities.

Some systematic procedures are suggested to insure proper performance of preventive maintenance. Appropriate records should be kept for the various pieces of equipment, indicating the acquisition date, the cost of equipment, the periods of use and storage, the depreciation schedule applied, and the frequency of preventive maintenance inspection. Those assigned the responsibility would maintain these records on the basis of daily inspection. On the record, notation should be made of replacement of parts and other actions taken. With the necessary information provided by the records, it is important to have a periodical examination in order to control maintenance cost. The examination of the records and inspection reports should indicate any excessive maintenance costs and the frequency of breakdowns. A small plant cannot afford to tie up manpower or machine activity due to faulty equipment resulting from poor maintenance.

A related matter is good housekeeping in the plant. This activity is frequently neglected in small factories. Attention should be directed to clutter in the aisles, unsightly walls, dirty windows, visible waste material around the machinery, and the haphazard stacking of unprocessed materials at random locations in the plant. Needless to say, such practices do not contribute to high productive output. In fact, the conditions have a negative effect on the morale of the employees and interfere with efficient productive methods. Good housekeeping can have positive inputs, not only toward production, but also in terms of safety considerations.[2]

SUMMARY

Manufacturing is basic in terms of giving a product its character, quality, and acceptance. With regard to the profits of the firm, manufacturing is strategic in terms of the cost of production. Profits are enhanced by reducing the cost of production by efficient manufacturing methods.

In the free enterprise setting, with the attending competitive struggles, the planning and controlling of manufacturing through planning, routing,

[2]H. N. Broom and Justin G. Longenecker, *Small Business Management* (Cincinnati, Ohio: South-Western Pub. Co., 1975), p. 503-505.

scheduling, dispatching, and expediting deserve utmost concern by the management of a small business.

With the object of being competitive and profitable, the possible improvements through waste control, work simplification, work standards, time study, and inspection should all be inviting. Another dimension of considerable importance concerns the maintenance of plant facilities to insure delivery of product on schedule without unnecessary hazards to employees.

15
Marketing Dynamics and Profitable Operations

"Marketing is the distinguishing, unique function of the business."

Peter F. Drucker[1]

THE MARKETING CONCEPT

The marketing function has undergone dramatic change with the passing of time, particularly with reference to its primary thrust: current emphasis is on the "marketing concept," which has been defined as "a way of life in which all resources of an organization are mobilized to create, stimulate, and satisfy a customer, at a profit."[2] In making decisions, you should incorporate the significance of the marketing concept in order to maximize customer satisfaction as well as profits in your business. One way of stipulating the marketing concept is through the following three questions:

1. Who are my customers?
2. What do they want?

---

[1]From Peter F. Drucker, *People and Performance: The Best of Peter Drucker on Management* (New York: Harper's College Press, 1977), p. 90. Reprinted with permission of Harper and Row Publishers.

[2]Edward J. Green, "The Concept of Marketing Planning," *Handbook of Modern Marketing* (New York: McGraw-Hill Book Co., 1970), p. 73.

3. How can they best be satisfied?

A small paint business utilizing these three simple questions developed a product innovation which revolutionized the paint industry.[3]

Every businessman must be a marketer — especially the small-business person — because he is called upon to perform all of the managerial functions. One of the early statements of the new managerial philosophy, called the marketing concept, was provided in the General Electric Company's annual report of 1952. The firm announced a new strategy for business management.

> The Concept . . . introduces the marketing man at the beginning rather than at the end of the production cycle and integrates marketing into each phase of the business. Thus marketing, through its studies and research, will establish for the engineer, the design and manufacturing man, what the customer wants in a given product, what price he is willing to pay, and where and when it will be wanted. Marketing will have authority in product planning, production scheduling and inventory control, as well as in sales distribution and services of the product.[4]

Customer Analysis

Customers are, by definition, those who need what you can supply. They are the only reason for the existence of your business. Your greatest challenge is to identify them, analyze their needs, and satisfy their requirements. Building an ever-increasing list of satisfied customers is fundamental to the growth of profitable business operations. The following is a list of suggested leads:

1. Leads from advertising
2. Leads from trade shows
3. Leads from trade directories
4. Leads from representatives and employees
5. Leads from growth data bases
6. Leads from customers

A list of prospective customers can be used as a mailing list for direct mailing pieces, newsletters, new literature, company announcements, and

---

[3]William H. Day, "The Marketing of Colorizer Paint" (Doctoral Dissertation) (Columbus, Ohio: The Ohio State University, 1953).

[4]1952 Annual Report (Schenectady, N.Y.: General Electric Co., 1952), p. 21.

new price lists. The important thing is to make regular contact. You may want to keep your list in two parts, the mass list and the "top one hundred." Keep the list up to date. To insure this, delegate the responsibility to one person in the company.

How to Keep Customers Satisfied

Customers are priceless assets; yet, many small-business men ignore existing customers in preference to new ones. Actually, the process should be reversed, for existing customers require much less effort and cost to sell additional volume. Satisfied customers can boost sales. Every means should be utilized to satisfy existing customers before turning your energies to the chase. Here are some helpful suggestions:

1. Make personal contact occasionally to make sure everything is O.K. Determine what competition is telling him and what he thinks about company salesmen and your product.
2. Insure rapid field service when required. Establish follow-up procedures to make sure the problem was actually solved.
3. Get involved personally in any negotiations involving a substantial purchase or cases involving deviation from normal specifications.
4. Examine accounts receivable occasionally to make sure that petty items, such as spare parts or service bill backs, are not creating irritation with the customer.
5. Remember the customer. There are various ways to remember this, and one of the best ways is to use a note of appreciation. When the opportunity presents itself, compliment him. Sometimes a small gift may be appropriate, providing it is not contrary to company policy. Another possibility is occasional entertainment to build personal rapport.[5]

How Do You Effectively Handle the Problem Customer?

Every company has some problem customers. Sometimes it is difficult to balance benefits to the business against the time, aggravation, and petty cost of doing business with problem customers. Types of problem customers are listed in the following classes:

---

[5]Gordon B. Baty, *Entrepreneurship: Playing To Win* (Reston, Va.: Reston Publishing Co., 1974), p. 220.

1. The slow payer (slow paying is his way of doing business)
2. The specs changer (feels that until delivery he has the right to keep on making changes in the specifications at no cost)
3. The backroom lawyer (he will find loopholes in your contract just to find eternal free service, exclusivity with his firm, product return privileges, etc., etc., etc.)
4. The wheeler-dealer (he has found another supplier to supply the same product as you for about 60% of your price)[6]

THE MARKETING SUBSYSTEM

Marketing activities represent a subsystem in the business for delivering merchandise or service to customers. The system involves the performance of several functions, such as buying, selling, transportation, storage, standardization and grading, risk bearing, financing, and marketing information. It is the level of efficiency in executing these functions that determines whether or not a profit will be made, and if so, how much.[7]

Buying

The secret of success in this functional area is to have a plan before you start spending money. To avoid overspending or acquiring the un-related merchandise, develop a buying plan. Base the plan upon a sales forecast for the period carefully divided among merchandise classes, using size ranges to fit your customers' needs. Avoid being like a certain son of a grocer, who took over the family business: within a few months he had shifted the inventory holdings into an array of foreign gift imports. That's right, the gifts did not sell; and because the grocery offering was insufficient to satisfy regular customer demand, he arrived at the bankruptcy court in short order. It is important to say no when the merchandise does not fit your merchandising plans. You will undoubtedly be exposed to a large number of salesmen seeking a market for their products. You will have

[6]*Ibid.*, p. 223.
[7]Theodore N. Beckman and William R. Davidson, *Principles of Marketing* (New York: The Ronald Press Co., 1967).

opportunities to buy almost daily; but remember an old adage: "Goods well bought are half sold."

There are some businesses where success depends upon buying unique merchandise or particularly good values. The type of business or kind of merchandise will dictate somewhat the buying practices to be followed. When you buy from a wholesaler, you can expect to have the same products carried by other competitors in the same trading area. This situation may be satisfactory in some lines of business, but it may be economic suicide in others. For example, a women's ready-apparel store would have difficulty trying to satisfy customers with the identical dresses available in other stores in the shopping area. Success with fashion merchandising depends on the buyer's ability to obtain garments that are different, sometimes unique, at good values. There are business lines such as grocery, drugs, or hardware where dealers handle much the same kind of merchandise, and buying through a wholesaler may be adequate for the operation.

Effective buying requires careful determination of several factors: the right kind and assortment of items; the level of quality that best meets the needs of your customers; the appropriate quantity to be purchased — which should be correlated with your sales objectives (forecast); the choice of dependable sources; and the establishment of sound buying procedures.[8]

Because of the importance of buying the right merchandise for your customers, careful consideration should be given to the buying alternatives. Would it be to your advantage to visit a regional or central market, or a special trade show? Can you afford the expense of buying trips? If you cannot afford to go for each season, would it be advantageous to make a biannual visit for a "direct view" of current developments.

Considerable buying is done on the buyer's premises. This is usually accomplished through mail orders or from sales representatives. The latter is doubtless the most important form of buying. Independent dealers in convenience goods buy a large part of their stock from wholesalers' sales representatives who visit the store. A sizable amount of style merchandise is purchased from manufacturer sales representatives who visit the store with samples.

The actual buying procedure may vary from one item to another. However, remember to incorporate the following: inspection of merchandise; sampling, where the product standardization and quality control

---

[8]Note detailed discussions of these items in Chapter 12.

warrant; and buying on description, where quality can be guaranteed on the basis of grade, brand, or specification.

Success in your buying activities will be facilitated by taking the necessary time to make an effective buying plan. Plan your buying and buy according to your plan.

Selling

Selling is the complement to buying in the system of distributing goods. As a primary marketing function, selling has the purpose of arousing, stimulating, or directing a prospective buyer's conscious or dormant desire for satisfaction. The two principal methods used are personal selling and advertising.

Selling is of paramount concern to small-business people, whether they engage in manufacturing, wholesaling, or retailing. As a manufacturer, you would be concerned about selling your plant output. What are your alternatives? Direct sales to consumers may be costly and uneconomic for a single product. Perhaps you can sell your product through an effective marketing organization.

Some of the types of middlemen involved in the selling function include wholesalers, who take title and provide many services to both manufacturers and retailers. There are certain types who specialize, such as brokers who facilitate sales transactions by bringing buyer and seller together. They receive their compensation as a fee or commission, usually paid by the seller. Jobbers represent another group, as do cash-and-carry wholesalers, selling agents, and manufacturers' agents. These various middlemen may operate as small businesses where the selling function is of utmost importance.

The most common of all middlemen involved in selling are the retailers. Most small businesses approach selling at this level. While manufacturers and wholesalers also respond to the needs and wants of customers, it is done differently in retailing.

To maximize profits, the selling function of your business should be planned to the Nth degree in both personal selling and advertising. Because of the importance of the selling function, the following two chapters are devoted to the subject. The correlation of sales to profits was succinctly stated in these words: "You cannot make a profit without a sale."

Transportation

A small-business person may overlook the importance of transportation and its effect on profits. True, the small business will not have a staff specialist for transportation. However, there are a few points to remember that can result in worthwhile additions to profits. One lesson quickly learned is the difference between c.l. and l.c.l. rates (railroads) or between t.l. and l.t.l. rates (trucks). The c.l. and t.l. refer to "carload" and "truckload," respectively, and the rates are almost half the cost of shipping l.c.l. or l.t.l., which represent "less than carload" or "less than truckload."

How can small-businesspeople avail themselves of the benefits if their company shipments are too small? One possibility is to ship less often, but in greater quantities. Another involves the use of a freight forwarder, a transportation specialist who makes a business of consolidating shipments of small shippers. The savings generated would add to profits. An investigation of shipping by commodity or class rates may offer added cost savings in the transportation bill. If transportation represents a significant amount in operating costs, it may justify the use of a transportation expert to analyze and recommend the efficient, economical, effective transportation methods to utilize.

Storage

Do not build a warehouse if you can obtain one for less cost. To obtain does not necessarily mean to purchase. Storage requirements for a business frequently peak at seasonal periods, and the additional storage requirements are only temporary. Therefore, it would be unnecessary to invest large sums in a warehouse. Instead, temporary space can be obtained in a public warehouse by means of a short-term lease or monthly rental.

By following such a program, the storage costs can be directly related to the needs of the business without adversely affecting the effective use of business funds. One additional consideration is the possibility of combining the use of a bonded warehouse, and thus provide a means of financing inventory by means of a warehouse receipt as collateral for the loan.

Standardization and Grading

Modern marketing is facilitated by means of standards and grades of the merchandise involved. Determine the specs that will be used in the particular business. Customer satisfaction can be assured and repeated more readily by selecting and using standards or grades. Pursuing such a course will also facilitate the financing of inventory and the protection of risks.

Risk Bearing

Whenever title passes with merchandise, the risk inherent in ownership also passes. Hence, risk bearing is an accepted part of operating a small business. The details of meeting this business need effectively are treated fully in Chapter 9.

Financing

The financial requirements of the business are dealt with at length in Chapter 6. Insofar as marketing is concerned, the matter of financing is largely that of providing merchandise inventory. Securing favorable terms of sale is a prime consideration. After determining the standard discount rate and net period, negotiate extended dating terms — which will permit the sale of some merchandise before the invoice must be paid. Buying on consignment is a financial arrangement whereby payment is made as the merchandise sells, and it obviates investment in the inventory. This is not always possible, but is worthy of investigation, particularly for the new firm. Another way to help build profits through financing is to secure quantity and cumulative discounts. Ask for special discounts for large orders. Annual commitments are sometimes made on a blanket order, and delivery is made periodically. The discount rate should be based on the total quantity involved in the order. In some cases it is possible to base the quantity discount on the cumulated purchases for one year or for another set period. Astute financing can and does contribute to profits.

Market Information

Knowledge is Power. Businessmen do not usually make mistakes by having too much information, but the reverse is usually the case. Marketing information relates to profits in a special and direct way. To fully apply the "marketing concept" requires pertinent data about customers.

Marketing research has evolved as a viable arm to marketing, and is especially needed by the small-business person.

> Any owner-manager must recognize that regardless of how enthusiastically he feels about his product or service, without customers, he has no business. It is imperative, therefore that the market be defined, that a market strategy be developed, and marketing tools be chosen when the business plan is incomplete and the overall business strategy is faulty.[9]

Why marketing research? The answer is simply to obtain information for making better and more objective decisions. The following checklist will prove beneficial in pointing up areas where market research may be needed in your business to more effectively apply the marketing concept and thereby to maximize your profits:

Marketing Information Checklist

1. Is the product right? How can it be improved? What new or additional features would customers or prospects like to see incorporated in it?
2. Is the product priced right? Could we get additional profitable volume if price were lowered? Do we suffer any disadvantage from prices of competitive products?
3. Is the product packaged properly? Could service or style features be built into the product or packages?
4. Is the product distributed through the proper trade channels? Do distributors make sufficient profits to warrant their pushing our products? Are there any defects in service to customers by the trade that handicap sales? Would sales be increased if we altered our distribution setup and sold through other outlets?
5. Could the selling season be lengthened if we emphasized new values to the trade and consumers? If so, how?
6. Is our line of products too long? If so, what slow-selling items should be eliminated? How much effort should be concentrated on the popular items?
7. Do we have a "leader" in our line which helps the sale of other items? If not, would it be advisable to create one?
8. What are the facts about our present customers? To whom are we now selling profitably?
   a. Where do they live?

---

[9]V. A. Grieco, *Management of Small Business* (Columbus, Ohio: Charles E. Merrill Pub. Co., 1975), p. 45.

      b. Why do they buy?

      c. When, how much, and how often do they buy?

      d. Where do they buy?

      e. What price do they pay?

      f. Why do they not buy in larger quantities?

      g. What age, sex, and educational, social, economic, and occupational factors influence our present customers?

      h. What brands of competitive products are also bought? Why?

      i. Is the need for our product clearly defined? Only vaguely present? Or dormant?

9. What are the facts about our potential market?

      a. Are there other people to whom we might profitably sell?

          1. Why do they not buy now?

          2. How could they be influenced to buy?

      b. What methods are necessary to induce them to buy from us?

          1. What sales promotion might be used to appeal to them?

          2. Are there special obstacles which make selling to them unprofitable or impossible?

10. What of our competition? Is it gaining on us? If so, why? What effects are competitors' sales and advertising activities having on our profits? On our prestige with the trade and with customers?

11. What other products or lines could be sold profitably through the present distribution channels? Would such a policy of expansion be advisable? What effect would it have on our present trade relations?

12. Should the line of products be further diversified to alleviate seasonal or style factors or sever market slumps due to effects of other factors?

13. What defects exist in the present selling strategy? Are our salesmen underpaid? Are territories too large or too small? Are we building potential volume in new markets so as to maintain our competitive standing in the national market now and in the future?

14. What long-range market trends as to products, sales policies, and customers' preferences are discernable? What changes are needed to keep pace?

15. Is the sales-promotion program (national advertising, radio, direct mail, etc.) really understood by the trade, our sales force, and consumers? Is it being actively merchandised to the trade by our salesmen? What can be learned in advance of the release of our promotional campaigns by pre-testing so as to assure maximum results?[10]

---

[10]From *Effective Marketing* by Walter Rohe. Copyright © 1938 by McGraw-Hill Book Co. Used with permission of McGraw-Hill Book Company.

THE MARKETING MIX

The term "mix" has been attached to marketing to signify the importance of proper balance of the factors involved in marketing activities. This concept is much the same as properly mixing ingredients in order to prepare delectable foods. The marketing mixture comprises a combination of activities which have become known as the four P's: Product, Price, Place, and Promotion.[11]

> *Product.* You should develop the correct product or service for the market segment selected in terms of quality, packaging, standardization, and grading.
> *Price.* Establish a fair price on the product or service for the customers, with a fair profit for your company.
> *Place.* Make the product or service available to your customers by properly using the marketing functions of transportation and storage.
> *Promotion.* Inform your customers about the product, using personal selling and advertising.

It is important that you provide a quality good or service. However, this may not be enough, for the product must be sold at a profit in order for your business to survive.

PRICING PROFITABLY

If you purchased merchandise that cost $3.00 per item and wanted to use a 40% markup, what would be the selling price? The usual answer is $4.20 per item. How much profit would that make? The fact is that there would be no profit, but a loss of 30¢ on each item. You cannot make a profit unless the merchandise is priced right. Although there are formulas to follow, if desired, understanding two basic concepts regarding pricing would also help insure profitable pricing.

One concept involves pricing based on the selling price, commonly referred to as retail or mark-up pricing. The important thing to remember is that the selling price is the base and is equivalent to 100%. Therefore, the cost plus the mark-up will total 100%.

[11]Hal B. Pickle and Roy L. Abrahamson, *Introduction to Business* (2nd ed.) (Pacific Palisades, California: Goodyear Publishing Co., Inc., 1974), p. 375.

Cost 60%	=	$3.00
Markup 40%	=	$2.00
Selling Price 100%	=	$5.00

Assuming 30% operating expenses ($1.50), the $5.00 price would yield a profit of 10% ($.50).

Another concept involves pricing based on cost, commonly referred to as markon pricing. Using this method, the base is the cost of merchandise and is equal to 100%. The percent of the markon is added to the cost, and the selling price is always in excess of 100%. Using this cost method with the pricing data above, the answer would be as follows:

Cost 100%	=	$3.00
Markon 66 2/3%	=	$2.00
Selling Price 166 2/3%	=	$5.00

The cost is the same. The markon is the same as the markup in dollars and cents, but the markon is always a higher percent. The selling price will be the same with either method. Understanding these two basic concepts on pricing is important, even though the businessperson may elect to use a pricing chart, markup wheel, or template to determine the amount of mark-up to add to cost for the selling price.

TABLE 15–1
Table of Markup Equivalents

Markup % on Cost	Markup % on Retail
5.3	5.0
10.0	9.1
11.1	10.0
14.3	12.5
15.0	13.0
17.6	15.0
20.0	16.2/3
25.0	20.0
30.0	23.1
33 1/3	25.0
40.0	28.6
42.8	30.0
50.0	33 1/3
60.0	37.1/2
66 2/3	40.0
75.0	42.9
100.0	50.0
150.0	60.0
300.0	75.0
400.0	80.0

BUSINESS IMAGE AND PRICE POLICY

Price policy of the company can have a definite impact on the image projected to its customers. Three cases including image are: exclusiveness, high quality, and low price.

Exclusiveness

The idea of exclusiveness is usually promoted by a high-price image. This policy is predicated on the price-quality relationship. Highest quality merchandise is branded and usually sold on an exclusive basis (such as Oxford brand men's suits). Other examples are the designer dresses which carry an elevated price with the image of exclusiveness.

High Quality

Some firms follow a high-price policy in order to convey the image of quality merchandise. While this may be assumed under the price-quality relationship, it may not always be true. An inverted example of the quality relationship involves one situation of pricing a new ballpoint pen. The manufacturer determined that based on cost the pens should sell for 19¢ each. However, in the market this was not successful in generating desired sales volume. After a careful review of the market demand and pricing of products, the ballpoint pen was raised to 69¢. Successful sales volume resulted. A considerable portion of the extra margin from the higher price was used for promotion, which further helped to multiply sales volume.

Discount Price Policy

The term *discount* is associated with a bargain: it conveys to the public the idea that they will receive a high-quality product at a lower price. The motive for saving is a strong one; and discount stores have had great success on the American business scene. A civil promotion is often directed at the "discount" theme of the outlet. However, under the caveat emptor (let the buyer beware) principle, it is well to compare the prices in discount stores with those in regular retailers. In some cases the discount prices are even higher than those of the regular retailer. For example, a well-known brand fishing reel was listed at a discount store; under the listed price of $25.00 on the price ticket, with a red line marked through, the words and price written below were "Our Price $12.05." The customer, in making comparison at a nearby national chain store, found the identical product at a regular retail price of $11.95.

As indicated in the table below, to maximize profitability it is vital to know the price-volume relationship. The concept which is important to understand is that maximized profit does not necessarily mean the highest unit profit, but rather the total profit—a combination of sales prices multiplied by the units sold. The answer is not always apparent, and frequently necessitates some experimentation to ascertain. For example, in the data presented below, the experimentation proved that the maximum profit was neither the low price of $23, nor the high price of $25. But the greatest profit was obtained, in this case, at the middle price of $24.

A Price-Volume Relationship

	$25.00/item	$24.00/item	$23.00/item
Price			
Volume	3,500 units	4,500 units	5,000 units
Total Sales	$87,500	$108,000	$115,000
Cost $16/item	$56,000	$72,000	$80,000
Profit	$31,500	$36,000	$35,000

SUMMARY

Your business profits will correlate closely with your ability to apply the marketing concept. Be alert to customers, analyze their needs, and satisfy their requirements. Perfect your skills in keeping customers satisfied. Examine all of the functions in the marketing subsystem for opportunity to exercise efficiency and effectiveness, thus adding more profit to your business operations. Evaluate your marketing mix. Can the blend of the 4 P's be improved? Verify the pricing methods and policies. You cannot make a profit unless the merchandise is priced right. Determine the image you want the business to project, and pursue this on a consistent basis.

16

Generating
Sales Income

*"The salespeople
keep the smoke in the factory chimney."*

W. H. Day

One of the most positive steps to a profitable business is the development of an effective selling function. Recognize quickly that it is through the sales effort that business income is generated. Without income, you cannot have a profit from business operations.

You may have great ability as a salesman, but if your business is to generate profitable income, you need to multiply yourself through others. Many small businessmen are shortsighted when it comes to managing the income producers in their business: the profit maximizers, the people who make the bank deposits possible—your salespeople, of course. How could it be otherwise? This chapter will help you generate more income through efficient sales administration.

HOW TO CONTROL SALES INCOME

The key to control is the initial establishment of sales objectives. Fundamental to the process of sales control is the establishment of the sales fore-

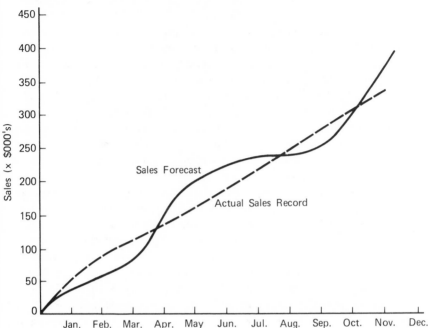

Figure 16–1.
Comparison of Forecasted and Actual Sales Performance.

cast, which becomes the cornerstone of the entire budget process for your business. Revise your sales budget as necessary, in the light of current sales conditions and operating facts, so that it can provide a yardstick for comparison with actual sales. Any variances between budget and actual sales should be particularly noted in the control reports. Significant variances should be given immediate investigation as to their cause, and appropriate remedial action should be taken promptly. Control charts may prove more useful in the matter of exercising control than may reports filled with numerous numbers. Major facts and trends are more easily perceived in a visual chart than in a list of numbers. (See Fig. 16–1 illustrating a simple line chart in which the budget or sales forecast line is noted as well as the actual sales performance for the period indicated.)

Design a Sales Strategy

To maximize profits through sales it is recommended that there be a balance between sales tactics and sales strategy. These terms should be clearly differentiated. Strategy represents the activities involved in preparing the product for market, preparing the market for the product, and creating customer confidence in the firm. Tactics on the other hand, involve the particular sales technique used.

Whereas sales strategy involves a plan for achieving the overall objective, it is the sales tactics that provide the step-by-step implementation of the necessary action to insure the accomplishment. A particular sales strategy may call for the invasion of a new market, whereby sales may be increased 10 percent from the new market share. However, the sales tactics would involve the decisions with regard to (1) the utilization of market research, (2) the method of selling, (3) the type of packaging for the product, (4) the amount of advertising budget, (5) the choice of advertising medium, (6) the size and composition of sales force, and (7) the sales force compensation plan.

It is essential, therefore, to not only design an effective sales strategy, but to provide the implementation through a carefully developed tactical plan, all of which should enhance the profits of the operation.

In order to adapt to changing conditions, the technique may vary from time to time. To plan an effective sales strategy it is necessary to have plural market knowledge and a means to secure this (this is discussed under the topic of marketing research). Effective sales strategy results from properly combining the knowledge of market, customers, and past sales performance, and the utilization of effective sales promotion in conjunction with selling programs. Time and effort invested in designing your sales strategy will pay dividends in greater profits.

MAXIMIZING PROFITABLE SALES THROUGH EFFECTIVE SALES ADMINISTRATION

There are three significant considerations about the job of salespeople. First, salespeople perform a market contact function—they represent your company to the customer. Second, salespeople usually have considerable freedom in planning their activities and carrying forth their responsibilities without direct supervision. Third, salespeople frequently find themselves with responsibility, yet without commensurate authority. These three factors give rise to important differences so far as motivation is concerned.

To insure an effective sales force, careful consideration should be given to employing, developing, and compensating them, and using tools and techniques for maximizing sales.

Employing "Income Generators"

If you would be satisfied with mediocre income, hire mediocre sales-people. Admittedly, "income generators" are a special kind of sales personnel. The very best are hard to come by. Learn how to distinguish, and capitalize on your experience.

Because of the multiplicity of different kinds of selling jobs in the wide spectrum of small businesses, it is imperative to first of all determine the nature of the selling job to be done. Carefully analyze the selling job for the purpose of identifying the primary responsibilities and tasks. Put them in written form and you will have a job description or statement describing what the selling job responsibilities entail. Based on the description of selling job requirements, a statement of desired qualifications and characteristics could be enumerated as a guide to selecting the best qualified persons. After determining the sales job to be performed with necessary qualifications for effectiveness, the next task is selecting the best person for filling the job. How many salespeople do you need? If you are operating a retail store, you can accomplish this by estimating the number of customers by the days of the week and relating this to the approximate time spent with each customer. You simply estimate the number of customers that can be anticipated in relation to the number of customers that can be handled by a particular salesperson, and arrive at the number to be employed. Pay attention to the fluctuation in customer traffic to insure an adequate number of salespeople for peak periods. Avoid being over-staffed during slack periods. Utilize competent personnel available on a part-time or temporary basis. This practice will facilitate more effective customer service, resulting in more sales income. It will also minimize salary expense. There are many top-notch people available to work the rush period between 11:00 a.m. and 1:00 p.m. and others who would like to work part-time in the evenings.

For outside selling, you can determine the number of salespeople needed by considering the number of accounts to be serviced, the frequency of calls to be made for each account during the year, and the length of time to be spent on each call. Make allowances for time—waiting time and time for unexpected delays—in arriving at the average time for sales calls.

This information will enable you to calculate the total amount of selling time needed. Dividing total selling time by the amount of selling time per salesperson will give you the number of salespeople required. Make allowances where salespeople are required to do weekly paperwork in the office, attend sales meetings, and other nonselling activities.

The Recruitment Effort

The type of salesperson being sought determines largely where to conduct the recruiting effort. In the case of a sales trainee, perhaps a local high school, junior college or university placement office will produce satisfactory results. For people with limited experience in sales or related work, perhaps a display advertisement in the classified section in the daily newspaper would be effective. However, to secure a seasoned professional with worthwhile experience it may be advisable to place the advertising in an industry trade journal. It is recommended that personnel agencies and consultants be used only as a last resort.[1]

The Selection Process

Avoid making a mistake by hiring the first candidate to apply for the job. Allow yourself sufficient time for responses to your recruiting efforts. Rather than leaving the details of each individual applicant to your memory, prepare and use an application form so that pertinent information can be put down for future reference. References should be carefully checked before hiring to make sure that the applicant's personal life as well as emotional and environmental stability are consistent with doing an effective selling job. It is imperative to know in advance about drug or alcohol problems and the attitude of the spouse with reference to the prospective job requirements. In making a judgment, it is important to consider the individual's motivation and integrity as well as his social skills.[2]

---

[1] John V. Petrof, et. al., *Small Business Management* (New York: McGraw-Hill Book Co., 1972) p. 289.
[2] *Ibid.*, p. 290.

DEVELOPING EFFECTIVE INCOME PRODUCERS

Don't expect your salespeople to be able to do everything you want when they are employed. You will probably have some definite ideas on the way you want things done.

Sales training should be provided in order to give proper orientation and education for each individual's needs and also to motivate the sales force according to the needs of the company. To insure best results from a training program, be certain to set training objectives. Basically, these would project what you want salespeople to do for your company. Whatever is necessary by way of training to communicate these expectations should be incorporated in the training program. For some employees it will be necessary to cover the fundamentals of selling; for others it will be necessary to include information about product knowledge; and all employees should be trained with regard to company policies and procedures.

One of the important considerations in training salespeople is the factor of motivation. Effective motivation of the sales force correlates directly with increasing sales income. The training program should stress the importance of customer relations. Outside salespeople should be instructed and assisted in routing and scheduling of calls to do this work effectively and minimize company sales expense.

Do Your Salespeople Know How to Sell?

Someone said children are not born with a knowledge of the multiplication tables. Neither are they born with a knowledge of how to sell. You need to be sure that sales personnel understand these fundamental steps in selling:

1. How to open a sales interview — The approach
2. How to deliver the sales message — The presentation
3. How to show the merchandise — The demonstration
4. How to handle questions — The objection
5. How to terminate the interview — The close

All of the above steps are essential. However, the most critical is knowing how to close. The difference between a conversationalist and a salesperson is the ability to close the sale.

Some suggested closing techniques follow.[3]

Closing on a choice. "Would you prefer the red pickup or the white pickup?" When the customer indicates his choice of color the sale is closed. The question posed to the customer may be a choice between a color, a size, a particular kind of material, a difference in model, or any other product feature.

The assumption close. Much like the previous close, the major buying question is assumed to be resolved, and it is a matter of clearing up the details. By posing the following type questions the salesperson can bring the sale to a close:

1. How much do you want to pay as a down payment?
2. When do you want this to become effective?
3. Do you wish to pay cash, or charge this purchase?

The single feature close. This closing procedure is coupled with the fact that the product is exceptional in having a particular feature that competition does not meet. By emphasizing the special feature, the salesperson attempts to close the sale.

Disposing of the single obstacle. When the salesperson has obtained agreement by the customer on every feature of the product except one, then it is that one single obstacle which is utilized as the feature of this closing technique. It is important for the salesperson to insure that there remains only the single objection. This may be tested by raising questions such as: "Is this the only reason you do not wish to make this purchase? Is there anything else that may stand in the way?" Once the single objection has been confirmed the salesperson may say, "That was the only question, wasn't it?" Upon careful definition of the objection the salesperson should proceed to dispose of this objection satisfactorily; having made a judgment as to this being accomplished, the salesperson would proceed to close the sale.

Reviewing the five buying decisions. Based on the premise that the customer only buys after the five buying decisions have been affirmatively met, the object of this closing technique is to review those five buying

---

[3]C. A. Kirkpatrick, *Salesmanship* (Cincinnati, Ohio: South-Western Pub. Co., 1971), pp. 332–37.

decisions. Establish the need, assure that the product fills the need, explain that the particular salesperson or company is the proper source, that the price is satisfactory, and finally that the time to buy is now. When the five buying decisions have been answered affirmatively the salesperson should have made the sale. It is suggested that as the salesperson reviews the five buying decisions additional facts and convincing proof be added to assist the customer in making an affirmative decision.

Summarizing the benefits. The object of this closing technique is to review for the customer the particular product benefits which have been made during the presentation, emphasizing those which seem to have particular appeal to the customer. As you begin this closing technique it may be prefaced by a statement: "Let us review the benefits which this product offers you." When the salesperson ascertains that the customer is in agreement on all of the benefits, the salesperson may then wish to write up the order by proceeding with the mechanics of closing the sale.

The emotional close. In sales situations where customers are agreeable to all but the fifth buying decision—the decision to buy now—the emotional close may be effective by appealing to the customer's desires for affection, self-esteem, etc.. In other words, having obtained agreement on the question of need, product, source, and price, it is necessary in order to close the sale to have the customer agree to the purchase at that particular time. The appeal to the emotions may be the key to closing the sale for that particular customer.

The "standing room only" close. This closing technique is based on the human tendency to want things other people want, desiring things which are hard to obtain, or simply desiring things they can't have or should not have: thus the designation "standing room only" close. To illustrate, in this type of close the following claims are frequently made by the salesperson: (1) Prices will be increased next week, (2) Our medical examiner turned down your friend last week when he applied for insurance, (3) This product supply is limited, or (4) The premium offer will expire next week. It is suggested that this technique will be more strategic if used late in the sales interview; otherwise it may detract or weaken the presentation by the salesperson.

The direct appeal close. This closing technique carries more risk than those mentioned previously; consequently, it should be used only as a last resort technique. Essentially, this closing technique is useful where there has been a long-standing relationship with the customer, so that the reliability and prestige of both the company and the salesperson have already been established. Under these circumstances the salesperson outlines the benefits of the product in satisfying the prospect's need and reassures the customer of the advisability of the purchase, relying upon the recommendation of the salesperson and the long-standing relationship. After making the sales presentation the salesperson would then raise questions, introducing the direct-appeal close as follows: "Would you like me to draw up the contract now?" or "When should we send our installers to measure your requirements?" or "Would you like me to submit your order today?" or "Seeing how much you appreciate the benefits of this new product, would you please give me some information for my report?"

Below is an example of how this closing technique might be used by a salesperson in introducing a new product to a wholesaler.

> "Mr. Wholesaler, my company has spent two years and $200,000 designing and testing this new item. We know it is right, we know it will make money for you, and we know you will not be taking any chances with it. You and I have been doing business for five years, and you know I have never given you bad advice. I can't afford to run any risk with you now. Because I know this is a good deal, I am going to include one dozen cases in this order of yours."[4]

The special concession close. This closing technique is also referred to as the special-inducement close because the buyer is given some additional or special reason for making the purchase. The concession may take the form of a free gift or a special price reduction. In selling to wholesalers or retailers, the inducement may be a special advertising allowance when a certain quantity is purchased by the buyer. Another possible inducement may be a trial order which would be less than the original amount suggested.

Caution is advised in using this technique, for the reason that when a concession is made the buyer may proceed to seek more concessions before consummating the sale. There is also the danger of raising the question about the desirability of the product when announcing a special inducement with the purchase. The small-business person must also remember that the inducements reduce his profits and therefore should be used sparingly. A final suggestion in using this closing technique involves the question of impartiality with customers: in other words, salespeople should not play favorites. To do so is unethical and may even be illegal under certain conditions.

---

[4]*Ibid.*, p. 336.

To help you increase the effectiveness of your sales force, reading *Secrets of Closing Sales,* written by Charles B. Roth and published by Prentice-Hall, Inc., is recommended.

Equipping for Effectiveness

The purpose here is not to specify the actual equipment for the sales force, but to suggest the idea of using equipment that would enhance the effectiveness of the salesperson. Don't let initial costs discourage your use of sales equipment without carefully examining the difference it would make in total sales over the next year or longer. The effect of an audio-visual presentation in terms of holding the prospect's attention and providing a professional presentation may multiply sales income so as to absorb equipment cost quickly. Think about the needs of your salespeople. This could be another means of generating more income.

Use the Know Yourself—
Employee Evaluation Technique

This will help each salesperson to know how he impresses customers. Important considerations include personality, manners, intelligence, poise, integrity, and physical appearance. The following is a list of negative factors which tend to alienate customers:[5]

Employees are slow in greeting customers
Employees appear indifferent and make customers wait unnecessarily
Personal appearance of employees is not neat
Salespeople lack knowledge of the store's merchandise
Customers complain of employees' lack of interest in their problems
Mistakes which employees make are increasing
Qualified employees leave for jobs with the store's competitors

The salespeople can be made to know themselves better through effective training. Sales training is good business and it pays dividends.

---

[5]Bruce Goodpasture, "Danger Signals in a Small Store," *Small Marketers Aids, No. 141* (Washington, D.C.: Small Business Administration).

COMPANY KNOWLEDGE

A part of the training effort should include a background of the company, to give employees a proper orientation of where the company came from and what it is presently striving to accomplish in terms of objectives, policies, and methods of operation.

PRODUCT KNOWLEDGE

It is difficult to sell without knowing something about the products. Sales effectiveness can be noticeably increased by adding this dimension to the training program. Get the product facts, instead of glib generalities, to the customer.

CUSTOMER KNOWLEDGE

Teach salespeople empathy—the key to effectively satisfying customers in the selling process. Ascertain customer interests, needs, desires, price and quality differentials, and maximize sales by providing the most suitable merchandise. Many helpful suggestions are included in the following list:

1. *Greeting:*
   Be friendly, courteous, prompt, businesslike.
   Learn consumer's name and use it.
   Make customer feel important.
   Talk favorably about merchandise.
2. *Presentation:*
   Ask questions, listen, learn what he wants.
   Place customer's interest first.
   Suggest merchandise which best fits his need.
   Demonstrate as in actual use.
   Give at least three benefits for each item.
   Let customer handle the merchandise.
   Don't talk too much.
3. *Close:*
   Help customer to decide.
   Ask which item customer prefers.
   Remove unwanted merchandise from sight.
   Use utmost tact.
   Assume sale has been made.
   Write all details on the order.
4. *Pleasing:*
   Assure satisfaction.
   Show a related item.
   Show it is a pleasure to serve him.

Keep all promises to customers.
Be cheerful whether you make the sale or not.
When a customer returns, he has been well served.[6]

COMPENSATION METHODS FOR SALESPEOPLE

The first objective is to provide a compensation plan tailored to the type of selling job and the results desired. The method selected should correlate selling effort with results. A second objective would be to insure that customers receive proper treatment. A third objective would consider a compensation plan that facilitates control of the salesperson's activities. The activities of the salespeople should be coordinated with company objectives. More effort may be required to sell one line as compared to another; more time may be required for promotions to taking inventory or soliciting and developing new accounts. By selecting the proper compensation plan, emphasis can be placed with regard to these different considerations. In any event, the plan should motivate the salesperson to work hard. Undoubtedly, there are many situations where salespeople never work to their full potential because of the absence of incentive. By using various incentives you can motivate salespeople and maximize sales income.

A prime consideration in designing a compensation plan is to make sure it will attract and keep competent salespeople. When the compensation rate is too low, the people attracted will likely not be too productive. You must be willing to pay the price for good salespeople. Compensation is only one factor in attracting good salespeople, but it is an important one. Unless the compensation plan provides a competitive income, the better salespeople will be lost to competitors and you will have forfeited the opportunity to maximize your profits.

The ideal compensation plan provides two types of income—regular and incentive. The regular income should permit control over the salespeople and insure an adequate minimum wage. It is for the incentive portion of compensation that a person is motivated to work harder, to obtain coverage above minimum compensation. Provisions should be

[6]L. T. White, *Strengthening Small Business Management* (Washington, D.C.: Small Business Administration).

made whereby salespeople receive some additional income for every sale consumated. Remember also that it is important that the salespeople understand and calculate their own earnings. Each salesperson should know what to expect on payday; the plan should be simple and easy to understand. It is depressing for salespeople to be left in doubt about their compensation.

Another dimension of a good compensation plan is economic sales costs. Are your sales costs comparable to other firms' in similar situations? Are your sales costs competitive? Above all, the compensation should be fair to you and your employees. There must be no favoritism. Salespeople with similar assignments should be compensated in a similar manner. Obviously, conditions will vary as to time, territory, and products. There must be flexibility to adjust to these differences. When changes are necessary to keep the plan fair, they should be made; but the changes should not be made so frequently as to keep things unsettled.

Straight Salary

Under this plan, compensation is based on the amount of time an employee works. Compensation by straight salary is predicted on time spent and does not allow for the amount of work accomplished. Therefore, compensation does not fluctuate in terms of calls made, sales, or anything else. These are advantages of the straight salary plan:

1. Simple and easy to understand.
2. Provides management with great control over salesman.
3. Assures regular income.
4. Develops loyal, satisfied salespeople.
5. Useful during the training period.

The straight salary plan also has disadvantages. A straight salary fails to provide a direct incentive, since earnings are not related to selling effort. However, this weakness can be overcome to some extent by giving merit raises periodically. Because of the lack of direct relationships between sales cost and sales revenue, some problems of cost control can develop for management. Another drawback is the fact that the businessperson sets the salary rather than having the salespeople set their own salary based on their own efforts.

This method may prove useful with new salespeople or in a new territory where sales are being generated. Straight salary also has merit in situations where large technical items are being sold, requiring considerable time being spent with the customer before and after each sale. Where "missionary" sales effort is undertaken, the straight salary is a satisfactory compensation plan.

Straight Commission

Under straight commission, compensation relates directly to performance. The plan has two parts:

1. The units on which the performance is measured.
2. The rate paid for each unit.

These advantages are cited for a straight commission plan:

1. Provides direct incentive.
2. Selling costs are directly tied to some base (sales or profits).
3. Simple to operate, easy to understand.
4. Attracts better quality salespeople.

One of the weaknesses of straight commission is the tendency of the salespeople to feel that they are in business for themselves, which precipitates money-control problems. Salespeople are usually reluctant to do any "missionary" work when paid by straight commission. Caution must be also exercised with regard to the tendency for salespeople to load up customers with merchandise without regard to their needs.

Straight commission is recommended when a business is weak and sales are paid for when they are made. The plan has merit when great motivation is needed and when supervision is hard to administer. It has merit for part-time salespeople. High-caliber salespeople prefer straight commission compensation. Salespeople like this plan when conditions are good and sales are easily made. Problems can arise under the straight commission plan involving split commissions—where more than one salesperson is involved in the sales.

It is sometimes necessary to have a drawing account so that income can be provided to meet current needs and pay advances against future commissions. Exercise caution here, and avoid undue advances over extended periods of time. A policy should cover the disposition of house accounts and call-in orders from the field territories, and avoid these potential problems.

Combination Plans

A variety of compensation plans are available. The object is to incorporate the advantages of straight salary plus the incentive of the commission plan. Four major types of combination plans are suggested:

1. Salary plus commission. A straight salary is paid with a commission on all sales above a specified level.
2. Salary plus bonus. Incentive is not as strong under this method, but the control factor is greater. It is useful for a short-term incentive where extra money is offered for each unit or type of merchandise sold. Sometimes called "push money," it may be offered to retail salesmen by manufacturers of particular merchandise. Mattress manufacturers may, for example, pay $5.00 extra for each unit sold.
3. Commission plus a guaranteed drawing account. As in the salary plus commission plan, the salesmen is permitted to draw against unearned commissions. However, at the end of the year all is wiped out as the account is balanced.
4. Commission plus bonus. This may be used to supplement a straight-commission program and alleviate some of the ills. A bonus can be provided for use in encouraging missionary work or pushing certain merchandise items.

Avoid being penny wise and pound foolish in compensating sales personnel. You may become alarmed by the increasing income of competent sales personnel, particularly those working on a commission basis. While the income becomes high for the salespeople you may be prone to forget that they are generating income (profit) for the company. Frequent attempts to renegotiate (downward) result in the loss of strategic sales personnel, much to the disadvantage of the business. *A competent sales force is one of the great assets of any business, and every effort should be made to compensate fairly, equitably, and adequately.*

ANALYZING AND CONTROLLING
SALES INCOME

The follow-up work after sales are made helps insure maximizing profits in a business. Do you know where sales are being made? Who are the customers? Where are they located? Which products are selling? Where should future efforts be directed?

A situation frequently encountered is called the "80–20" principle. Where 20 percent of the customers provides 80 percent of the business, or 80 percent of the customers accounts for only 20 percent of the business. This principle generally holds true for salespeople, products, and territory. Actual percentages may vary per company, but the principle is generally valid.

One purpose of sales analysis and control is to identify misdirected effort. Sales effort and cost tend to relate to the number of salespeople and customers, rather than to the actual sales volume or profit. In other words, selling costs are the same for a salesperson to sell and process a $100 order as they are for a $1,000 order. Wherever possible, match effort to performance. However, this does not mean getting rid of the 80 percent of products and customers, but rather allocating effort which is appropriate to each.

Another matter in sales analysis and control is the verbal "iceberg principle." The iceberg which is 10 percent visible and 90 percent obscured is analogous to some sales situations — where net sales which are satisfactory in appearance may, upon more careful consideration, reveal products and territories which are in difficulty. These are the parts which are not visible, and detailed analysis of data is required to identify them.

It is not enough to recruit, select, and develop a sales force. There remains the continuing responsibility to control the selling effort. It is imperative that you measure progress toward the objectives that have been set, in order to reach your profit goals. To this end it is important that a plan be established whereby the potential for each salesperson is established and provides sufficient work to keep them busy. By designating routes for the salesperson to follow, time will be minimized and back tracking avoided. These methods have proved helpful to small-business people in operating a sales force. A sales quota for each salesperson is a useful device.

Analyzing Sales by Product

You need to determine which products are selling and which are not. Data should be collected from internal records on individual products or groups of products. Comparison with past years' sales will show the trend of each product. Attention should be given to products with increasing sales so that they can be maximized; those declining should be further evaluated for corrective measures, and should be deemphasized or dropped.

Comparison with industry figures may be beneficial, whether the industry has been growing or declining. It may seem well that the company sales are keeping pace with industry sales. However, while the industry is growing, sales may remain constant or may decline, and a problem may be apparent.

A strategic comparison made frequently is actual sales versus the sales forecast. When sales performance falls below the estimate, analysis should be made to explain the difference, and prompt corrective action taken. Analyzing sales of product by territory and customer may generate clues as to why performance is less than desirable.

Analyzing Sales by Territory

Besides knowing which products are selling, you should ascertain the territory from which the sales are generated. After obtaining sales by area, and comparing differences, you can extend the comparison by using *Sales Managements Buying Power Index.* A percentage of total national buying power is given for each particular area. If your business distributes nationally, these figures can be used to determine your percentage of sales in each area. If distribution is limited to a few states, the figures in those states can be used to work out an analysis for the particular business (by using the total of the states combined to equal 100 percent). If your business is local, figures may be obtained from the local newspaper or Chamber of Commerce. Having obtained an index figure for an area, the index is multiplied by the total company sales for a period to determine the goal for each area. Thereafter, actual sales in the area can be compared to the goals for the area to measure variations which may exist. Comparison can be based on a percentage or on dollar sales (a small percentage deviation in a large area could represent a large amount of dollar volume). You will also want to compare actual sales in each area with budgeted sales from the forecast.

Analyzing Sales by Customer

Having collected and analyzed the data on which products are selling and where they are selling, you will want to determine who the customers are. A few customers sometimes account for the largest percentage of business. You may find a number of accounts that are marginal or even unprofitable. Upon a closer examination of customers you may find that the business is appealing to a certain economic or ethnic class.

A manufacturer should determine which channel of distribution is being used to reach customers. A comparison of alternatives may be effected to determine the best method of distribution for reaching desired customers.

Customers may also be analyzed in terms of products purchased and area of location. Such a cross-reference will enable you to determine how the overall pattern fits together. One large customer could explain why a territory's sales are high, while the territory as a whole may actually be slipping.

Analyzing Sales and Routing

A salesperson's call potential can be determined from past performance. First, determine the number of calls each salesperson can make during an average week or month. Figures may vary from one person to another, depending on age, physical condition, experience, and ability. Consider the types of accounts each person now handles, since different accounts require different call frequencies and can affect the size of their present territory, their prospect file, and competition. Time spent in credit investigation, project development, and customer service should be allowed. Secure answers to the following questions: What is the length of the average call? How are accounts classified? How should the territory be arranged to maximize calls per salesperson? The frequency of calls for each account classification should be determined by considering customer requirements. Upon determining the frequency of calls according to the importance of each account classification, a breakdown may be provided (see next page).

With a call potential of 11,000 or even 11,500 calls per year, the above data is within acceptable limits.

After the customer load for each salesperson has been determined, the area is split into territories of the proper size for routing. Each territory should be of such size that each salesperson can give it full coverage, but

Account Classification	Number of Accounts	Planned Call Frequency (calls/year)	Total Calls
A	50	30	1500
B	100	20	2000
C	200	15	3000
D	250	10	2500
E	300	5	1500
	Total planned calls per year		10,500

not too large for them to cover without just skimming the cream off the top. The well-designed territory is one which lends itself to efficient routing. Proper routing will insure regular calls and prevent unnecessary travel. Careful planning will enable salespeople to cover a territory in a logical pattern without excessive travel. The pattern should be set up to keep them on the road no more than necessary, and to avoid back tracking and in-and-out travel. Mileage should be determined beyond which salespeople should remain overnight in the territory. A successful routing plan should insure regular calls, which are important for products purchased on a regular basis.

Evaluate with Sales Quotas

Sales quotas are simply sales goals or other quantitative goals assigned to each salesperson. The sales quota can be derived directly from the sales forecast. It is used to measure the performance of salespeople and to encourage them to reach predetermined levels of performance. Salespeople tend to strive for improvement in their work and tend to produce increases in efficiency when their performance is being measured against an objective. Using the sales quotas will help identify leading performers, and can be the means of improving your overall sales program. The effectiveness of quotas as control measures depends largely upon the quality of sales forecasting and budgeting, and upon the territorial design. Performance differentials can be highlighted by comparing individual breakdowns of territorial quotas with similar breakdowns of actual sales statistics. Sometimes quotas are used solely for inspirational purposes. In such cases, however, little attempt is made to relate the growth to sales potential. Caution is suggested in those cases where quotas are set on the basis of subjective judgment, particularly where they are unrealistically high: as a consequence, much of the inspirational value is lost.

QUOTAS SHOULD BE ACCEPTABLE

Basic to the use of a sales quota as a measuring tool are the requirements that it be specific, realistic, obtainable, and accepted as such by the salespeople being measured. Acceptance of the objectives by the salespeople is important. It may be obtained either by their participation in setting the sales objectives or by explaining the quota to the extent that they are acceptable.

The basic ingredients for a successful use of a quota program include simplicity, fairness, and two-way communication.

The starting point for setting fair quotas should be the overall performance of the business — the total business divided by the total market. It seems reasonable to expect each territory to equal the average of the company, providing market opportunities and conditions are the same between all territories. Good judgment is important in adjusting territory sales expectancy to the sales quota. When making comparisons of actual sales for the territory with expected average penetration, some disclosure of variation of factors may be indicated, requiring adjustment in some territories.[7]

SUMMARY

The strategic importance of adequate sales income in the profitable operations of a small business cannot be neglected. Insuring adequacy of sales income will be enhanced by establishing objectives and utilizing sales forecasts to sharply focus the task.

Too frequently, the development of those responsible for sales income is neglected — not intentionally, but simply by overlooking the real potential. Sales income suffers accordingly. Recognize the importance of the selling process, especially the final step — the close. Ten proven methods for closing sales have been presented. How much more income (profits) could be

---

[7]*Ibid.*, p. 300.

obtained by raising the effective level of closing sales by 25 percent or 50 percent or even 100 percent?

Answer these important questions: Do the salespeople know how to sell? What is their level of knowledge about the company, the products, and the customers? Do the methods of compensation help to motivate sales personnel?

To discover additional sources of income, evaluate the present sales in terms of product, territory, customer, etc. Generating more sales income may be the key to managing your business more profitably.

17

Using Advertising, Promotion, and Publicity Effectively

"Ideas won't keep:
Something must be done about them."

A. N. Whitehead[1]

Expertise in the use of advertising, sales promotion, and publicity can strategically develop increased profits for the small business. The object of this chapter is to examine possible ways to employ these marketing tools more effectively.

ADVERTISING OBJECTIVES

Too often it is observed that advertising by small business seems to be on a hit or miss basis. Acting upon the assumption that every business should advertise, many small businesses advertise a little now and a little more later on. Such a program lacks objectivity.

---

[1]From *Dialogues of Alfred North Whitehead* (1953). Recorded by Lucien Price.

A starting place should be a statement of the objective of an advertising expenditure. When advertising is approached in this way, the essential elements can be coordinated — including budgeting, media selection, creative strategy, scheduling, and analysis of results. It is important to develop advertising in terms of a campaign, so that it will be a continuous and sustained activity rather than a one-time event.

The following questions may help in the definition of your advertising objectives. Are you:

- introducing a new product?
- attempting to penetrate a new market?
- opening a new store?
- desiring to increase the use of a product?
- attempting to increase quantity purchases?
- desiring to command a premium price?
- drawing attention to the superiority of your products or
- service?

Advertising can be classified under two major types: (1) Product advertising, which has to do with the special efforts designed to increase the sales of particular products or service; and (2) Institutional advertising, which involves efforts to build the reputation of the business. Your decision with regard to the type of advertising to use will depend upon the nature of your business, the objectives of your business, the practices in the industry, and the availability of particular media.

Figure 17-1 presents schematically the principal elements involved in the marketing of a product (manufacturer, wholesaler, retailer, and consumer) and the kinds of components that are combined to make an effective marketing program. Success depends on the effective coordination of the personal selling effort in conjunction with the advertising program.

ADVERTISING BY MANUFACTURERS

The manufacturer in Figure 17-1 typifies the small factory that usually aims the advertising in two directions — to the ultimate consumers and to the retailers (dealers or business users) of the product. Whether the manufacturer is selling consumer goods in a local market or industrial good in a broader geographical market will dictate the type of advertising

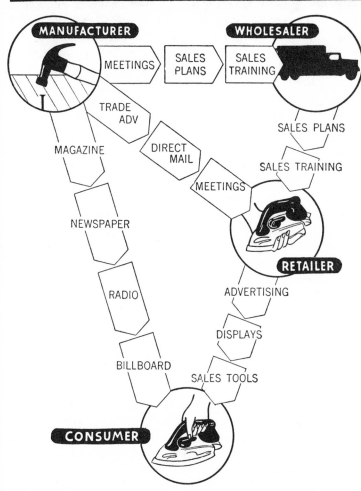

medium which would be effectively used. The actual advertising medium selected should be based on the planned objective for the advertising program. Figure 17-1 suggests various ways advertising can be used by a manufacturer to enhance the marketing effort for retailers and consumers.

What media, the total expenditure, and the advertising schedule should be structured to the needs of the particular product involved. It should not be a stereotyped program, but flexible and adjusted to changing factors affecting the marketing program.

A regional paint manufacturer, marketing on a national cooperative advertising program, made a rather strategic observation in connection with the national magazine advertising campaign for the product. It seems that the full-page ads being run for the benefit of the paint dealers was scheduled at the usual time in the spring of the year. However, the weather was colder than usual and it delayed the usual spring clean-up and paint-up activities in the primary markets. It was concluded that the advertising so spent was virtually wasted. Thereafter it was decided to shift the budget for the national magazine advertising over to cooperative advertising with retail dealers in their local markets—in the form of colored newspaper ads when the weather was right for the advertising.

Smaller manufacturers selling through dealers or to other businesses rely heavily on the use of direct mail and trade publications that are read by their prospects. If the market area is larger—regional or national in scope—advertising in trade journals offers another possibility. In addition to having selective circulation, the rates are relatively low. Frequent insertion of small advertisements may be most effective for the small manufacturer. The object of the advertising is to secure inquiries and leads for use in follow-up efforts (by means of direct mail, sample distribution, or contact by sales representatives).

When prospects are few in number and represent a rather selective group, direct mail is suggested. In preparing the list for direct mail advertising, they should include present and former customers in addition to prospective customers. Because of the lack of standard ratios to serve as guides (such as are available for retailers), the manufacturer has a particularly difficult problem in budgeting the amount to be spent for advertising. It will be helpful in this regard to make a careful estimate of the amount of the selling job which can be done by advertising, and to compare it with the results expected through the sales force. The important thing is to set a budget figure for the advertising program and to carefully allocate it over the budget period.

While radio is used less frequently than direct mail by small manufacturers, "spot" announcements can be effective in getting a new product off to a good start.

To enhance the effectiveness of the advertising program for the small manufacturer, it is recommended that a theme be selected as a guideline for planning the advertising efforts. The following have been suggested: (1) The product, when it is new or superior to competitive products; (2) The packaging; (3) The price, if it is more favorable than competitive prices; or (4) Service, in terms of prompt deliveries and proximity to customers. These things are merely suggestive. Others may be developed that will have particular relevance for a manufacturer's product.

ADVERTISING BY WHOLESALERS

As a rule, small wholesalers do not engage in extensive advertising. The expense for personal selling ranges from ten to twenty times as much as the amount spent for advertising (for most wholesale lines, large and small firms combined).

When small wholesalers do "floor selling," the buyers visit the sample rooms or the selling floors and inspect the merchandise. Most of the buyers are small retailers. By utilizing appealing displays, the wholesaler can both increase immediate sales and demonstrate to the retailers how to present the merchandise effectively in their own stores. When small wholesalers do engage in external advertising it is directed to the trade rather than to ultimate customers. Most wholesalers utilize signs as a form of advertising, either on the store front or on the roof or side of the warehouse. If a wholesaler has an exclusive line or markets his own brand, he may resort to consumer advertising.

Manufacturers usually provide catalogues, price lists, sales lists, and some dealer-aid material as forms of advertising used by wholesalers. The object of these materials, of course, is to enhance the effectiveness of personal selling by minimizing the time required on sales calls. Wholesalers rarely undertake direct merchandise advertising.

ADVERTISING BY RETAILERS

Primary advertising considerations for retailers include selection of a theme, choice of merchandise to advertise, coordinating sales effort, timeliness, and effective window and internal displays.

Selecting a Theme

What advertiseable features does the merchandise have? Some merchandise will suggest its own theme, such as fashionability, economy, or popularity. It is most helpful to know the *real* reasons why customers buy the particular merchandise.

Choice of Merchandise to Advertise

Since only about 15 to 20 percent of merchandise stock is suitable for external advertising, the choice of the right merchandise is of paramount importance. The advertised articles are depended upon, not only to cover the direct cost of advertising, but also to attract customers to the store to buy unadvertised products. The object of the advertising would be to build the volume of regular customers, rather than simply to attract bargain hunters or specific item buyers.

In choosing the merchandise to advertise, consider merchandise which is representative of the store's character. Reference to past sales, want slips, and customer complaints may also be useful in selecting the type of products to advertise.

Coordinating Sales Effort

Once customers have been attracted to the store through the advertising, the amount of purchases may be multiplied by the use of attractive displays, point-of-purchase advertising, circulars, handouts, and informative signs placed in convenient locations throughout the store. Besides coordinating the internal advertising of the store with the external advertising of the store, it is extremely important that the sales personnel be informed so that they may respond appropriately to the advertised items requested by customers.

Timing

The timing of the advertising by a particular store depends upon the type of merchandise handled and the acceptance level of the merchandise, e.g., the position on the "fashion cycle." The more exclusive stores representing fashion leaders in a community usually advertise heavily during the initiation of the selling season. Those catering to the middle class usually place their advertising before the peak of the selling period. The "economy" stores release their ads just after the crest of the selling period.

The situation is different with regard to staple merchandise and/or special sale promotions. In these cases, advertising would be timed to synchronize with paydays and also with the shopping habits among customers of the stores serving the lower- and middle-income groups. For those stores catering to the upper-income groups, the timing of such activities would be more in line with tax dates and the preferences of customers.

Window Displays

Since window displays are at the point of sale, they serve as effective "reminder" advertising, in addition to stimulating impulse buying. Effective window displays are an indispensable advertising medium for enhancing the sales volume for the store.

When sales volume fails to reach expectations with regard to merchandise being displayed in windows, the displayed merchandise should be replaced immediately, even in the middle of a busy selling day. The choice of substitution merchandise should be carefully considered in order to produce desired results. Besides being the most valuable advertising space in the store, window display space should be utilized to project the desired "store image" on the customer traffic. It is generally considered advantageous to coordinate displays with national advertising, if possible.

Interior Displays

The use of price cards and informative signs will enhance the effectiveness of interior displays. It may be well to inquire of manufacturers and distributors concerning the availability of display cards and other dealer aids which can be utilized as a part of the interior store display. These sources may also provide helpful information as to the selection of the proper location for interior displays, and they frequently supply props and fixtures to use with the display to make it most effective.

ADVERTISING—WHEN, WHERE, AND HOW MUCH?

Advertising should be budgeted along with the other operational expenses. As a general guide, you may want to consult the figures supplied by trade associations or other sources of information that indicate the percentage of sales usually spent in similar businesses. You may use such figures as guides, but may wish to modify the amount spent based on the objectives which you have determined.

In reaching your decision on how much to spend on advertising, you may consider the following factors:

1. *Size of store compared to size of community.* A small store needs more advertising in a large community.
2. *Size of trading area.* Some businesses draw customers from several counties, and they need to advertise accordingly.
3. *Competitive advertising.* Carefully assess the competitive advertising situation.
4. *Store location.* A neighborhood establishment needs more advertising then a store located in a popular shopping center.
5. *Age of the store.* A new retail business requires more promotion than one that is well established.
6. *Store policies.* A men's clothing store needs more advertising than an ice cream store in a shopping mall.
7. *The type of media used.* The availability of media and the cost of media are important considerations.
8. *The stage of the business cycle.* Most businesses advertise more when they have more money to advertise with.

When you have decided how much should be spent, the next question deals with when the advertising should be committed. Fluctuation in sales from month to month reflect fluctuations in consumer buying habits, which are related to conditions of climate and to special calendar events—holidays such as Mother's Day, Father's Day, and Easter. Table 17-1 gives a schedule of special events for consideration in establishing the advertising program for a retail business.

You may also develop special promotional events for your particular store. It could be very helpful to supplement the schedule with a monthly plan, using a form similar to that presented in Figure 17-2.

TABLE 17-1
Schedule of Retail Promotion Events

Month	Climatic	Calendar	Traditional
Jan.	Clearance of winter merchandise; resort wear.	Inventory clearance.	White goods sales, drug sales.
Feb.	Advance showing of spring merchandise.	Lincoln's Birthday, Washington's Birth-day, Valentine's Day, Boy Scout Week, Lent.*	Furniture, piece goods, housewares.
Mar.	Spring clothes.	Girl Scout Week, Easter gifts,* St. Patrick's Day.	Home furnishings.*
Apr.	Spring cleaning, garden supplies and outdoor furniture, fur storage.	Baseball season open-ing, Do-It-Yourself Week, Baby Week.	Spring Anniversary Sales.*
May	Spring clearance, summer sportswear, air conditioning.	Mother's Day, camp wear.	Bridal promotions.
June	Summer wear.	Graduation gifts, Father's Day, vacation needs, barbecue needs.	Housewares, drug sales.
July	Summer clearance.	4th of July, inventory clearance.	
Aug.	Advance showing of fall merchandise.	Back-to-school needs.	Furniture,* piece goods, fur sale, housewares.*
Sept.	Fall clothes.	Christmas layaway promotion, back to school.	China and glass, draperies and curtains.
Oct.	Fall clothes and accessories.	Columbus Day, Halloween	Fall Anniversary Sale,* woolen piece goods.
Nov.	Fall clothes and accessories.	Election Day, Thanks-giving, Christmas opening, toys.	Linens, china, and glass.
Dec.	Winter clothes, resort wear.	Christmas gifts, evening wear.	

*Subject to variation.
Source: Peter Bowles, *Small Marketers Aids, No. 56,* (Washington, D.C.: Small Business Administration).

The next important question is where to advertise. Ideally, the small-business person will utilize the advertising that will provide the greatest

Figure 17–2.
Advertising Planning Form. *Source:* Bernard Smith, *Small Marketers Aids, no. 60* (Washington, D.C.: Small Business Administration).

Week date	Sales	Dollars for advertising	Window (items)	News-paper (items)	Mail (items)	Other (radio, T.V., and so on)
	Last year_____ This year_____	Last year_____ This year_____				
	Last year_____ This year_____	Last year_____ This year_____				
	Last year_____ This year_____	Last year_____ This year_____				
	Last year_____ This year_____	Last year_____ This year_____				
	Last year_____ This year_____	Last year_____ This year_____				

return for the advertising dollar. While some business advertising may be successful through concentrated utilization of a particular media, other businesses may benefit from a combination of media. In selecting media, care should be exercised to avoid overreaching the trade area and customers of the particular small business, with the resulting higher cost of advertising usually charged for the larger circulation or geographical coverage.

Generally, the media used in advertising include the following: (1) newspapers; (2) radio; (3) television; (4) magazines; (5) billboards and signs; (6) public transportation; (7) Yellow Pages; (8) specialty advertising (such as shopping bags, calendars, pencils, and matchbooks); (9) direct mail; and (10) other media (handbills, samples, catalogs, etc.)

Television stations in big cities are not very appropriate for small businesses. The large city newspapers are expensive media for a business that only services a fraction of the city. Most magazines have coverage in excess of the needs of a small business. Radio advertising in the large metropolitan areas usually results in paying for unused coverage. For businesses located in small towns and cities, a local radio station and/or newspaper may provide an effective means of advertising.

Signs and billboards are effective when used near the site of a small business. Specialty advertising is another medium which has proven effective for many small firms: whether you use a pencil, matchbook, or calendar, the firm name, address, and phone number should be clearly displayed.

Public transportation vehicles have proved effective for small firms when it is possible to coordinate the vehicles with the firm's market.

Direct-mail advertising offers many advantages to the small firm. It is adjustable to any size firm: it is inexpensive, flexible, and capable of being selective in coverage. You can also measure its effectiveness. The challenge is to do an outstanding job on the direct mail advertising; otherwise, it will be tossed in the nearest wastebasket.

MAKE YOUR ADVERTISING EFFECTIVE

Good advertising doesn't just happen. It is planned. In planning your advertisements, take into consideration the following suggestions for making them more effective.[2]

Make Your Ads Easily Recognizable

Try to give your own copy a consistent personality and style.

Use a Simple Layout

In printed media, your layout should carry the eye through the message easily and in proper sequence, from art and headline to copy and price and to signature.

Use Prominent Illustrations

Featured merchandise should be shown in the prominent illustrations. Pictures emphasizing the product in use are good.

---

[2]Charles T. Lipscomb, Jr., "Checklist for Successful Retail Advertising," *Small Marketers' Aids No. 96* (Washington, D.C.: Small Business Administration, February 1973).

Get the Main Benefit to the Reader or Viewer

Prospective customers want to know "what's in it for me?" Emphasize the main reason why readers or listeners should buy the advertised item.

Give Complete Information

Give all essential information about the item, such as the manufacturer, model, and various sizes and colors. Your description should have a warm, sincere, and enthusiastic tone.

State Price or Range of Prices

Don't be afraid to quote a high price. If the price is low, support it with statements which create belief, such as clearances or special purchases.

Specify Branded Merchandise

If the advertised merchandise is a known brand, say so. Take advantage of advertising allowances and the pre-selling which the manufacturer has done. As one smart marketer says, "Cooperative advertising is one of the most valuable types of programs available to me from suppliers."

Be Sure to Include Store Name and Address

Check every ad or commercial to be certain you have included store name, address, telephone number, and store hours.

You may also obtain useful ideas from the ads provided by suppliers, trade associations, and trade publications. Newspapers and radio stations often provide aid and counsel. As a small-business person, you may find helpful assistance from a group of freelance specialists dealing in copywriting layout, commercial art or illustration, display work, research, and photography. The services are usually contracted on a fee basis, and such a staff of part-time specialists could prove a valuable asset in developing your small business advertising program. Those specializing in the use of handbills, signs, circulars and other direct mail pieces may provide the expertise related to these advertising medium.

You may also wish to utilize the aids provided by manufacturers or commercial services—"mats" for use in your advertising activities. The effect of the mats is to give you the illustrated part of the advertisement so that it can be adapted to fit by adding your store name, price, etc.

ADVERTISING AGENCIES

In the beginning, you may not need a regular advertising agency, but a good part-time artist and layout specialist who may have had advertising agency experience. The right expertise will be helpful to you in designing letterheads, literature, a logo, and scheduled advertising.

When your business progresses to the point that an advertising agency seems justified, shop around. There are many advertising agencies, and they are motivated to do many things for you. Your object is to have an agency that is hard working and cost conscious—one that takes a practical approach to accomplish what is needed for you at a price you can afford to pay. In choosing an agency, select an agency in which you will be one of the largest accounts. Regardless of how small your business, there are agencies to fit your category. The relationship should be complementary. As your business grows, you will have a larger advertising budget to spend, and this in turn will help to increase the size of the agency. Pay attention to the growth rate of your business in comparison to the agency. The agency may grow faster, and you may suddenly find yourself not getting the attention you need because you have become one of their small accounts. If so, you need to start looking for a new agency.

Your advertising agency may wish to handle your public relations and publicity. This is not recommended, because editors and reporters prefer to talk to the owner of the business. It is also more likely that product releases written by yourself will be easier to generate, cheaper, and better in quality. The important thing is to *do it*.

You should have a definite understanding about the compensation of the agency for its services. Remember that the advertising agency is paid a commission by the media. Bearing this in mind, you should carefully work out the details of your business relationship.

ANALYSIS OF RESULTS

It is desirable, when possible, to evaluate the effectiveness of each advertising program. Perhaps you have read about the old advertising story which states that doctors' mistakes are buried, lawyers' are in jail, preachers' are in hell—but the ad men's mistakes are in 4-color, 2-page spreads in some magazine. The moral of the story is that you cannot always predict the response to your advertising. It is true that advertising programs cannot be measured precisely. However, there are some suggestions which may be helpful in measuring some degree of their effectiveness. Where applicable, the following ideas may be utilized:

1. By advertising one item per ad only, and without reference to the item on the sales floor, you can count the calls and requests which result as a measure of effectiveness.
2. Observe the results in sales after a new advertisement has been placed.
3. In the case of a continuous advertising project, by omitting the regular advertising for intermittent periods a change in sales volume may give some indication of advertising effectiveness.
4. Use separate marks of identification in an ad which appears in two or more places. By asking the reader to bring the ad to the firm in order to obtain a special price or premium, you can determine how many ads come in from each source, which is another means of appraising effectiveness.

Because of so many uncontrollable factors affecting advertising, such as the numerous forces affecting customers and their behavior, the changing business conditions, and the continual change of competitors and their advertising, evaluation of advertising is complex and difficult to measure.

In the long run, the important thing is to know your market, your customers, and the best means of reaching them. Your efforts in understanding your customers will pay a high return. Two important words to remember in advertising—it must be *consistent* and *continuous* to achieve the objectives which you have set.

SALES PROMOTION EFFORT

Sales promotion is a special kind of effort designed to increase income. According to the Committee on Definitions of the American Marketing Association, sales promotion includes

> those marketing activities other than personal selling and advertising, and publicity that stimulate consumer purchasing and dealer effectiveness such as displays, shows and expositions, demonstrations, and various non-recurrent selling efforts not in the ordinary routine.[3]

Among the possibilities within the province of sales promotion, the following are included: (1) Trading stamps; (2) Free samples; (3) Premiums; (4) Special sales; (5) Contests; (6) Coupons; (7) Store window presentations; and (8) Displays at point of purchase.

The effective utilization of the above possibilities represents a challenge to your initiative and ingenuity. Sales promotion should not be overdone. With appropriate utilization, it should be effective in enhancing the profits of your enterprise.

PUBLICITY

The object of publicity is to enhance the public opinion about the business and its products. The formation of public opinion has two major facets. First, there are the many separate impressions which people form from the day-to-day contacts with the small-business person. This is most important— it is the performance record of the businessman. It is a composite of his record as a purchaser, seller, supplier, employer, and as a member of the local community. The effect is aptly stated in these words: "What you are rings out so loud, I can't hear what you're saying." Second, public opinion is influenced by the communications containing information about the firm and its performance. The implication of this second dimension of

---

[3]Committee on Definitions, *Marketing Definitions: A Glossary or Marketing Terms* (Chicago: American Marketing Association, 1960), p. 20.

public opinion is that while performance is necessary, it is not sufficient; therefore, communications efforts should be supplemental.

Publicity is information which is circulated through mass media, but which does not require payment by the sponsor. Therefore, it represents the most profitable opportunity for influencing public opinion. The small-business person should capitalize on the distinct advantages of using publicity for generating positive public opinion.

Third-Party Endorsement

When something newsworthy is presented by the editors and reporters in local media, it has the effect of a third-person endorsement. Unlike advertising, which is generated by the firm, the publicity influences the public opinion from a third-party vantage point.

The Ripple Effect

This amounts to amplification coming from the people who are ac-quainted with the businessperson or the business firm. The fact that media publicity leads to word-of-mouth publicity makes it probably the most valuable form of communication to the small business.

The Unlimited Scope

While advertising is directed specifically to the small-business cus-tomers, publicity enjoys a much greater scope. The information generated may interest a large spectrum of people, such as manufacturers, middle-men, bankers, creditors, employees, and competitors. The impact of favorable publicity can project a comprehensive picture for the entire organization.

One of the concerns about publicity is the fact that it is not controlled by the small-business person. Therefore, there is some hazard in the possibility that the publicity could project unfavorable aspects of the business. In addition to this reservation, there is the danger of the informa-tion publicized being distorted. Even though the medium may be willing to provide corrections, such actions may not satisfy the injury caused. A final caution: avoid having too much publicity, for this may be almost as bad as not having publicity at all.

A good publicity program should not be left to chance. It will likely not materialize. However, because it can be of strategic importance, good publicity should be carefully planned and encouraged as a valuable means of increasing profitability.

SUMMARY

Advertising, promotion, and publicity all suffer (as do most activities) from lack of clearly defined objectives and carefully planned programs. The effective utilization begins at Step 1 — What are the objectives? Other questions to be answered include: When, where, and how much? The money expended should be controlled as your other operating expenses by using a budget system.

Most small business operators have not had experience with advertising, promotion, or publicity. Therefore, it would be advisable to secure some professional assistance, which is usually available through the staff of a proven successful advertising agency. Warning: when you find an acceptable agency, don't give carte blanche — be on guard to the fact that the more advertising used, the more the agency is paid by the media. Keep in close touch with this phase of your business to keep it profitable.

18

The Credit Decision

"Words pay no debts."

Shakespeare

Should you extend credit to your customers? If yes, what kind of credit—open account or credit card? Would there be sufficient advantage to warrant the risk, the capital investment, and the time? Bad-debt expense is a fact of life for firms granting credit. What should your policy be on extending credit? There are many businesses with profitable operation without the use of credit: coin-operated laundries, convenience stores, barber shops, and beauty salons, to name a few. Dun and Bradstreet failure statistics include many firms that extended credit unwisely.

As you consider the question of extending credit to various customers, you may want to review carefully the C's of credit as they have become known—*Character, Capacity, Capital, Collateral, Circumstances,* and *Coverage.* A convenient formulation using the first three C's is as follows:[1]

Character + capacity + capital = good credit risk

---

[1]Theodore N. Beckman and Ronald S. Foster, *Credits and Collections: Management and Theory* (8th ed.) (New York: McGraw-Hill Book Co., 1969), pp. 90–91.

Character + capacity + insufficient capital = fair credit risk
Character + capital + insufficient capacity = fair credit risk
Capacity + capital + impaired character = doubtful credit risk
Character + capacity − capital = limited success
Capacity + capital − character = dangerous risk
Character + capital − capacity = inferior credit risk
Capital − character − capacity = distinctly poor risk
Character − capacity − capital = inferior credit risk
Capacity − character − capital = fraudulent credit risk

The use of credit is usually justified where the unit price of the product is large and the customer is not prepared to pay the full price upon purchase. Some merchants take a down payment, with the understanding that the account would be paid in full in sixty or ninety days, without interest payments. However, the large retail merchandisers have changed their credit policy considerably over the years. Formerly they allowed a cash discount on the payment of the thirty-day charge accounts as an incentive for prompt payment (2/10 n/30). However, with the rise of installment buying and the accompanying service charges, the cash discounts have disappeared and the customer is automatically charged interest if the thirty-day account is not paid on time. The use of credit is not only encouraged, but actually promoted, because of the additional income generated by the 1½–2 percent carrying charges added to the unpaid balances of revolving charge accounts.

Small businesspeople are often found long on risk, short on capital, and using excessive time on credit business without compensation. Make a careful decision concerning the use of credit in your business. If your decision on the use of credit is affirmative, you need a policy to implement the decision. Answer the questions of credit: to whom? how much? schedule of payments? carrying charges?

Some businesses extend credit using the nationally recognized credit cards (MasterCharge, BankAmericard [Visa], American Express) and accept the creditability of the customer based on his credit card. There are other small businesses that elect not to use the national credit cards, and must therefore make a judgment on the creditability of the customer.

In fact, some small businesses issue their own credit based upon the customer already having another credit card. A few years ago some independent service stations used signs indicating that all credit cards were honored, to induce the customer to make a purchase. At that time the card of the major oil company had the name and address on the card, so the independents could send the customer an application form to secure one of their cards. The major oil companies terminated the practice by printing the name of a customer and the charge account number, but no address.

In extending credit to customers there is a wide and varied practice among small businessmen. Some simply judge the customer by appearance along with name and address, only to regret having made the sale. Perhaps it would be well worth the cost to acquire a credit application form, such as the example in Figure 18-1, to receive pertinent information before extending credit. In verifying a customer for credit, a local credit association may be helpful. Although there is a charge for the service, it can be more than offset by eliminating a bad credit risk.

GROWTH OF CONSUMER CREDIT

Data in Table 18-1 indicate that *consumer* credit has steadily increased since 1950; but the rate of increase has been decreasing since the period of greatest increase — 1950-1960. Also revealed in the data is the increasing importance of installment credit as the major kind of consumer credit. In 1950 it represented 68.4 percent, which increased to 82.1 percent in 1974. The rapid expansion of consumer credit underscores its importance in business. Therefore, credit policy for the small firm is an important decision.

TYPES OF RETAIL CREDIT

There are two main types of retail credit, generally designated regular charge account and installment account. In recent years there has been a refinement in the charge account from the customary thirty-day charge accounts to the revolving charge accounts. They both differ from the installment credit account in that they do not have a chattel mortgage involved in the purchase of merchandise. Customers using a thirty-day charge account are expected to pay for their purchases at the end of the month. Statements issued to customers usually show a due date, and the

TABLE 18-1
Consumer Credit: Selected Years (Billions of Dollars)

Type of Credit	1950	%	1960	%	1970	%	1974	%
Charge Accounts*	5.0		8.6		15.5		18.6	
Single Payment Loans	1.8		4.5		9.4		13.2	
Total Noninstallment Credit	6.8	31.6	13.2	23.4	25.1	19.7	31.8	17.9
Percentage Increase				+94.1		+90.1		+26.7
Automobile	6.1		17.7		35.2		50.3	
Other Consumer Goods	4.8		11.5		31.5		46.5	
Personal Loans	2.8		10.6		31.3		41.5	
Home Repair and Modernization	1.0		3.1		5.1		7.4	
Total Installment Credit	14.7	68.4	43.0	76.6	102.1	80.3	145.8	82.1
Percentage Increase				+192.5		+137.2		+42.8
Total Consumer Credit Outstanding	21.5	100.0	56.2	100.0	127.2	100.0	177.6	100.0
Percentage Increase				+161.4		+126.3		+39.6

*Credit issued by service firms and professional individuals.

Source: Statistical Abstract of the United States, Supt. of Documents (Washington, D.C.: U.S. Govt. Printing Office, 1974), p. 461.

account is not charged interest if the payment is received on time. However, there has been another development in recent years, known as "cycle billing," which has as its purpose the elimination of the peak work load in connection with the monthly billing at the end of the month. The accounts are divided alphabetically and segments are processed every three to four days so that the process of billing and collection is spread more evenly over the entire month.

Revolving Charge Accounts

These differ from the thirty-day accounts in that they are not required to be paid in full: a portion of the amount of charges due is paid, and interest is charged on the remainder. The interest is computed on the average daily balance—which is calculated by totaling the balance outstanding for each day of the month, and dividing by the number of days in the billing period. A customary rate of 1.5% per month is charged, making the annual equivalent 18%. In the interest of controlling customer credit, most stores place a set maximum for each revolving account customer. The maximum does not exceed $500 unless some special arrangements are made. Customers with high credit ratings may have a running balance of several hundred dollars with no payments required monthly, but interest is charged.

Credit customers are usually issued a card for identification when making purchases on credit. Some community credit groups issue a common card and have it nitched or punched with the identifying marks of the participating stores. Purchases are also permitted on credit by firms honoring the national credit cards circulated by companies, such as BankAmericard, Master Charge, Diners Club, and American Express. The volume of business done on credit cards issued by banks reached $4.6 billion in 1972.[2]

Installment Credit

This assists the customer purchasing a large ticket item and desiring to pay over several months or years. Furniture, appliances, and recreational equipment are commonly purchased with the use of installment credit.

---

[2]*Statistical Abstract of the United States* (Washington, D.C.: U.S. Govt. Printing Office, 1973), p. 455.

The monthly payment is figured on the basis of the total purchase price less the down payment, plus interest on the balance for the payment period, divided by the total months involved. Length of the finance period varies with the item purchased, ranging from one to three years for a home appliance or recreational equipment to twenty to thirty years for a home. The normal procedure is to prepare an installment sales contract to be signed by the customers. The contract sets forth the terms specifying the amount financed, rate of interest charges, amount of interest to be paid, total number of payments, and the date of initial payment. Specific provision is made for the item purchased to be pledged as collateral for the financing. Those firms with sufficient funds may choose to finance their own contracts. However, many smaller firms use financial institutions to facilitate installment credit sales by selling or discounting the contracts.

CREDIT INFORMATION

Credit information about customers is usually obtained from credit application forms and reports from credit bureaus. It is not a difficult thing to secure necessary information at the time the customer is seeking credit. You may use a specially printed form to suit your particular needs, or a standardized form which may be obtained from an office supply store. Figure 18-1 exemplifies the type of form which is commonly used to obtain vital information from a customer seeking credit. You may also wish to affiliate with the local retail credit bureau, whose *raison d'être* is to supply its members with pertinent credit information. This type of venture requires your cooperation in supplying information of value to other members, and they reciprocate similarly through the means of the credit bureau. Over time much useful information is accumulated in the files, which facilitate your receiving vital credit information in a matter of minutes over the telephone. Detailed reports can also be obtained, as can trade clearance reports that summarize recent customer activities concerning purchases and payments at other stores. If your local bureau belongs to the Associate Credit Bureaus, it can supply information on a national scope. Dun and Bradstreet is another name associated with credit and business ratings, and subscriptions are available to their publications. The occasional user may find assistance in the use of this information through his banker.

Figure 18–1.
Application for Credit. *Source:* From Clifford M. Baumback, Kenneth Lawyer, and Pearce C. Kelley, *How to Organize and Operate a Small Business,* 5th ed. Copyright © 1973 by Prentice-Hall, Inc., Englewood Cliffs, N.J. Reprinted with permission of Prentice-Hall, Inc.

GUARD YOUR CREDIT AS A SACRED TRUST

APPLICATION FOR CREDIT

International Consumer Credit Association
OFFICIAL RECOMMENDED APPLICATION

MR.
MRS.
MISS ____ WIFE'S NAME ____

HOME ADDRESS ____ CITY ____ STATE ____ HOW LONG ____ OWNS RENTS ____

PREVIOUS ADDRESS ____ CITY ____ STATE ____ HOW LONG ____

DATE OF BIRTH ____ NO. OF DEPENDENTS ____ TEL. NO. ____ SOCIAL SECURITY NO. ____

EMPLOYED BY ____ ADDRESS ____

POSITION ____ HOW LONG ____ MONTHLY SALARY ____

FORMER POSITION ____
(if employed less than 1 yr.)

WIFE'S EMPLOYER ____ ADDRESS ____

POSITION ____ HOW LONG ____ MONTHLY SALARY ____ SOCIAL SECURITY NO. ____

LANDLORD OR MORTGAGE HOLDER ____ ADDRESS ____ MONTHLY RENTAL OR MORTGAGE PAYMENT $ ____

NAME OF NEAREST RELATIVE AND RELATIONSHIP (OTHER THAN HUSBAND OR WIFE)

____ ADDRESS ____

BANKS ____ CHECK OR SAVINGS ACCOUNT NO. ____ ☐ CHECKING ☐ SAVINGS ☐ LOANS

ADDRESS ____

MAKE OF CAR ____ YEAR ____ FULLY PAID: YES ____ NO ____ BALANCE DUE $ ____

MAKING PAYMENT TO ____ ADDRESS ____

CREDIT REFERENCES

NAME OF FIRM	ADDRESS	TYPE OF ACCOUNT		ACCOUNT IS NOW	
		CHARGE	BUDGET	OPEN BAL.	PD. IN FULL

MEDICAL REFERENCES

HOSPITAL ____ ADDRESS ____ BALANCE DUE $ ____ PD. ____

DOCTOR ____ ADDRESS ____ BALANCE DUE $ ____ PD. ____

DOCTOR ____ ADDRESS ____ BALANCE DUE $ ____ PD. ____

LIST ON REVERSE SIDE OF THIS APPLICATION ANY UNPAID BALANCES ON INSTALMENT ACCOUNTS AND MONTHLY PAYMENTS THEREON.

THE ABOVE INFORMATION IS FOR THE PURPOSE OF OBTAINING CREDIT AND IS WARRANTED TO BE TRUE. I AGREE TO PAY ALL BILLS UPON RECEIPT OF STATEMENT OR AS OTHERWISE EXPRESSLY AGREED.

I HEREBY AUTHORIZE THE PERSON OR FIRM TO WHOM THIS APPLICATION IS MADE, ANY CREDIT BUREAU OR OTHER INVESTIGATIVE AGENCY EMPLOYED BY SUCH PERSON, TO INVESTIGATE THE REFERENCES HEREIN LISTED OR STATEMENTS OR OTHER DATA OBTAINED FROM ME OR FROM ANY OTHER PERSON PERTAINING TO MY CREDIT AND FINANCIAL RESPONSIBILITY.

PLEASE READ BEFORE SIGNING APPLICATION.

SIGNATURE ____

DATE ____

CREDIT LIMIT	APPROVED
$	

CREDIT BUREAU

IN FILE ____ DATE ____

FIRM	SINCE	HIGH CREDIT	TERMS	LAST PURCHASE	PAYS

FORM NO. 1063B

The *Truth-in-Lending Law* was enacted in 1969 as the Consumer Credit Protection Act, with the principal purpose of insuring better information to the customer on what credit costs. Businesses are required under the Act to advise customers in writing—10-point type, .075 inch computer type, or elite-size typewritten numerals—about the finance charge and the annual percentage rate. The finance charge includes all costs paid by the consumer for credit—all interest, carrying charges, cost of insurance premiums if required for credit protection, and credit investigation costs. The annual percentage rate is the percentage interest rate charge expressed as an annual rate, and must be reported to the nearest quarter of one percent. A publication of the Small Business Administration entitled *Understanding Truth-in-Lending* outlines specific requirements as follows:

RE: *Revolving Charge Accounts.* Before the account is opened the following information must be disclosed:

1. Conditions under which a finance charge may be made and the period within which, if payment is made, there is no finance charge (such as "30 days without interest").

2. The method of determining the balance upon which a finance charge may be imposed.

3. How the actual finance charge is calculated.

4. The periodic rates used and the range of balances to which each applies as well as the corresponding Annual Percentage Rate—for instance, a monthly rate of 1½ percent (APR, 18 percent) on the first $500, and 1 percent (APR, 12 percent on amounts over $500.

5. Conditions under which additional charges may be made, along with details of how they are calculated. (This applies to new purchases, when charges are added to the account.)

6. A description of any lien (secured interest) you may acquire on the customer's property—for instance, rights to repossession of a household appliance.

7. Minimum periodic payment required.[3]

Each and every monthly statement sent to the customer must include the following information in the correct terminology indicated in bold-face type in the quoted material following.

1. The unpaid balance at the beginning of the billing period (previous balance).

2. The amount and date of each purchase or credit extension, and a brief description of each item bought if not previously given to the customer.

3. Customer payments (payments), and other credits, including those for rebates, adjustments, and returns (credits).

---

[3]"Understanding Truth-in-Lending" (Washington, D.C.: Small Business Administration, November 1969).

4. The finance charge expressed in dollars and cents (finance charge).

5. The rates used in calculating the finance charge, and the range of balances, if any, to which they apply (periodic rate).

6. The annual percentage rate which must be expressed as a percentage after January 1, 1971 (annual percentage).

7. The unpaid balance on which the finance charge was calculated.

8. The closing date of the billing cycle, and the unpaid balance as of that date (new balance).[4]

RE: *Installment Contracts.* The law specifies certain information be provided the customer usually printed on the installment sales contract or printed form containing the following:

1. The cash price (cash price).

2. The downpayment including trade-in (cash downpayment, trade-in, or total downpayment — as applicable).

3. The difference between the cash price and downpayment (unpaid balance of cash price).

4. All other charges, itemized but not part of the finance charge.

5. The unpaid balance (unpaid balance).

6. Amounts deducted as prepaid finance charges or required deposit balances (prepaid finance charge) and/or required deposit balance.

7. The amount financed (amount financed).

8. The total cash price, finance, and all other charges (deferred payment price).

9. The total dollar amount of the finance charge (finance charge).

10. The date on which the finance charge begins to apply (if this is different from the date of the sale).

11. The annual percentage rate which must be expressed as a percentage after January 1, 1971 (annual percentage rate).

12. The number, amounts, and due dates of payments.

13. The total payments (total of payments).

14. The amount you charge for any default, delinquency, and the like, or the method you use for calculating the amount.

15. A description of any security you will hold.

16. A description of any penalty charge for prepayment of principal.

17. How the unearned part of the finance charge is calculated in case of prepayment (Charges deducted from any rebate must be stated).[5]

---

[4]*Ibid.*
[5]*Ibid.*

COLLECTION POLICY

Bad debts and collections correlate directly with the wisdom in selecting credit customers and the efficiency of methods for collecting accounts. A small-business person should keep close tabs on the status of his accounts receivables. Knowing the customers will be invaluable in pursuing the appropriate course in collection. To give a general indication the bad-debt ratio will be helpful, and may be had by dividing bad debts by sales. Decide what is a reasonable ratio for your business, check the ratio regularly, and quickly ascertain the cause for any variance. One of the most skillful decisions to be made in managing a small business concerns credit policy—to be liberal enough to secure maximum sales on credit and yet conservative enough to minimize excessive losses.

The owner of a high-priced, exclusive, ladies' ready-to-wear business always cautioned the credit manager that if bad-debt losses were too low, he was turning away too many credit customers. In other words, he expected to lose some money in credit business. Properly managed, however, he knew it was possible to add additional increments to profits through wise credit management.

One of the most delicate areas involves the decisions dealing with the collection of overdue accounts. The small-business person has the advantage here if he elects to use it: individual knowledge of the customer. Knowing the customer is a guide to the timing and methods to use. Different stages are suggested in collecting accounts, from a gentle approach progressing to a more stern approach, culminating in legal procedures, if necessary.

Computerized Billing

Computerized billing has become feasible for small businesses. By serving a number of accounts on a fee basis per account, computer services can extend the benefits where they would otherwise be uneconomic. You may want to investigate the availability of the service in your community or nearby and consider the cost/benefit factors involved. In addition to billing the credit accounts, it is possible to include payroll, inventory, and general accounting statements.

Aging of Accounts Receivable

This should be done regularly by the small-business person. Table 18–2 provides an example of a statement. Note that the first two columns give the customer name and current balance. In the remaining columns the balance is shown according to the time it was charged. Remember the axiom: the longer an account is on the books, the more likely the failure of payment in full. Therefore, prompt action should be taken by activating well-conceived collection procedures when an account becomes past due.

TABLE 18–2
The Profit Company, Aging of Accounts Receivable, June 1, 1977

Customer Name	Current Balance	Number of Days on Account				
		0-30	31-60	61-90	91-120	Over 120
H. Black	$125	$ 25	$ 50	$ 50		
J. Christensen	360	300	60			
E. Davis	150	100	–	–	$ 50	
A. Edwards	30	15	–	15		
B. Frank	80	20	20	40		
R. Goddard	425	125	100	100	–	$100
W. Harris	600	50	150	100	200	100
R. Ingram	65	–	–	–	65	
P. Johnson	225	–	125	100		
TOTALS	$46,000	$24,000	$9,000	$7,000	$4,000	$2,000

Source: Adapted from *Small Business Management Fundamentals* by Dan Steinhoff. Copyright © 1974 by McGraw-Hill, Inc. Used with permission of McGraw-Hill Book Company.

In the situation represented in Table 18–2 $46,000 is the balance of accounts receivable. The remaining columns also add up to $46,000. This statement shows the owner that $24,000 is the amount of current month charges with $9,000 less than 60 days old, $7,000 less than 90 days old, $4,000 more than 90 days, and $2,000 over 120 days old. The probabilities are not too good for collecting the $2,000 over 120 days old, and he may want to list that amount as charged off to bad-debt loss at the end of the year. If the accounts are eventually paid, they can always be reported as income.

As you proceed with collection procedures you may use different tactics on customers like Christensen, Harris, and Ingram in Table 18-2. In a small business a personalized approach will undoubtedly pay dividends. Most large firms have to rely on standardized, impersonal approaches because of the volume of accounts involved.

Accounts Receivable Turnover

The relationship of the credit sales made during the year and the average amount of accounts receivable carried on the books provides an indication of the accounts receivable turnover. The actual calculation can be made as follows:

$$\frac{\text{Credit Sales for the Year}}{\text{Average Accounts Receivable}} = \frac{\text{Accounts Receivable}}{\text{Turnover}}$$

Where seasonal variation in credit sales is a factor, the accounts receivables should be averaged to provide a more representative indication of turnover. Notes receivable should be included in the computation where firms are selling to one another on this basis. This figure can be useful in managing the credit policy for the firm. When the turnover figure is increasing, it indicates that customers are paying more quickly. However, when the turnover is decreasing it is indicative of slower payment by customers and/or that the credit department is granting unjustified credit. The following example illustrates the computation of the turnover figure and its use in evaluating performance.

The ACE Clothing Store sells to many of its customers on a 30-day credit account. In 1976 total credit sales were $600,000 with average accounts receivable on the first of each month at $100,000, producing a turnover of six times a year. In other words, it took one-sixth of a year (60 days) to collect the average amount of receivables on the books. If customers had paid their accounts on the first of the month in line with the 30-day policy, the turnovers should have been twelve times. Some appropriate action should be taken to move the turnover upwards toward twelve. The credit policy may need revision with new restrictions placed on granting credit. Collection policy needs review, as the average accounts receivable figures would suggest some accounts are above and some below the average figure.

Procedures for Calculating Credit-Control Indices[6]

Rejection percentage:

$$\frac{\text{Number of applications for credit declined}}{\text{Total number of credit applications received}} = \text{rejection percentage}$$

Trend in number of credit accounts:

$$\frac{\text{Net gain or loss in number of accounts}}{\text{Total number of accounts at beginning of period}} = \begin{array}{l}\text{percentage trend in} \\ \text{number of accounts}\end{array}$$

Change in credit sales volume:

$$\frac{\text{Net gain or loss in credit sales}}{\text{Amount of credit sales in previous period}} = \begin{array}{l}\text{percentage change in} \\ \text{credit sales volume}\end{array}$$

Ratio of credit sales volume to total sales:

$$\frac{\text{Credit sales for period}}{\text{Total sales for period}} = \begin{array}{l}\text{ratio of credit sales volume} \\ \text{to total sales}\end{array}$$

Change in accounts receivable outstanding:

$$\frac{\text{Net gain or loss in accounts receivable outstanding}}{\text{Accounts receivable outstanding for previous period}} = \begin{array}{l}\text{percentage change} \\ \text{in accts.}\end{array}$$

Collection percentage:

$$\frac{\text{Collections for period}}{\text{Accounts receivable outstanding at start of period}} = \begin{array}{l}\text{collection} \\ \text{index}\end{array}$$

Accounts receivable investment index:

$$\frac{\text{Total credit sales}}{\text{Average accounts receivable outstanding}} = \text{accounts receivable turnover rate}$$

$$\frac{360 \text{ days}}{\text{Accounts receivable turnover rate}} = \text{number of days accounts are outstanding}$$

$$\frac{\text{Actual collections of accounts receivable for a period}}{\text{Average accounts receivable outstanding}} = \begin{array}{l}\text{accounts receivable} \\ \text{investment index}\end{array}$$

---

[6]Donald P. Kohns, *Credit and Collections* (Cincinnati, Ohio: South-Western Pub. Co., Inc., 1968), p. 25.

ADMINISTERING A CREDIT PROGRAM

Some of the vital steps you will want to include in your credit program are listed below:

1. Have a prospective credit customer fill out an application similar to the example given in Fig. 18-1.
2. Check the record of credit with credit agencies or bureaus. Ascertain the limits of credit granted. How does the applicant rank on the 4 C's of credit (character, capital, capacity, and conditions)?
3. Based on the data gathered, decide on the amount of credit to be granted or the type of credit account.
4. Your decision should be communicated clearly to the customer, explaining the details and expressing appreciation for the business.
5. New accounts should receive close follow-up on a regular basis. Proven credit customers may be offered better credit terms in the future, and they should be so advised.

SUMMARY QUESTIONS ON CREDIT DECISIONS

1. Do you need credit sales to have a profitable business?
2. Would credit sales increase profit? By how much?
3. What kind of credit should be used?
4. What procedure should be followed in granting credit?
5. What controls (indicators) will be used to insure profitable use of credit? .

THE
FUTURITY
PHASE

19

Maintaining a Profitable Enterprise

Sometimes small-business operators make a profit in spite of themselves and because of fortuitous circumstances. One could say that it was profitable more because of luck than good management. But in the spectrum of small-business activities there are mostly those who achieve desired profits by careful planning and a lot of "hard work." The object of this chapter is to consider those functions and procedures that would maintain a profitable enterprise on a continuing basis.

NET PROFIT VERSUS CONTRIBUTION

Net profit under usual accounting procedures refers to the bottomline figure on the profit and loss statement (which begins with a statement of income minus cost of goods sold, minus the operating expenses, equals the net profit for operations). It is too frequently unrecognized that certain products, merchandising lines, departments, and branch operations may in fact be unprofitable. If the small-business operator is content with the bottom-line figure on the P & L statement, he may overlook the opportunity to maximize the profitability of the business.

Would it not be advantageous to know the profitability of the various important components of the business? It is possible to do so by establishing procedures in record keeping which separate the income according to desired categories, and also to maintain a record of expenses (direct costs) for each category. Fixed costs are excluded under the contribution concept. The deliberate purpose is to ascertain how much "contribution" is made by the respective categories, after deducting operating costs. Comparisons can then be made on the basis of the amount of the contribution (either in dollars or by percentage of the respective categories) toward meeting the fixed-cost obligations of the business. By adopting this method of profit analysis, you may be surprised to see the variance in the contribution to net profit. This type of analysis may uncover problem areas, the solution of which will not only enhance profits in the short run, but will ensure to a large extent the maintaining of a profitable enterprise.

INCOME ANALYSIS

Most small-business operators consider current sales income as the best single indication of current business performance. However, it is easy to err in the use of sales income data. In fact, it is a mistake to consider only gross sales income movements and fail to analyze sales income data in conjunction with standards of performance, competitors' sales income, and operating expenses. There are six elements which characterize every sales transaction and provide basic income data. The sales transaction is an order: (1) of a particular customer; (2) for a particular quantity; (3) of a particular company product; (4) from a particular sales representative; (5) on a particular date, and (6) under particular terms. By utilizing the information from the sales transactions it is possible for a small business to analyze the sales income in the following ways: (1) by customer, (2) by sales representative, and (3) by products.

Certainly the kind of reports and the number of reports deemed necessary for the profitable management of a particular business is a decision for the owner/manager. The following list of reports are suggestive of possibilities that might be derived from the sales income data:

1. Monthly report of sales by products (dollar volume)
2. Monthly report of sales by products in physical units
3. Daily record of sales, product, and inventories in physical units by products
4. Monthly sales to house accounts
5. Monthly reports on sales and commissions of each salesman
6. Monthly comparison between actual sales and projected sales by products in physical units
7. Monthly department sales by zones
8. Quarterly report on sales to key accounts in total and by products
9. Occasional study of sales by sizes of account
10. Occasional reports on the proportions of total sales made to different types of buyers

Your first reaction may be that to have all those reports would take too much time and cost too much money. In yesteryear that may have been true, but modern, electronic data processing equipment makes all of the information possible in a speedy, economic manner. You say small businesses cannot afford a computer. True, but there are many firms that offer data processing services especially designed to serve the needs of small businesses. You will have to decide what reports you consider necessary to maintain a profitable enterprise. It is certainly advisable to have a clear insight as to the source of income on a continuing basis.

The analysis of sales income is not very meaningful unless it is compared with projected sales. Through the process of goal setting (objectives) the expected income from recognized sources would have been established. In fact these projections could be made on the basis of customer, sales representative, and products. Having projected this information as standards of performance, analyses and comparisons are facilitated by adding the current data.

Some business operators measure success in terms of their sales performance in relation to a competitor's. You may or may not wish to choose this as a barometer. Nevertheless, it is important to track the performance of competitors. Analyzing market share is one approach to tracking competitor performance.

By determining your share of the market, it may be possible to have an effective comparison with other markets from information obtained by suppliers. Brand preference studies which are conducted in some markets are an indirect gauge of market share among competing brands in a specified market area.

Competitive behavior has a bearing on your current profit picture, and should be carefully considered as a viable factor in maintaining a profitable enterprise.

The third factor involving operating expenses, and more particularly marketing costs, will be discussed in more detail later in the chapter.

A Control Book

To help you see more clearly the current status and trend movements of your business, it is suggested that selected strategic data be presented in graphic form. A picture is worth a thousand words, according to the Chinese proverb. One glance at a sales map, expense chart, or income trend graph would be more meaningful than hours spent studying columns of numbers and figures.

A control book would simply be a loose-leaf binder with a compilation of the selected visual material that you prepare to assist you in controlling business operations. The preparation of the materials need not be costly. Graphs and charts can be prepared quickly on paper with a ruler and pencil; and by taking a few moments to plot the data as it becomes available, the picture can be clearly seen.

One approach in helping you set up your control book is to take the sales forecast and budgeted expense items and put them on a chart at the beginning of the year. By providing location for the monthly performance data, the actual record can be plotted on the projected performance; any variance can be quickly noted and analyzed, and appropriate action taken.

Comparison Data—Ratio Analysis

An additional section which can be added to your control book may include the results of applying the various ratios that may be found in the Dun and Bradstreet publications or from your trade association. By selecting the appropriate ratios for your business and calculating them, the answers can be recorded in your control book for reference, analysis, and utilization.

Ratio information may be useful (1) to compare your business with its own record of performance, and (2) to compare your business with other similar businesses in the particular industry classification. You will have to take the responsibility for developing the first comparison. By obtaining data from your trade association, or by utilizing the information published by the Industries Studies Department of Dun and Bradstreet, Inc., you may make the second application. To illustrate, please note the data obtained from Dun and Bradstreet publications as presented in the following paragraphs.

So that you may understand how the various ratios have been calculated, a list of the important ratios are provided next, with an explanation for their calculation.

Current Assets to Current Debt. Current Assets are divided by total Current Debt. Current Assets are the sum of cash, notes and accounts receivable (less reserves for bad debt), advances on merchandise, merchandise inventories, and listed federal, state and municipal securities not in excess of market value. Current Debt is the total of all liabilities falling due within one year. This is one test of solvency.

Net Profits on Net Sales. This is obtained by dividing the net earnings of the business, after taxes, by net sales (the dollar volume less returns, allowances, and cash discounts). This important yardstick in measuring profitability should be related to the ratio that follows.

Net Profits on Tangible Net Worth. Tangible Net Worth is the equity of shareholders in the business as obtained by subtracting total liabilities from total assets, and then deducting intangibles. This ratio is obtained by dividing Net Profits, after taxes, by Tangible Net Worth. The tendency is to look increasingly to this ratio as a final criterion of profitability. Generally, a relationship of at least 10 percent is regarded as a desirable objective for providing dividends plus funds for future growth.

Net Profits on Net Working Capital. Net Working Capital represents the excess of Current Assets over Current Debt. This margin is the cushion available to the business for carrying inventories and receivables, and for financing day-to-day operations. The ratio is obtained by dividing Net Profits, after taxes, by Net Working Capital.

Net Sales to Tangible Net Worth. Net sales are divided by Tangible Net Worth. This gives a measure of relative turnover of invested capital.

Net Sales to Net Working Capital. Net Sales are divided by Net

Working Capital. This provides a guide to the extent the company is turning its working capital and the margin of operating funds.

Collection Period. Annual Net Sales are divided by 365 days to obtain average daily credit sales; the average daily credit sales are then divided into notes and accounts receivable, including any discounted. This ratio is helpful in analyzing the collectibility of receivables. Many feel the collection period should not exceed the net maturity indicated by selling by more than 10 to 15 days. When comparing the collection period of one concern with that of another, allowances should be made for possible variations in selling terms.

Net Sales to Inventory. This involves dividing annual Net Sales by Merchandise Inventory as carried on the balance sheet. This quotient does not yield an actual physical turnover; rather, it provides a yardstick for comparing stock-to-sales ratios of one concern with another or with those for the industry.

Fixed Assets to Tangible Net Worth. Fixed Assets are divided by Tangible Net Worth. Fixed Assets represent depreciated book values of buildings, leasehold improvements, machinery, furniture, fixtures, tools, and other physical equipment, plus land, if any, and valued at cost or appraised market value. Ordinarily, this relationship should not exceed 100 percent for a manufacturer, and 75 percent for a wholesaler or retailer.

Current Debt to Tangible Net Worth. Derived by dividing Current Debt by Tangible Net Worth. Ordinarily, a business begins to pile up trouble when this relationship exceeds 80 percent.

Total Debt to Tangible Net Worth. Obtained by dividing total current debts plus long-term debts by Tangible Net Worth. When this relationship exceeds 100 percent, the equity of creditors in the assets of the business exceeds that of owners.

Inventory to Net Working Capital. Merchandise inventory is divided by Net Working Capital. This is an additional measure of inventory balance. Ordinarily, the relationship should not exceed 80 percent.

Current Debt to Inventory. Dividing the Current Debt by Inventory yields yet another indication of the extent to which the business relies on funds from disposal of unsold inventories to meet its debts.

Funded Debts to Working Capital. Funded Debts are all long-term obligations, as represented by bonds, mortgages, debentures, term loans, serial notes, and other types of liabilities maturing more than one year from statement date. This ratio is obtained by dividing Funded Debts by Net Working Capital. Analysts tend to compare Funded Debts with Net

Working Capital in determining whether or not long-term debts are in proper proportion. Ordinarily, this relationship should not exceed 100 percent.[1]

Analyze Your Performance

Yes, it will take some time to prepare your control book and to calculate the ratios. But this could well be one of the most valuable investments of your time. After visualizing your performance and computing the ratios, take time to analyze the results carefully. Don't be satisfied if things look well: you may neglect the opportunity of maximizing profits by simply being satisfied with profits. The question should always be raised, how can we improve the performance? At times you may be disappointed with the results and reflect seriously as to the underlying causes for adverse results. Whether the results are profitable or unprofitable, analyze the reasons and capitalize on the knowledge derived from your investment of time in analyzing the performance of your business.

THE PROFIT AUDIT

The term *audit* is not new in the business vocabulary. There are a variety of audits identified and used: the accounting audit, which is conducted to verify the records of the business; the inventory audit to establish the amount and valuation of inventory; the personnel audit, which is conducted to gain better insight into the human equation; and the marketing audit, which is undertaken to measure the effectiveness of the marketing function, per se. Perhaps the combination of these audits would add up to a profit audit. But (in line with the emphasis of this book) the audit with which we are most concerned is the profit audit. Audit is defined by Webster as "a formal or official examination and verification of an account; a methodical examination and review." This definition is applicable to our interest in the profit audit. In a sense, profit audit is a more comprehensive term; it includes all of the other audits which may have a contribution to

---

[1] Reprinted by permission of Dun and Bradstreet, Inc.

the understanding of the factors which contribute to the profitable operation of the business.

WHAT IS A PROFIT AUDIT?

A profit audit is an independent evaluation of the entire operations of the business, covering the objectives, programs, implementation, organization, and control for ascertaining what is being accomplished, appraising what is being accomplished, and recommending what should be accomplished in the future. A primary purpose of the profit audit is to develop an independent judgment of the quality and direction of the business activities. The audit may be accomplished both from an extensive viewpoint and an intensive viewpoint. In the extensive viewpoint, all functions of the business should be examined with emphasis upon the relative importance of each of the functions in contributing to profits. This dimension of the profit audit would be interfunctional. The intensive viewpoint would single out a particular function (such as marketing or production) and, through a searching study, would consider the contributions of the function toward profits. The extensive approach might also be considered a system-level profit audit. From an organizational standpoint, it would be a horizontal analysis. The intensive viewpoint could be considered an activity-level profit audit. From an organizational standpoint, it would be a vertical analysis.

Components of a Profit Audit

OBJECTIVES

The starting point of the profit audit is to consider or obtain a current statement of the objectives of the business. In fact, one of the first benefits from the profit audit may be exposing the fact that there is a lack of specific objectives clearly stated. Someone said, "If you don't know where you're heading, you probably won't get there." Objectives should be timely in view of the continuous changes taking place in the business environment. Another advantage of the audit is to review and relate the business objectives in terms of present and future expectations.

PROGRAM

Examine your program for its achieving objectives. What is the level of resources being used by the company to reach objectives? Are the available resources sufficient to meet the company objectives? What is the allocation of the total company budget in terms of the different functional areas as they relate to generating profitable operations? Are the programs of the different functions balanced, coordinated?

IMPLEMENTATION

This phase of the audit is concerned with the decisions and procedures to execute the program. In a sense, the implementation of the program covers the "tactics" used by the business to accomplish the desired objectives. When we speak of tactics from an organizational standpoint, we are moving down in the organization to where the action is. This would apply to each of the important functional areas of the business. In the marketing discipline, for example, consideration would be given to such matters as the choice of compensation scheme for salesmen, the choice of advertising media, and the choice of advertising agency; in the accounting function, the choice of inventory evaluation, and the depreciation schedule; and so, the process of evaluating tactical decisions would be carried on throughout the business. In caring for this phase of the audit, a consideration should also be given to what alternatives were available, why choices were made, and what the consequences of those choices were. In appraising the procedures followed by the company, the questions of who does what, when, and how should be answered.

Some of the procedures which affect the effectiveness of marketing actions are those used for developing current sales and cost information, handling and expediting customer orders, forecasting sales, and preparing marketing plans. The audit should examine the more critical procedures involved in each of the company activities to see whether they are the best available.

ORGANIZATION

An appraisal of the organization involves a consideration of: the formal lines of authority and responsibility; the impact of the informal organization in terms of power and status relations; the primary bases for allocating assignments; the adequacy of company personnel as a group; and the adequacy of specific individuals in terms of their key jobs. The kinds of questions to be used in appraising the organization of the businesses are the following: Have the important functions of the business been centralized in terms of one person having the responsibility and authority? Is the organization of the company structured in the most effective way (function structured, product structured, geographically structured and customer structured)? Is there sufficient coordination among the heads of the different departments in the company to facilitate proper communication? What steps should be taken to upgrade the qualifications and capabilities of company personnel?

Who Should Conduct the Profit Audit?

A number of factors will affect the answer to this question. The size of the company and the funds available for the purpose of conducting the audit are primary considerations. The value of the audit will correlate with the quality of the work done. The return for the effort expended should provide valuable inputs for increasing profits.

Assuming the company is well developed organizationally, it may be desirable to give the responsibility for conducting parts of the audit to different department heads, who may take the responsibility for auditing other departments in the company. Another approach would be to have the key management personnel audit the subordinate activities, either in their own functional areas or in other functional areas of the business. Still another possibility might be the utilization of the auditing office (should the company be developed to the point where they have an auditing office).

For the smaller company as well as the largest companies there are three additional considerations for conducting the profit audit. The first of these might be called the task-force audit, which is simply an assignment to two or more individuals to conduct the audit. This could be a team effort (even for the small firm) of the key personnel to work together in making an audit of company operations.

Still another possibility is to engage an auditor from the outside. The use of the so-called outside audit would represent a cash outlay; but if the regular personnel are usually quite busy, it may be well worth the investment—not only from the standpoint of available time, but also from the standpoint of having an outside view of the company operations. As the saying goes, "Sometimes we are so close to the forest we can't see the trees," which could well be a drawback of using in-company personnel for making the audit.

As a final consideration, the audit could be conducted by yourself as you review, analyze, evaluate, reconsider, redefine, ways and means of maintaining a profitable enterprise vis-à-vis the profit audit of your company.

THE PROFIT CONTROL PROCESS

As indicated in the beginning of this book, the emphasis here is profits. Maximizing profits is not a matter of taking what is left over after operations are completed. It is deliberately planning a profit objective and taking whatever action is necessary in the course of operations to insure the realization of the profit goal. In the control process involved in achieving desired profits, these are four elements common to all control systems.

Establish Goals and Standards

The details of goal setting have already been discussed in Chapter 2. As important to establishing a means of controlling the achievement. We have already discussed in this chapter some steps which should contribute to this end. Various standard control charts should be useful, such as those developed for the control book.

Program

What will it take to reach the goals? The answer to this question should be a carefully developed program encompassing all phases of the business. The program for each functional area should be detailed, and provision should be made for the intercoordination between departments in accomplishing the company goal. The resources of the company should be carefully budgeted for each of the functional areas for the specific program, designed to contribute in a maximum way to the profitable operations of the enterprise. Another dimension of the program is the importance of the time frame being planned to progress from the inception of operations on through to the completion of the program (which is tantamount to the arrival at the goals set).

Information

The performance of the company will be gauged from the information assembled. It should be established who needs what information, when, where, and in what form. The comparison of information gathered may be made continually—as from daily cash reports, or intermittently—as from quarterly income statements. If you avail yourself of a computerized accounting system, comparative information can be provided showing actual performance against standards set as a part of the regular data output.

Corrective Actions

Control implies achieving desired performance. When the information indicates that the performance is less than desired the deviation requires corrective action in order to put the operation back in a state of control. There are two types of control systems. (1) In the *closed-loop* system, comparisons are made through established rules or special devices which are capable of automatically revising the inputs as necessary to bring about more conformance between outputs and established standards for performance. (2) In the *open-loop* system, managerial personnel make comparisons between outputs and established standards and use personal discretion concerning whether any action is desired, and if so, what kind. It may be possible for both systems of control to be utilized effectively in taking corrective action to maintain control of business operations.

COMMON CAUSES OF FAILURE

The purpose of citing causes of failure is to alert you to the situations which may preclude maintaining a profitable business. Most of the factors listed below are usually the result of the failings of management. It is important to be sensitive to the possible causes of failure, so that corrective action may be taken promptly to avoid irreparable situations developing. These are the most common causes of failure:

1. Incompetent management
2. Lack of experience
3. Low sales performance to potential
4. High operating expenses to sales
5. Insufficient capital
6. Inventory problems
7. Unnecessary fixed costs
8. Credit problems
9. Competition
10. Locational matters
11. Expanding prematurely
12. Fraud and neglect

GROWTH VERSUS STAGNATION

It is very unlikely that the business will arrive at an operational plateau and perpetuate itself at that level. Many factors impinge on business operations, continually changing results. When a business is not expanding it may be in danger of contracting. The expansion and growth of business is not necessarily an automatic process, but a progressive management will plan and effect desired expansion and growth.

There are positive reasons for stimulating the growth of a business. First and foremost is the opportunity for increasing profits. A small business does not usually enjoy the benefits of specialization and economies of scale associated with larger enterprises. Therefore, another reason for growth is to move in the direction of growth, reaping the advantages of specialization and economies of scale.

Growth is frequently associated with more strength. Because of a stronger organization through its larger size and stronger position, growth is encouraged as a means of being more capable of warding off economic fluctuations.

One of the most important factors in growth is the capability of the management to grow. While the business grows it also facilitates personal development and opportunities for employee development.

What Are the Growth Opportunity Factors?

PLANNED GROWTH

Perhaps the most common form of growth for most small businesses results from the expansion of the existing business. By devising a deliberate plan for growth of the business, the necessary steps to implement the achievement of the plan can be identified, implemented, and insured with greater probability than to leave growth unattended. Take time to project where you want your business to be in three years, five years, even ten years in the future. Such planning might even suggest the necessity for acquiring a future building site as an essential part of the growth plan.

INNOVATIONS

A well-conceived innovation can have a salutary effect on profits and growth for a small business enterprise. While innovations may not occur too frequently, if at all, the probabilities for innovation can be increased by encouraging their development by way of new or improved products, by improving or developing new production processes, by developing better and improved transportation methods, by developing a unique or improved credit plan, or by developing promotional techniques which are innovative.

Mention was made earlier in this book about the Colorizer Paint Company, whose innovation developed as an application of the marketing concept, and provided unprecedented growth for the company. Certainly, innovation is a pertinent factor for company growth.

PROFICIENT MANAGEMENT

A very productive way of stimulating growth is to employ proficient management. By means of proficient management, the business may receive some dynamic inputs, fresh ideas, new approaches, or "new blood" to energize the growth possibilities for the firm. Keep your eyes peeled for such an individual who may be brought into the firm.

Government Contracting

The government has already taken steps in various programs to assist small business. There are opportunities for small businesses to bid contracts to supply the government. Care should be exercised and caution taken with regard to the amount of the business that is conducted on the basis of government contracts. Nevertheless, this may provide the opportunity to use excessive plant capacity and facilities to a good advantage. Certainly, it can be a viable means for supplementing growth and profits for the firm.

It is recommended that assistance be obtained through the S.B.A. in acquiring government contracts for use by small business. By means of the S.B.A. field offices you can obtain information about the government agencies that are purchasing products or services which may be supplied by your company. You may also arrange for being placed on the approved list of bidders, and may obtain the necessary drawings and specifications for the purposes of preparing bids.

ACQUISITION AND MERGER

One of the frequently used routes of growth involves the acquisition of other small businesses or branch operations. A marketer of petroleum products may desire to increase his market, and may buy service stations and facilities in adjacent communities as a means of expanding operations. Two companies may desire to combine their efforts in the form of a merger to provide complementary benefits to each. One company may have the capability in the productive side of operations, whereas another firm may have a well-established marketing organization: by means of a merger, a more complete and competitive organization may result.

Information about possible acquisitions and mergers may be found in the classified section of daily newspapers under "business opportunities" or in various financial newspapers such as *Barrons* and *The Wall Street Journal*. Leads may also be obtained through trade associations, competitors, or sales representatives.

EXPORT MARKETING

With today's modern means of communication and transportation, even small businesses now effectively market products in foreign countries. This is another route which may be pursued as a means of growth for your company. While export marketing offers an opportunity for expansion and growth of the business, it should be explored carefully. To pursue this possibility, useful information and assistance can be obtained from the U.S. Department of Commerce. Knowledge about export opportunities and how to make the necessary foreign contacts can be facilitated in your contacts with the U.S. Department of Commerce.[2]

SUMMARY

With a bit of luck a small business operator may enjoy profits now and then. However, the real challenge is maintaining a profitable enterprise over time. Several things have been suggested to meet the challenge. By the contribution-plan approach to income (profit) analysis, the strong and weak spots can be identified.

Another suggestion is that you use a control book (compilation of useful operating data and statistics) to provide a visual tracking on charts and graphs of the movements and trends for the firm. Your control book could also include a presentation of ratio data, to focus attention on the plus and minus situations.

Perhaps the underlying key is to budget your time to permit a careful analysis of business operations, and thereby know the direction in which it is moving and determine what changes should be made to reach the profit objective.

One approach to follow in the evaluating process is a profit audit. The organization, structure, and procedure have been presented. If done properly, an audit should be well worth the effort. Recognize the causes of failure, and avoid them.

Bear in mind that your business will not likely reach a pleasant plateau and be perpetuated on that basis. Therefore, you should plan for growth and avoid stagnation.

---

[2]John Petrof, et al., *Small Business Management* (New York: McGraw-Hill Book Co., 1972), pp. 381–87.

20

Continuity Versus Termination

*"The genius of a good leader is to leave behind him
a situation which common sense, without the grace of genius,
can deal with successfully."*

Walter Lippmann
Roosevelt Has Gone, April 14, 1945

Sooner or later the futurity of your business will be determined either by choice or by circumstance. Unfortunately, the future of too many small businesses is terminated by circumstance, usually the unpredictable or unexpected circumstance that results in an unhappy circumstance for beneficiaries. It is by far more advantageous to plan the futurity of your business so that it may be done according to your wishes, and avoid unnecessary disappointments.

The purpose of this chapter is to bring your attention to some of the important considerations with regard to the futurity of your business, whether or not it should be continued or terminated.

SELECTING YOUR SUCCESSOR

Have you selected your successor? Will your successor be a member of your family, an employee, or a person from the outside? Sometimes members of the family are qualified but not interested—they want to do their own thing. Sometimes members of the family are interested but not qualified. Can they be qualified? Do they need additional experience, education, training?

Don't make the mistake of a groceryman who advised his son that he was retiring, and turned the business over to him. The parents decided to take an extended vacation out of state. The son and his wife assumed the responsibilities for the grocery store. The sudden thrust of full responsibilities was overwhelming. Through the exercise of poor judgment in extending credit and in buying improper merchandise, and through a general lack of control, the business became insolvent within six months. When dad and mom returned from the trip, the business had become a casualty.

When you have selected your successor, begin the transfer of responsibility to allow sufficient time for the necessary adjustments required for a transition in management. You will have to carefully consider how much time they will require. For some people, six months may be sufficient, but for others it may take longer. It would be essential for the successor to have the necessary information to manage operations. This information would include information about the administrative details of the company, financial data, and special information concerning technological and operational considerations. The information will be more understandable when your successor understands the objectives of your business.

Carefully review all of the matters which should be transacted before your departure from the business; and when you leave, be somewhat available for consultation on important questions. The safest transition would best be accomplished over a longer period of time to enable you to observe the assumption of responsibilities and management of your company. Depending upon the size of the business and the extent of the responsibilities, this process may take several years if handled on a gradual basis of increasing the responsibilities of your successor. By following this process you may be prepared upon your retirement to take a well-earned vacation, without any undue apprehension about the futurity of your business.

DISPOSING OF A PROFITABLE ENTERPRISE

There are two prime alternatives in disposing of a going concern: selling the business to many buyers—"go public" by selling stock or sell the business to a particular buyer. The first alternative includes the opportunity of possibly getting the highest price for the business; and if desired, you can maintain control by retaining over 50 percent of the stock. In deciding to proceed with the first alternative, it would be necessary to meet with the underwriters, who would be selling the stock, work out the particulars and to determine the best guidelines to follow. This endeavor would be dependent upon the conditions of the stock market, which could have a great impact upon your decision.

The sale of the business to a particular buyer is almost the reverse of the process of acquiring a going concern. A prospective buyer may be long on desire but short on cash. As the seller, you may find difficulty in finding a desirable buyer, since prospective businesspersons often consider that beginning from scratch may be cheaper than purchasing a going concern.

Assuming that you can find a desirable buyer, the next major question to be resolved is the price at which the business is to be sold. What is the value of your business? The answer may be approached from two determinations. In the first instance, the minimum value of a business would be the market value of assets less any liabilities against these assets. What then would be the value of the business in terms of the market value of the assets — the plant, the equipment, the inventory, the accounts receivable, any intangibles such as copyrights and patents, etc.? For you to sell at less than the market value of assets would be a case of foolishness, indeed.

Another means of ascertaining the value of the business is to capitalize the profits. Actually, the buyer is probably more interested in acquiring a "profit-making" enterprise than in simply purchasing assets. Suppose that the buyer would desire a 20 percent return on the investment in a business, which would indicate a rate for capitalization of 20 percent. At this rate of capitalization, a buyer should be willing to pay $250,000 for a business which would produce $50,000 profit. ($50,000 ÷ .20 equals $250.000)[1]

At this point the seller has two problems: (1) to determine the true profit potential of the business, and (2) to sell the rate of capitalization to the prospective buyer. While it may be helpful to show the historical record of past achievements, the more vital subject for the prospective buyer is the projected profits of the future. It would therefore be more advisable to concentrate on the profit prospects of the future rather than on the past track record.

---

[1]Richard H. Buskirk and Percy J. Vaughn, *Managing New Enterprises* (New York: West Pub. Co., 1976), p. 436.

Bear in mind the risk factor in the enterprise, remembering that the higher the risk the higher will be the rate of capitalization. In some instances a rate of 50 percent may be desired on a risky deal — in other words, two times the earnings. More secure types of businesses may only command a 20 percent capitalization rate, or five times the earnings. However, the more usual situation approximates three to four times the earnings rate of the enterprise, and some dispositions of businesses are for less.

Having ascertained a price that is agreeable, attention should next be shifted to the matter of negotiating the terms of sale. Before accepting terms it would be well to carefully analyze the possible consequences. Certainly, you want a sufficient down payment to protect you from losses if the buyer fails to maintain the enterprise. If you allow the buyer to take over and operate your business without a sufficient down payment, you are assuming a great risk. How are you willing to take payment — as a royalty on each unit of product sold? Or will you hold a mortgage on the property as security?

While you may be impressed by the potential capabilities of the new operator, you would best protect your interests and protect yourself from disappointment by maintaining control of the hard assets. You may wish to retain ownership of the primary assets of the business and to make them available to the new owner on the basis of a rental agreement. Should the new operator be unsuccessful, you would still retain ownership of the hard assets. In the meantime you would have the advantage of a rental income; and that would also be an advantage to the buyer in lowering the price of acquiring the business.

Before making your final decision you should consult your tax advisor and carefully consider the transaction in terms of its tax implications. It may be more advantageous for you to accept payment over a longer period of time. However, there is a lot to be said for having all the money in hand for the business when it is sold. Some people are inclined to make a poor business deal because it appears to be a better tax arrangement. For some it would be good advice to take the money, pay the taxes, and take a vacation.

When you have made the decision to sell your business, use judgment in expressing yourself on the subject. By appearing to be too eager to sell, you will weaken your bargaining position. Be wary of business brokers who try to get into the act. It will cost you as much as 10 percent to engage their services. Their services often leave much to be desired. In fact, it may simply tie your hands if you sign an exclusive contract. Selling a sick business is a lot more difficult than selling a healthy enterprise. Prospective buyers may be few and far between. In fact, an uninterested buyer is a person who is able to see beyond the present difficulties and appreciate potential possibilities. The buyer gets a bargain if the business failure can be turned into a success.

In disposing of a failing enterprise, it is important to know the proper time to "get out." If you wait too long, it may be too late. For one thing, do not publish your difficulties or trouble all over town, for such news will adversely affect the opportunities to sell the business.

All sorts of schemes and devious practices have been attempted in an effort to sell a failing business. However, the best advice is to *be honest.* Falsifying records of a losing concern is fraud, and the buyer has his legal rights against the seller.

In seeking to find a buyer, it may be productive to contact competitors or let it be known to them that you may be ready to dispose of your business. Competitors frequently see an opprtunity for growth and expansion in acquiring other competitors' businesses. In fact, what appear to be two competing businesses are sometimes owned by the same person.

Another possibility for resolving the problem of an unprofitable business may stem from the conversion of the business from its present form — modifying a store building into an office building or modifying a plant building into a warehouse building. The conversion process could be the means of changing the business from failure to success. If you still want to dispose of the business after the conversion, it may be more profitable to do so from the vantage point of success instead of failure. Carefully consider the question: What do you have to sell and who might be inclined to give the best price?

Let Someone Else Operate the Business—Rent

If you are unable to obtain a buyer it may be advantageous to find someone who would operate the business and take it off your hands. Certainly, the value of the business will be preserved when keeping it in an operating status. When it terminates, the values are greatly reduced. Another consideration in closing the business is the impact upon creditors. So long as creditors see the business operating, they have hopes of collecting their accounts. But when the doors close it usually starts a stampede for the courthouse, and your difficulties are multiplied.

In letting somebody else operate, you would retain the title to the assets. In a sense, you would rent the use of the assets to the operators, and arrange a payment for the business.

Exchange the Business for Stock

In order to make an exchange of your business for stock in another corporation, it is necessary to set the valuation of your business. One of the encouraging factors in this transaction is that the trade of stock for stock is a tax-free transaction. Another aspect which prompts sellers to move is the opportunity of obtaining the asking price for the business. The catcher is that the stock you're trading may be inflated to more than offset the value of your business. Furthermore, the buyer may stipulate that you are not allowed to sell the stock for a specified time period—so you really don't know what value you are getting for your business. In other cases you may try to sell the stock, but find that the market is weak and the buyers are few, again compounding the difficulty of receiving a suitable payment for your business. The best stock-for-stock trade is where you are dealing with a large corporation that may have reason to acquire your business, and where the stock received can easily be sold and the market price easily determined.

Because of the manifold legal aspects involved in disposing of a business, it becomes necessary and advisable to utilize your lawyer. However, impress upon your lawyer the importance of the sale and of handling it with care, so as not to overdo the legal aspects—to the extent that the deal may be scuttled amidst all the legal maneuvering between the lawyer of the seller and the lawyer of the buyer. One of the important legal aspects would be compliance with the bulk sales law in the disposition of a business in total (bulk). Accordingly, all creditors should be notified so that their claims may be satisfied. Should the claims not be satisfied, they may be held against the assets which are transferred to the new buyer.[2]

There are those who strongly advocate that the best arrangement in disposing of the business is to take the cash and pay the taxes. Should it be necessary to arrange financing, make sure you have a suitable amount of front money and that the title to the property is retained by you until payment has been made in full. This arrangement will give you protection in the event that it becomes necessary for a legal repossession of the business.

[2]*Ibid.*, p. 438.

Estate Planning

This important matter of planning the estate is frequently neglected. Somehow, it is always put off until tomorrow, and sometimes that is too late. Recently, a wife received a telephone call from the emergency room of a hospital advising her that her husband had been killed in an automobile accident. He owned and operated a heating and air-conditioning business with two other employees. The husband left no instructions whatsoever. The wife nearly suffered a nervous breakdown trying to pull together all the loose ends of carrying the business forward. She was not even sure of the amount of insurance and whether or not it would be sufficient to meet some of the obligations outstanding. How helpful it would have been to have had these matters detailed on a list of instructions for such an un-anticipated event.

In many cases, after years of hard work in building a large successful business, the estate is dissipated in taxes for failure to plan wisely for the death of the business owner and/or his wife. After the lawyers and executors complete their work, some otherwise satisfactory estates have dwindled down to relatively small proportions. If your business is a successful business, where will the money come from to pay the taxes upon your death? What will happen when your wife dies? So often the executors are forced to sell the successful company in order to meet the tax obligations.

From the day you begin your business you should consider the matter of estate planning. One of the advantages of incorporating is the ease it makes for the establishment of your estate. By issuing stock to your children (less than the controlling amount) you can preclude the necessity of your business paying heavy taxes at a later date. If you fail to do this planning, the consequences may negate your good intentions and carefully planned objectives.

Do you have adequate personal life insurance? If your insurance program is inadequate, another possibility would be to sell some of the corporate stock, or possibly go public, to raise funds to meet IRS obligations upon your demise. However, this process is complicated and may not prove very satisfactory, except for the larger small businesses.

Another way to establish an estate is called the family annuity. It is simply establishing a large portion of your business for your children by means of transferring it to them. This amounts to selling the business to your children under contract whereby they pay a certain sum as long as you live. Upon your death the payments stop, and they own the stock which each one has been purchasing. This type of private family annuity has been used for years by prominent families in England. It is suggested that part of the annuity income be treated as a return on capital, with no tax or with capital gain at the low rate. Should your death come before recovering your cost basis, you would escape the capital gains tax entirely.

This family-annuity plan would provide a larger (installment type) annuity payment than if you sold your business, paid a capital gains tax, and then converted the net proceeds to a commercial annuity. The effect is to remove a portion of the annuity payments from your taxable income. For details check Section 72, Revenue Ruling 239, 1953–2CB–53 (as modified by the 1954 code). This plan completely eliminates gift taxes, providing that the business is sold at a fair price in the contract.[3]

There are several matters to be given special consideration with regard to planning a family annuity program for your business. It is recommended that your attorney proceed carefully in the development of the necessary papers and documents to effect this program for you. Under this plan there will be no taxes on the appreciation of the value of your business as it grows and becomes more valuable in the future. Therefore, if your business is successful and growing, perhaps you should dispose of it as soon as possible to your desired heirs; otherwise you may not be able to afford to die.

Remember that lawyers like to handle large estates, and usually on a percentage basis. Because it is difficult for them to handle the private annuity, they frequently come up with reasons why this may not be for you. However, if you want to make your lawyer earn his keep, read Norman Dacey's book *How to Avoid Probate*.[4] This book sold over a million copies, and provides small-business people with excellent information.

Now might be a good time for giving stock in your company to your children, while you are comtemplating the details of this rather complicated subject. It is possible for you to give, tax free, $6,000 per year to each child if you are married ($3,000 if you are not). Remember, it usually does not help your tax situation to give your wife anything. She probably should have been on the payroll already.[5]

---

[3]Gardiner Greene, *How to Start and Manage Your Own Business* (New York: Mentor Books, 1975), p. 239.

[4]Norman F. Dacey, *How to Avoid Probate* (New York: Crown Publishers, Inc., 1965).

[5]For further details on estate planning refer to special sources as follows:

Robert Brosterman, *The Complete Estate Planning Guide* (New York: McGraw-Hill Book Co., 1964).

"Estate Planner's Corner," *Digest of Tax Articles* (November 1962).

SUMMARY

A business is fragile in the sense that the question of continuity is ever present and cannot be assumed. Even large corporations have had their obituaries announced suddenly by the press.

The terminations of small businesses are published regularly. Frequently, the demise of the business is correlated with the demise of its owner. In such a situation, how would you want things to go? The purpose of raising this question previously in this chapter was to show the need for you to make plans for the continuity or termination of your business. You cannot know exactly when you may step out of the picture.

A brighter possibility is your retirement. It is easier to dispose of a going concern — a profitable enterprise. Selling the business is almost the reverse process of acquiring a going concern, as discussed in Chapter 1. If you are unable to find a buyer, you may wish to continue operations to avoid the disadvantages of closing. Perhaps you can find someone to operate the business and keep things alive. Under this arrangement you would retain title to the assets and the operator would pay "rent" for the use of the assets.

One of the means of disposing of a business is to accept stock in another corporation. However, there are some pitfalls to watch for when taking stock, as have been explained in this chapter.

You should avoid neglecting the matter of planning your estate. Without careful planning, years of strenuous toil in developing a large and successful business could be absorbed by taxes upon your death. The matter of estate planning should be considered with the beginning of your business.

One of the final suggestions in this chapter deals with the use of a family annuity as part of planning the continuity of the business upon your termination. This approach has many advantages worth considering.

Excerpt from *Commerce Clearing House* — Paragraph 852-043 re: Private Annuity Transaction, *CCH Federal Estate and Gift Tax Reports.*

Robert L. Farmer, "Private Annuities," *Trusts and Estates* (New York: Fiduciary Publishers, Inc., January 1962).

Peter F. Mancina, "The Private Annuity," *Taxes* (April 1965).

Leigh B. Middleditch, Jr., "Mechanics of the Private Annuity as an Estate Planning Device," *Tulane Tax Institute,* 15th annual ed. (1965).

Burton G. Ross, "The Private Annuity as a Tax-Minimizing Instrument," *Commerce Clearing House* (April 1963).

Stanley C. Simon, "Tax Notes: Iconoclastic Thoughts on the Capitalization of Family Corporations," *American Bar Association Journal* (May 1962).

Joseph Tovay, "How to Use Private Annuities in Estate Planning," *New York Certified Public Accountant* (June 1962).

APPENDICES

Case
Studies

The case studies included were taken from actual small businesses. A variety of situations and typical problems were included to familiarize the reader with the business' situations. It was intended that cases would be selected as discussion material to supplement the study of the various subjects presented in the text.

A practical format which has been used successfully calls for an outline of the problem symptoms (facts), a succinct statement of the problem prepared as a question to be solved, a list of alternative solutions with analysis of pros and cons, and a decision statement indicating a choice of the best alternative solution with supporting reasons.

Assignments may be made individually or as a team effort, and presentations made orally, in written form, or both, if the cases will be used in classroom work.

As an adjunct and supplemental to reading the text, a set of "learning experiences" were prepared to give the reader some practical involvement. Further study of subjects covered will be facilitated through the bibliographic materials presented.

A AND B SPORTING GOODS

A and B was a sporting goods store located in North Tulsa, in a shopping center along with twelve other stores, all ranging about the same size.

It was originally established as a partnership between two well-known black businessmen in the North Tulsa community — Albert Able, an assistant manager for Stresscone Manufacturing Company, and Bob Baker, personnel director for Manpower Training Center. Both partners continued their regular jobs.

For years, the north side needed a conveniently located sporting goods store. A and B wanted to begin such a small business inside their community. They felt their small business would be more successful by dealing with people they both knew most of their lives.

Both A and B were college graduates. Able majored in Business Administration and minored in Physical Education. He was also working toward a Master's degree in Management. Baker obtained a degree in Physical Education with a minor in Management. Able gained experience in managing a small dairy hut for about five years. He was successful, until other food service competitors moved into the area, which slowed business considerably. Able was planning to move to another location, but he became ill and did not. Able also had experience as a part-time salesman for the Mantique Men's Clothing Store for two and a half years.

Baker had gained some experience by working at his grandfather's small theater. He often ran the theater and later handled the bookkeeping records with his grandfather. He never managed his own business, but he had been an assistant manager of a small maintenance company.

In December of 1970, a small shopping center located in the middle of North Tulsa was preparing to open by leasing space. When Able heard about it, he thought of opening a small clothing store, but he could not do so by himself. He thought there would be too many problems in a partnership. However, when his long-time friend came up with an offer, he could not resist. A company that had financed his grandfather's theater made them what they felt was a good offer. This took about two months to finalize. After they had decided on the building, they realized that the shopping center did not need a clothing store. Leased tenants included a men's and women's clothing store, two shoe stores, and a variety of discount clothing stores. Both partners felt that they should rule out the clothing store.

Able, who was an all-around athlete in high school and college, decided that the northside needed a sporting goods store. The nearest store was on 15th Street, five miles south — toward downtown. Able figured that with the large amount of schools in the black community and the surrounding Boys' Clubs in the area, a sporting goods store could be a very profitable undertaking.

Able pursued the idea by talking with some of the public school coaches and different coaches at Boys' Clubs, to determine how much sports-wear was purchased each season. He also made a few verbal agreements on uniforms and footwear with high school coaches.

Able went as far as asking their opinion on opening a sporting goods store for the area—whether it would be a good idea. Almost everyone agreed it would be a good idea and encouraged Able by offering to help in anyway they could.

Further checking into different high schools and colleges was continued, to find out what style and quality most athletes wear and to help guide in buying the right stock.

The sporting goods store was open in early July. After six months, both partners were well satisfied. Sales were great. The grand opening was advertised on the black radio stations and at different car washes in the area. Pamphlets were placed on telephone poles and an ad was placed in the *Oklahoma Eagle,* a black newspaper.

After being in the business together for about one year, Baker had family problems and decided that working two jobs was not for him. He offered to sell out to Able and pay off $1900, his half of a business loan.

After arranging an agreeable settlement, Able and Baker Sporting Goods was terminated. The new name is Able Pro Sporting Goods, now owned and managed by Albert Able, forty-seven years of age, married, with two sons and a daughter. Able planned to use his family to help as employees. His wife was a private nurse, and worked part time in the evenings. She was also a trained book-keeper. Both sons worked full time and when his daughter graduated, she would be full-time help.

After four more years in business, Able paid off his $2400 loan and saved enough additional funds to open another sporting goods store in another section of North Tulsa.

With the addition of the new store, Able felt the two locations would be more convenient to his customers and more profitable to him. But the second store was not selling as planned. The first store's sales remained essentially the same.

Able made each son an assistant manager at each store, so they could operate the stores most of the time.

Able remains perplexed about the results to date at the second store.

ROYAL CEMETERY

Royal Cemetery Trust was established more than thirty years ago by the father of one of the present trustees. The cemetery trust commenced operation with 180 acres of land which was held in the name of the trust.

The original plan was to sell trust certificates (with each certificate holder owning a percentage of the profits from the sale of cemetery lots) in proportion to the number of shares owned.

General trust certificates were sold or traded. But over the years the two present trustees acquired all of the existing trust certificates.

Of the original 180 acres, only 100 acres have actually been dedicated for cemetery purposes. The remaining acres adjoined a highway and was relatively valuable land for commercial purposes.

During the past ten years, the trustees have (1) attempted to operate the cemetery themselves, (2) retained professional cemetery operators, (3) allowed others to operate the cemetery under an operating contract, and (4) tried to sell their interest in the cemetery.

The trustees were both professional people who operated their own successful businesses. They do not have the time to physically operate the cemetery themselves.

Professional cemetery operators charge 60 percent commission on the sale of lots. Their commissions together with operating expenses made the operation unsuccessful.

At one point the trustees entered into an operating contract with an individual. This individual, after incurring several debts in the name of the cemetery trust, left the country.

The trustees then tried to sell their interest in the cemetery. They found that, as trustees, they were prohibited by law from selling the property belonging to the trust to themselves.

The cemetery was then operated by direct employees of the trust, under the supervision of the trustees.

As sole owners of all the existing trust certificates, the trustees were actually trustees for themselves. They have been advised that they could terminate the existing trust by a simple action in court.

They were also advised that the original trust had expired by its own terms more than ten years ago, and was renewed at that time. They were not sure that they were safe in taking profits from the trust of which they were the trustees, since the law prohibits "self dealing." Trust law also required that the trustees submit annual statements of profit and loss to the beneficiaries of the trust. They were required to withhold 10 percent of gross sales for a "perpetual care" fund, and they were audited by the State Banking Commission.

The trustees wanted to get their cemetery business on a profitable basis within the law. They were advised that if they formed a corporation for profit they would lose their *ad valorem* tax-exempt status as a cemetery trust. They were also advised that if they abolished the trust and operated the cemetery as partners, they would not only lose their tax-exempt status, but would lose the protection of individual immunity from the debts and liabilities of the cemetery, immunity which they enjoyed as trustees and as directors of a cemetery corporation.

The trustees were also interested in selling the remaining 80 acres for business and commercial development. A portion of the sale price of the land would be put back into the cemetery by way of permanent improvements such as fences, roads, landscaping, and possibly a chapel.

The trustees were advised that it they elected to abolish the trust, they would become the fee owners of the 80 acres of land that was not dedicated for cemetery purposes. They could sell the land, develop it themselves, or dedicate it for cemetery purposes.

The problem of tax consequences was another area of concern. The cemetery property was acquired in 1930 at a cost of $27.50 per acre. The 80 acres which the trustees wanted to sell was now appraised at $3500 per acre for commercial development. Although they would be able to take advantage of long-term capital gains, the profit from the sale would cost each of the trustees a minimum of $35,000 in income taxes.

A considerable tax saving could be had by separating the cemetery operation from the 80 acres of undeveloped land, then giving individual gifts to the cemetery as a tax deduction.

The problem was further complicated by the fact that a cemetery corporation may not own or hold real estate other than that which is dedicated for cemetery purposes. To gain tax exemption as a cemetery corporation, *all* of the net income from the sale of cemetery lots *must* be put back into the cemetery as a permanent improvement.

The alternatives available to the trustees were: (1) continue to operate as a trust; (2) form a cemetery corporation and transfer the assets of the trust to the cemetery corporation; or (3) abolish the trust and operate as a joint venture or partnership.

Under this set of facts we were asked to advise the trustees (who were also sole trust certificate holders) how they could best proceed within the law, bearing in mind the tax consequences, the desired sale of the 80 acres of undedicated land, and the continued operation of the remaining 100 acres as a cemetery.

RALPH'S DECORATING CENTER

Ralph's Decorating Center was opened in 1972. In August 1975 the business moved to the present location in order to expand floor space. The store was located on Main Street in Amarillo, Texas, across the street from TG & Y and the Sizzling Sirloin Restaurant. The business was situated on the corner and next to a stop light. Parking was sometimes a problem. There was a lack of adequate parking space; but in the present location there was nothing to be done about it.

The store was owned by Ralph Smith as a sole proprietorship. Ralph was involved in retail selling of paint, wallpaper, draperies and other small, miscellaneous items. He also sold some paint wholesale to professional painters. Ralph had had twelve years experience in this type of work, eight of the years with Sherwin-Williams Paint Company. For two years he worked as a credit manager, and then worked five years as a branch manager.

In previous years, Ralph had made most of his sales in the spring, summer and fall, and this money helped him out through the long winter months. This year, although total sales were up, the cash wasn't. In fact, Ralph had had to borrow some money to meet all of his expenses.

Several problems were recognized pertaining to his lack of cash. Individually, these problems might not have appeared to reduce the cash flow, but taken together they reduced it significantly.

Ralph kept no record of cash taken from the cash drawer. He withdrew money for lunch and kept no record of it. Also, if a small delivery of merchandise was made, he paid the freight charges out of his cash drawer. If he averaged taking just $5 a day it would equal $1500 a year. To a small business with an estimated net profit in 1976 of around $12,300, this was a fairly large chunk of money.

Ralph also had no set procedure for determining his accounts payable. He did not keep an up-to-date record of merchandise received, and thus he did not know exactly what he owed. He paid all bills received at the first of the month, regardless of the terms: thus he lost some of the cash discounts he could have received.

Advertising was a major problem area. Ralph did not have an advertising budget, and spent money on advertising when he felt it was necessary. Because of this, Ralph's advertising expense was much higher than it should have been. According to a trade journal of similar businesses, advertising expense should be less than 1% of total sales. Ralph's advertising expense for 1976 was 4.07% of total sales. In dollar terms, Ralph's advertising expense for 1976 should have been about $1400, but he actually spent around $3200.

Ralph kept no perpetual inventories. However, he should have kept a record on the paint in the stockroom. If he had, he would have known what paint was selling well and should have been reordered. By not buying slow sellers he could have kept his money from being tied up in slow-moving stock and also could have kept a better selling paint on hand to maximize sales.

Ralph purchased a new home in 1976, which needed some repairs. Since then his personal withdrawals have gone up greatly. This was his largest problem area. Ralph's estimated net income for 1976 was $12,326, but his estimated withdrawals from the business totaled $15,204, or a deficit of $2,878. This decreased his working capital and his investment in the business, and also reduced his cash flow.

Ralph had a good business, and he was a hard worker who was willing to put in the time necessary to make his business a success. The sales for Ralph's Decorating Center had gone up every year since it began. From 1975 to 1976 sales increased from $75,000 to $95,000, and Ralph planned to go over the $100,000 mark in 1977. Ralph had stated his future objectives. He wanted to own his own store building some day, to provide everything for the home, except furniture and appliances.

A-1 MANUFACTURING COMPANY

A-1 Manufacturing was a small manufacturing firm located in the rural town of Big Chief, Oklahoma. The business was owned and operated on a partnership basis by Bill Emery and Walt Barber.

The town has a population of 200, employed mostly at larger cities. The rural area consists of small farmers and ranchers. The only other businesses in the town were a lumber yard, a service station, a beauty shop, and a small grocery store.

Bill and Walt started the business in August 1976, and located it in a twenty-by-forty building rented from the lumber yard. A panel clip-truss machine, hydraulic press, and jig table were purchased and set up in the building. An old Chevrolet truck and a pole trailer were purchased to transport the lumber and finished product to the customer.

At first they worked from 5:00 P.M. to 9:00 P.M., after working at their regular fulltime jobs. Now, the hours of operation are from 8:00 A.M. to 4:30 P.M., Monday through Friday, on a demand situation. Bill's primary job was the business records and sales. Walt, a carpenter, handled the construction and delivery. Temporary employees were hired to help in the construction as needed. The temporary employees were carpenters who were used by Walt in his self-employed home construction and remodeling work.

The business offered a range of engineered, designed wooden trusses, primarily for the building of residential homes. Free delivery was offered within a fifty-mile radius, and a 40¢ per mile one-way charge was made for trips over fifty miles. A thirty-day credit was offered to selected customers — mostly the lumber yards and larger contractors, since it was found they could not afford to run credit checks on a large percentage of individuals. Also, a 3% cash discount was offered if paid in 10 days. Later, this was changed to 2%, since their profit margin was not large enough.

Financial Position

The only financial records kept were accounts payable and accounts receivable, using a voucher-type system. The initial investment was $1400 ($700 each). The Panel Clip Truss Machine and Clips were purchased for $1200 and $200 was retained for operating capital. A radial-arm saw was rented along with the building for $50 per month. Gross income for the first 5 months was $4500, while operating expenses, including inventory items, was $4500. In January 1977 the gross income, $4500, was equal to the previous five months. The price of the trusses were kept within a competitive range with a 20% markup.

Market Conditions

The nearest competitive business was located at Tulsa, sixty-five miles from Big Chief. The market area for A-1 Manufacturing Company included the northeast corner of Oklahoma, southeastern Kansas, southwestern Missouri, and northwestern Arkansas. Most residents of northeast Oklahoma were of low to middle income. Most were farmers and ranchers (do-it-yourself carpenters). Also, most towns within the fifty-mile radius were small.

With sales up in January, Bill and Walt felt the business had progressed enough to purchase a much-needed truck and trailer for deliveries. Not having any collateral for a one-year note, they obtained a bank loan for $9400 with a three-year monthly payment plan which, when paid back, would be $12,000.

Since no advertising had been done except by word of mouth, they decided to run an ad in the local newspaper. A temporary salesman was hired. The salesman was one of the temporary carpenters who had no sales experience either in school or on the job. He possessed a desire to do it, had a good personality, and met people well. His purpose was primarily to seek response from potential customers. The cost of the salesman would be $3.25 an hour plus 10¢ a mile for travel expense.

The business was now run on a demand situation, but Bill and Walt felt that if their projected goal of $100,000 sales was met, they could run it on a full-time basis.

INSULATION, INC.

Tulsa, Oklahoma was a fast-growing city with a population of approximately 350,000, located in the heart of the Southwest. Tulsa was strong in retailing and manufacturing with many industrial plants. However, the evolution of petroleum and its byproducts had concentrated many businesses, both large and small, in Tulsa.

In 1970 a small corporation was formed using the name Insulation, Inc. It was based on an application of thermal insulation for oil and gas pipelines. Bill Smart developed the idea. He had worked for several oil companies and was experienced in the marketing of petroleum byproducts. He developed the idea of a continuous-flow system of insulation after visiting a wrapping plant and observing how food products were wrapped. He wondered if such a system would be valid in the insulation business. At the time of this idea, Bill was working for Jim Sutter, who eagerly expressed an interest in the new concept. Bill had a limited amount of capital, but with Jim's help commercial merit could possibly be developed.

Several friends of Jim and Bill became interested in Bill's idea and through further investigation and development, the system proved worthy of marketing. Consequently, a small corporation was organized for marketing the system by means of monetary assistance gained through the sale of stock to friends. At the beginning of 1971 Insulation, Inc. started business. A patent on the system was secured, and a heavy sales program was initiated to make the insulation industry aware of the new application. Things were very slow the first two years of business. Many of the contracts that were available were beyond the financial range of the company; others were hard to obtain because of the reluctance of the contractors to use the new application. After a few small jobs, the company began to receive the recognition it deserved. A more stable financial position was obtained through small contracts, and larger jobs started to look more appealing. Further improvements of machinery and development of the system made the marketing of the application more attractive.

By 1976 the stock of Insulation, Inc. had appreciated approximately 300 percent. The par value of the stock in 1971 was $1.00 per share with 50,000 shares outstanding. The stock was spread between eighteen individuals, with no one person owning more than 20 percent of the total outstanding shares. Since 1971 90 percent of the par value of the stock has been paid back in dividends along with the 300 percent stock appreciation. The current ratio of assets to liabilities is 13 to 1.

The corporation with its eighteen stockholders has a Board of Directors of nine people. Jim Sutter was voted president of the corporation because of his great managerial talent and his capital contribution to the corporation. He owns 20 percent of the outstanding stock. Bill Smart was chosen vice president because of his knowledge of the application of the system and his marketing experience. He was granted 20 percent of the corporation's stock for the idea of the system.

As the contracts became larger, the company was finding it more difficult to provide adequate machinery and knowledge to complete these jobs. They finally came to the conclusion that being a licensee would be a lot less difficult and also more profitable. This would let the company handle multiple jobs at one time, simply providing the machinery and an engineer to help the licensed company perform the insulating of their pipeline. The rental of the machinery, engineer, and royalties for the insulation of pipe would be absorbed by the company wishing to insulate.

Good profits started to be enjoyed through licensing, but still there were bigger and bigger contracts of pipe to be insulated — which Insulation, Inc. was unable to handle adequately. The company had become fairly well known and many of the big producers of pipelines, such as Exxon, became interested in the system. Soon, knowledge of the new system was recognized to the point that Canada, Mexico, and even Brazil had taken an interest in the new insulation system. Previously, the company had financed many of their past jobs through bank financing. These obligations were paid, resulting in a favorable credit rating. The stockholders have been pleased with the returns on their investments and are very reluctant to sell more stock, for fear of spreading the wealth of the company and thereby decreasing their returns. Several jobs are now available, which would take considerable financing. The management is pondering how to finance these big contracts.

AVIATION SERVICE, INC.

Aviation Service, Inc. (A.S.I.) was a small company, with two aircraft based in Muskogee, Oklahoma, and one aircraft based in Dallas, Texas. The company contracted electrical-line patrol flights with electrical companies from Louisiana to Nebraska and Colorado.

The aircraft based in Dallas was flown by a hired commercial pilot. He covered Texas, Louisiana, and Tennessee. The two owner-operators covered the states from Oklahoma north to Nebraska.

The aircraft being used were Piper Super Cubs, and they were equipped with 150 h.p. Lycoming engines that were designed to burn 80 octane fuel.

The energy crisis caused a shortage of 80 octane fuel, and A.S.I., was forced to use 100 octane fuel instead.

The 100 octane fuel had a much higher lead content, and this caused the engines to operate at a much higher temperature than normal, causing fouled spark plugs (cost $12 each), burnt valves, and burnt rings. This situation greatly reduced the engine life. Before the energy crisis the engines were burning 80 octane fuel and could be expected to last 2000 hours between overhauls. But since they are burning 100 octane fuel the T.B.O. (time between overhauls) is down to 1,500 hours.

The cost of overhauling one of the 150 h.p. engines was approximately $2,200, and this was occurring much more frequently since they have had to use the 100 octane fuel.

The shortage of the 80 octane fuel had presented a very serious problem for A.S.I. The 150 h.p. engines in their aircraft were about worn out. A decision had to be made whether to purchase new 150 h.p. engines, new aircraft, or a different engine. If they bought new 150 h.p. engines, they would still have the same problem.

A.S.I. could buy new aircraft at $33,000 each. But this would not solve anything, since all new Super Cubs come equipped with 150 h.p. Lycoming engines. A.S.I. could buy new engines that were built to operate on 100 octane fuel, and have them installed with some modifications.

The 180 h.p. Lycoming engine could be installed with some changes in the cowling, and with new and different engine mounts. The new engine mounts were called dynafocal mounts and were mounted in rubber which greatly reduced vibration—a major cause of stress on the airframe and pilot. These mounts cost $30 each, and each engine required four.

The added horsepower was a needed feature because of the aircraft operating in higher elevations in Colorado. The aircraft fly approximately twenty feet above the electrical power lines, and must follow it when it goes up or down a hill in a roller coaster fashion so the pilot can spot broken insulators, loose wires, damaged poles, etc. The added horsepower would add a better margin of safety when these aircraft were required to climb steeply in mountainous country.

The 180 h.p. engine would also be laboring less than the 150 h.p. engine, and would actually burn two gallons *less* fuel per hour, which was a savings of about $1.50 per hour. In favorable weather these aircraft were sometimes airborne twelve hours a day, consuming approximately eight gallons of fuel each hour.

Records of other aircraft owners that were using the 180 h.p. Lycoming engine show that they were getting from 2,500 to 2,700 hours between overhauls. This was almost double what the 150 h.p. engine was getting. This would produce a savings of about $2,000 between overhauls.

The new 180 h.p. engines cost a little over $6,200 each, but this would be offset by the $2,000 savings of extended time between overhauls; and the savings on gasoline at $1.50 per hour would amount to $4,500 each.

A company in Muskogee, Oklahoma, said they would do the installation and accept the old 150 h.p. engines as payment for the job.

PETE'S PIZZA

Pete's Pizza has been in operation two years. It is located in a town which is the county seat and has a population of about 15,000. At the time of the opening, there was one other pizza business, Joe's Pizza, which has been there for about four years. It has since been converted into a Steak House. Pete's has some new competition, however: a new Pizza Hut has recently opened just down the street. Yet Pete's has had no decrease in business since the opening of the Pizza Hut.

Pete's was the place to go in town. People from all the neighboring towns go to Pete's, especially after the school games and after church. The need for a special place has been met. Everything from baby showers to family reunions have been held there.

Joe's Pizza was once the only pizza place in the county. Because of more successful advertising, much of Joe's business went to Pete's. From the beginning until recently, Pete advertised a great deal. A photographer roamed about taking pictures of people eating. These appeared in several local papers. Recently, however, the pictures have been less frequent, and it has been several weeks since the pictures have been in the local paper. The first thing people did when receiving the weekly paper was to look to see who had been photographed eating at Pete's. This was a very big hit with everyone.

A lot of advertising was done by the local radio stations. They played records; and whoever was telephoned and guessed the correct person singing the song or name of the record, or whatever, won a free pizza. This was done several times a day.

Both types of advertising appealed to the younger crowd, teenagers and younger children who talked their families into taking them. Pete had not limited his efforts to just this particular market. He was interested in all types of people coming to Pete's, and preferred to see more older people, the twenty-five to thirty-five age group, and more families.

On weekends the place was always full. The younger crowd came from all the neighboring towns. A slight problem occurred with people coming in for sodas, etc., and taking up space. When they ordered food, they would continue to take up space by coming in and out and staying longer than was necessary or proper.

Since Pete was involved in a second pizza place, Bud and Ron had complete control of the first pizza place. The policies have been set, and both Bud and Ron agree that there really isn't anything to do—the business just sort of runs itself.

All of the personnel hiring was done by Bud and Ron. They interviewed all the applicants. Their main concern was trying to find people with good personalities, who were willing to work hard. They tried to hire those who would get along with the customers well. Most of the applicants they had were young highschool girls and boys. They used a form that asked for address, other general information, and past work experience. Those applicants with some type of past experience in food service were preferred.

Pete had a long list of regulations and job requirements tacked on the wall in the kitchen. It took about three months for the personnel to learn all that was required. This was the average length of time that employees remained on the job.

The main reason employees gave for quitting was that they got tired of working nights. Young people would rather be out dating. Employers also get tired of working the late hours at night. Pete was open until twelve on Sunday through Thursday, and was open until two on Friday and Saturday. The weekends were very busy and the work was hard. All of the cleaning of the building and equipment was done by the cooks and waitresses.

The following list was a breakdown of the personnel at Pete's. All personnel, other than the two managers, received a minimum wage of $2.30 an hour. The managers were paid above $5.00 an hour.

Names	Position	Hours per week	Age	Student	Length of Empl.
Gerald	cook	30 evening	18	yes	5 months
John	cook	30 evening	18	yes	5 months
Bud	cook	30 evening	18	yes	1 month
Joe	cook	30 evening	17	yes	1 month
Leo	cook	45 days 1-11 & evenings	18	no	4 months
Linda	waitress	40 days	17	no	18 months
Dee D	waitress	27 days	19	no	6 months
Donia	waitress	40 evenings	18	yes	24 months
Sally	waitress	25 evenings	18	yes	6 months
Kathy	waitress	25 evenings	21	no	2 months
Kathy	waitress	25 evenings	17	yes	1 month
Vickie	waitress	20 evenings	17	yes	1 month
Vickie	waitress	20 evenings	19	no	8 months
Jo Ann	waitress	8 Sat. only	17	yes	4 months

SANITARY PLUMBING

In 1950 Carl Parker attended the Universal Plumbing School in Kansas City, Missouri, and completed the required courses in one year. After finishing school, he went into the plumbing field working as an apprentice plumber for various plumbing companies. In 1953 Carl passed the journeyman's test and became a licensed plumber for Pendergrass Plumbing Company. He was employed by this company for thirteen years, and worked his way up to supervisor of plumbing installation in commercial construction.

In July of 1965 the company was involved in a strike, and he did not work for a month. He had been considering going into business for himself, and he decided that if he did not try it at this time, he probably would not try at all.

He contacted a residential home builder and asked for a chance to plumb a house. The builder agreed to give him a chance, and he plumbed the entire house by himself. For the next job, he hired a backhoe operator and a helper, and they became his first employees. From then on the number of employees he hired was determined by his work load. Carl operates the business out of his home, and his wife handles all of the paper work, such as records, labor book, payment of bills, payroll checks and files, and she has done so since the business was started. Recently, Carl built a garage in back of his house to store plumbing supplies such as fixtures, fittings, copper tubing, plastic and galvanized pipe, and various other items for use in his business. This has enabled him to purchase supplies in larger quantities, thereby saving him quite a bit of money. Carl only works on residential construction. Very little service work or remodeling is done.

Carl's son had worked for him every summer since he was fourteen years old, and recently received his journeyman's license. He attended Okmulgee Tech for his training for two years in the school's plumbing program, and had worked for his father full time since he finished school. He was one of the youngest licensed plumbers in Oklahoma. Stan was a good asset to his father and the family business.

As in any business, there were problem employees. Some employees did not take their responsibilities seriously. Problems included getting to work late, not coming to work regularly, failing to take pride in their work, having a poor attitude toward working, and trouble working with fellow employees.

Recently, John called to say his wife was not feeling well and that he wanted to stay home with her. George called one day and said he was having family problems and wanted two days off. Carl agreed to this. However, without any further notice George did not come back to work for a week.

Carl had given his son the authority to oversee the men's work. But when Stan told a worker that he felt that a certain job could have been done with less material, the worker got mad and walked off the job. The employees find many excuses to leave work, such as cold weather, hot weather, etc. The employees want to leave at exactly the indicated quitting time, even though a few more minutes would be enough to complete a job and would therefore eliminate the necessity of having to make a special trip back to that particular job the next day. These incidents have all happened at a time when the work load was heavy and the employees were aware of it.

Carl would like a potential employee to have a desire to work, a willingness to learn, a desire to improve himself, an interest in the job, initiative, pride in his work, and be dependable. After he interviews prospective employees, he will hire them on a trial basis. From this point, Carl will take the time to train them. He feels that if he trains the worker for his own type of operation, he will have an employee better than one who was trained by someone else — plus he can stress quality work and a good attitude to his employee.

Carl's method of obtaining prospective employees were to leave word at the plumbing supply house, as most small plumbing companies do, and to go by word-of-mouth from other plumbing contractors.

ACE MANUFACTURING COMPANY

This company was established as a sole proprietorship in January of 1974. Ten months later the owners decided to incorporate, and were authorized to issue 3000 shares of stock. Up to this date 500 shares had been issued, owned in a ratio of 51%

and 49% for Mr. A and Mr. B, respectively. Both stockholders provided an initial investment of $5,000. Mr. A supplied the land and building free of charge for the company's use. He also owned another company doing similar type of work. These companies helped each other out regarding contracts (if one is not able to do it all) and they also shared equipment and machinery. Employees, when not busy with one company, helped the other business when needed. Records and books were kept separately for each company by part-time office help. A certified public accounting firm prepares financial statements and tax returns.

The company's main work consisted of manufacturing steel pipes to job specifications, with a lesser amount of time being devoted to producing regular sized pipes. Most of its customers were in the Tulsa area, consisting of utilities, construction and oil companies.

Both owners had many years of experience in their trade. Mr. A had success-fully operated a similar business for many years. Mr. B. before going into business for himself, worked for seven years as a craft mechanic and welder for a local company. Earlier, he operated a distributorship working as a route salesman selling soft drinks. After completing high school, Mr. A attended a business school and had various types of industrial training. Mr. A, the majority stockholder, leaves the complete operation and management to Mr. B, and concerns himself with his other business.

The company was located in an area of other small businesses, on a narrow residential street in the center of Tulsa, close to major expressways. The biggest disadvantage was the poor access for large delivery trucks.

Mr. B spent a great deal of his time in the shop, working and training his full-time employees to be shop foremen. At this time he hired other workers as needed for a particular job order. Mr. B realized that more and more time was required to manage the company, if his plans and goals for growth were to become a reality.

His part-time office helper took care of whatever she could, including cor-respondence with customers, bank deposits, reconciliation of books with bank records, depositing of receipts, payroll, and paying bills. All of these records had been turned over to a local CPA firm, which in turn supplied a quarterly profit and loss statement. In between these periods, Mr. B was not well informed as to what really took place financially. Keeping of records of sales trends and expenses, as well as comparing these with past performances, was not done.

For bidding on contracts Mr. B used a guide quoting the industry averages required for a particular job. Somehow it never occurred to him that conditions in his particular business may be completely different. He felt that formulas for establishing break-even point and factory overhead costs were time consuming. When establishing bids, he only figured materials, labor, and some down-time, but neglected to include factory overhead costs and a reasonable percentage for waste of materials. Some of his job bids fell considerably short of what they should have been, and they recovered only his costs, with no allowance for profit. See sample bid, Table A-1.

TABLE A-1
Sample Bid

ESTIMATED COSTS:		
Materials needed to complete	$1044.	
Labor, 115 hours at $22 p.hr.	2530.	
Total costs	$3574.	
BID PRICE		$4074.
ACTUAL COSTS:		
Materials		
Allowance for waste of materials		
Labor		
Allowance for labor cost		
Overhead costs		
Totaled		$4029.
NET PROFIT		$ 45.

Several of his accounts receivables were considerably aged, leaving him seriously short of working capital. This in turn led to the inability to pay all bills as they came due. Bills were paid when there was enough money left over, and the rest were carried over to the next month. Mr. B felt that there was not much he could do regarding these overdue accounts, as these were good customers accustomed to paying only two or three times a year. Various small, everyday expenses like paying the mailman were paid by Mr. B, out of his pocket, without any receipts.

The company had no advertising plan, and got its customers by "word-of-mouth." Mr. B wants to increase his sales, but felt that advertising was too expensive. He worries that he might receive orders too large for his company to handle. Union work required on larger contracts keeps him from bidding on these more profitable contracts. He seriously considered borrowing money to expand his operation and possibly establishing a union shop to handle contracts requiring union labor.

BEST WELDING SERVICE

Best Welding Service was started in January 1973. The business was first a partnership. The partnership consisted of two partners, Earl Hand and Don Petty. The partnership was equal, with each investing $6000. The money was invested in a welding truck and all the welding equipment needed for the business to be mobilized. Earl Hand had five years previous experience welding for other welding shops, but decided if he was ever going to make any money it would be better to go into business for himself. Hand had learned from previous welding jobs that some of the customers needed welding done on their property: it couldn't be done in the shop. Petty had also been doing welding for other shops. Since both men had been working for others, neither partner was experienced in the handling of the business's money.

Neither partner was prepared in the handling of credit customers. When the business was first getting started, both partners were so eager to have their own business that they began doing a lot of welding for people who would say, "We'll pay later." This was very hard on the business's capital account. The business was new, and they also had to build their credit with their suppliers. Sometimes the business would need supplies to finish a job, and they had to finish the job before they would get their money.

Subsequently, the owners decided to use local advertising and it really paid off. Opportunities increased to bid for contract jobs and to work for subcontractors. The work was good, but they found that it was a lot more working hours than they had expected. While the weather was good, they had to get in as much work as possible. When the weather was bad for two or three days the work would have to be completed at a later date and after hours in order for the job to be finished on time.

To do contract work for the highway department they were required to take a certification test. Both owners took the test and passed, which resulted in more jobs. These jobs required dealing with inspectors and bosses.

Petty got a better job offer in February 1976, and the partnership was dissolved. The business was established as a proprietorship owned by Earl Hand. Petty sold his share of the business to Hand.

The business had grown considerably and the credit had decreased some, but there was at least $500 a year still out for uncollectible checks written to Best Welding Service.

The debt to volume was approximately 1% of sales.

COLE'S D-X SERVICE STATION

Cole's D-X Service Station, located in a small town in eastern Oklahoma (population 2000), was owned and operated by Mr. Cole. The local economy was based partly on agriculture, and on a fairly large segment of limited-income people such as retirees and welfare recipients. There were some industrial workers, however, who were employed in other towns, since there were no factories in the town. The outlying rural areas also contributed significantly to the income of the little Oklahoma town.

This station was an existing business when Mr. Cole purchased it in 1972. It was a four-pump gasoline facility which could accommodate two cars at the same time. He also had a two-bay car-servicing area, a two-bay self-service car wash, and rest rooms. Inside, there was an office for customer service, accessory display, and a back room for storage and tires.

Three men operated the station: Mr. Cole, his married son, and a full-time employee. Their hours of operation were from 7:00 A.M. to 7:00 P.M. six days a week, Mr. Cole's son was a qualified mechanic, which enabled the station to offer tune-up jobs, tire changing, maintenance services, oil changing, flat-fixing, and motor overhauls.

The business was located on a through highway within a block or two from most of the businesses in town. The station itself faced the thoroughfare, and was situated in the northwest corner of the busiest intersection in the town.

The financial facet of the business was briefly summed up in Mr. Cole's words: "Three of us have made a living out of it." This was his way of saying that he, his son, and one employee derived enough from the business to warrant remaining in it. He had made a $900 mortgage payment on the service station. The business had no cash reserves to rely on, should adverse conditions arise.

When Mr. Cole first bought the station and started operating it he knew he would have to double its existing volume in order to survive. To attract customers, credit was extended to people known to be poor credit risks, in order to reach the "double-the-volume" objective.

Mr. Cole was operating the station with one-third of the business volume on accounts receivable and two-thirds on a cash basis. Some credit customers had large amounts owing. Some of these accounts had become large over a period of several months. Even though these customers had run up a large bill at the station, when they did not pay after a few months they stopped buying altogether. Mr. Cole would much rather have the past-due customer keep doing business with him than to not come back at all. Eventually, he would hope to absorb the credit loss for that individual, although it would take quite some time to accomplish this. People who continued to do business with him in this manner usually paid off their delinquent accounts over a period of time.

Mr. Cole now has a delinquent account in the sum of $600 with an individual to whom he had extended credit over a long period of time. This man at first ran up a bill of $150. He then paid the $100 on his account. At the next accounting the bill was $250. He told Mr. Cole he had a job and was working. After working six weeks, he paid $75 on his account, and continued to run up his indebtedness to $600. Thereafter, he never returned, although he still resided in the same place.

Another customer from whom Mr. Cole had sought payment was a woman who had owed $130 for three years. She had made payments in the amount of $2.00 or $5.00 monthly at her discretion. Once, when she sent $5.00 to pay on her account, Mr. Cole would not accept it because it was such a small sum. He told her he wanted $20.00 per month. He said he was not trying to make it difficult for her, but—knowing how much her income was—he felt she was able to pay much more on her account.

At times, Mr. Cole was hard pressed to meet his own obligations, because of the many delinquent accounts at his station. If he had had some surplus back-up money, it would not have been so difficult, and it would also have given him more time to collect from delinquencies.

Still another customer with whom Mr. Cole was still doing business, was a man who only paid when Mr. Cole personally pressured. This man would run up a $250 bill over a six-month period, and then he would stop trading at Mr. Cole's station. When Mr. Cole would personally collect the money from him, the man would then come back and begin doing business on a credit basis again. Thus it would go for another six months. It was a kind of cycle.

Mr. Cole usually waited until he was hard pressed for money before going out and trying to collect the money owed him by the delinquent customers. After waiting a long time, he sent the delinquents a threat from the Small Claims Court. This sometimes brought in money that he otherwise would not have obtained. Recently, by a threat to delinquent customers, he collected $260.

Mr. Cole found that if customers have agreed to pay their bills on the first of the month, he should go to see them about their accounts if payment has not been made by the third of the month. However, at that time of the month he was exceptionally busy because of the increased activity at the station, due to payday. Mr. Cole did not send out monthly statements. However, if a customer does not come in and pay each month, he would send him a bill. He just did not have that much time for the paper work. Mr. Cole felt, however, that requiring early account payments would make a better customer relationship.

J. D. ADAMS, JEWELER

Jones Jewelry, presently J. D. Adams, Jeweler, was owned and operated by Mr. and Mrs. Robert Jones for twenty-six years. The store was located in downtown Springdale, a small town in northwestern Arkansas. Mr. Jones purchased the business from his father-in-law who kept very little stock and did most of his business repairing watches. Mr. Jones rented the building and made some improvements on the interior. He also built up the reputation of the store with his friendliness, fairness, and honesty, along with the stock, but watch repairs represented a large percent of business. In 1973 Mr. and Mrs. Jones were ready to retire, and began looking for prospective buyers. He received several offers, but wanted to find someone who would take care of his long-time customers and friends.

J. D. Adams was born and raised in a small town near Springdale, but had lived and worked in Tulsa for the past nineteen years. His wife was an English teacher in Jenks, and was currently teaching English at Springdale High School. They have two children, one of which was living at home. At the age of thirty-seven, he attended Okmulgee State Tech, and graduated three years later with the sole intent of moving to a small town and purchasing a going concern. On hearing of the Jones' store being for sale, Mr. Adams looked into the possibility of purchasing it.

The stock was paid for with the agreement that Mr. Jones was to be paid a set amount of money per month until the entire amount was paid. Money was borrowed from the local bank to build up the stock.

After purchasing the business, Mr. Adams made a few more improvements on the interior. He laid carpet and added a few showcases. At first, he rented the building as Mr. Jones had done. Later, he got the chance to buy it and the one next to it, and did so.

Mr. Jones left a good size stock, but Mr. Adams had a source to get some of his ring stock from someone other than a wholesaler. Therefore, he was able to enlarge the stock at a lower cost.

He employed one full-time employee and one part-time employee. At Christmas time, the busiest time of the year, his wife and daughter also helped.

The business was located in the middle of downtown Springdale, which had a population of 2,500. Springdale, the county seat, was surrounded by a number of other small towns from which is secured a good percentage of business. At least 45 percent of the population were farmers and ranchers — 30 percent were low-income people over age fifty, on welfare and Social Security, and 25 percent were entrepreneurs and people employed by them. Business was usually best the first week of each month, due to the large amount of people who received welfare and Social Security checks. Also, every Wednesday the ranchers and farmers came to the sale at the stockyards, which made it the busiest time of the week. The store was the only jewelry store within a forty-five mile radius.

Because of its large stock, good service, and low overhead, not only did it serve customers from towns that did not have a jewelry store but, it also got business from people from several towns that had a jewelry store. People had traveled from Oklahoma City and Tulsa to shop at Mr. Adams's after having shopped in the larger stores in the larger cities. They had reported that Adams had a wider variety of merchandise of better quality and lower prices than the larger stores.

Mr. Adams had worked hard at establishing a reputation for honesty and fairness among his customers, and dependability at backing up his merchandise. He had even gone so far as to do small jewelry repair jobs without charge, and had eliminated charging for cleaning rings and other jewelry.

He was president of the Chamber of Commerce, a member of the local chapter of the Lions Club, a member of the City Council, and he supported various local clubs and organizations.

Mr. Adams ran ads in several weekly newspapers. He had two billboards at each entrance into town on the main highway. He frequently had spots on at least two local radio stations.

Mr. Adams entered the business without any accounts receivable, because Mr. Jones took all of them with him. In his four years of business, he had rarely refused credit to anyone, and had inevitably suffered the consequences. He had lost approximately $4000 in accounts receivable, all of which were over one year old, (the oldest being 3 years and 3 months old). The percentage of uncollected accounts over collected accounts was around 37 percent. An undetermined amount of money had been spent on statements and stamps in an effort to collect the uncollected accounts. These unpaid accounts had caused a reduction in profit.

EL MEXICANO RESTAURANT

Before coming to Coweta, Oklahoma Tom Norse and his wife, Pam, lived in Las Vegas, Nevada, where they operated a small motel for five years. Business was good enough to give them a modest income and a savings of about five thousand dollars. Tom wanted to get out of the motel business and open up a restaurant, but Vegas was not the place to do it. Restaurants were a dime a dozen there.

In 1961, while visiting relatives in Coweta, Oklahoma, Tom decided that this was where he was going to open his restaurant. The town had a population of about six thousand people, and showed signs that it was going to grow. An industrial park south of town was bringing in new industry and labor every day. Also, a solid industry was already established there, and there were many people engaged in farming. Downtown Coweta was relatively new because of rebuilding after a tornado that had leveled everything in the 1940s. All indications led to the conclusion that this town was going to grow.

Realizing this, Tom started checking established restaurants. To his amazement, there was only one — besides the hamburger stands. The other three or four restaurants seemed to experience changes of management frequently. Only one restaurant was going to be his main competition, and he set about trying to figure how he was going to handle it. This place listed on its menu typical family dinners with an emphasis on steaks. Tom decided he would serve Mexican food. Mexican food was not served anywhere in town at the time.

Tom decided he would try to find a location downtown, and cater heavily to the people that worked downtown while on their lunchbreaks. By creating an informal atmosphere, he would draw on the family evening crowd.

In 1962 the El Mexicano Restaurant was opened in the middle of downtown Coweta. Seating capacity was about forty-five. The building was an older building, but decorated with many articles brought back from a short vacation in Mexico. The employees consisted of a cook, one waitress (full-time), and Tom. Pam helped serve and cook, and manned the cash register.

Pam had come upon an idea to entertain the customers in a subtle way. She obtained several snapshots of local people and businessmen taken in the 1940s and 1950s. These were arranged along each wall next to the booths. People seemed to enjoy trying to figure out who was who in these pictures. After a while this idea proved so successful that a contest was started, awarding a free dinner to the first person to recognize a particular snapshot.

El Mexicano proved to be a going concern. Business was good, the food was good, and Tom soon proved he had a way of making people enjoy themselves — and of course making them spend their money.

Tom and Pam spent less time at the restaurant after awhile, but were always there at opening and at the busiest times of the evening. Tom continued his skill in helping people to spend their money. Everyone agreed that Tom and Pam had a goldmine going.

Then, in 1976, personal problems developed between Tom and Pam, and a divorce ensued. Tom gave Pam ownership of the business and he left town. For awhile business remained as before. But Pam found it increasingly harder to retain the level of quality and efficiency. Personnel problems developed and food costs rose. Business was beginning to drop off seriously. Pam was trying to decide what to do with the business.

EASY-GROW SEED COMPANY

The Easy-Grow Seed Company of Mideast City was founded in 1909 as a subsidiary of James Seed Company of Tulsa. In 1946 Green Thumb was incorporated as a separate entity. The company managed to survive the war years. George Rollins became general manager of the company in 1950. The company was in poor financial condition when Rollins came. By diligence and good common business sense, Rollins managed to get the company back on its feet.

The company was divided into three functional divisions: 1) wholesale store, 2) retail store, and 3) seed cleaning and processing plant. The wholesale and retail stores sell garden seed, field seed, and various brands of garden tools and hardware items. In addition, the retail store sells house plants and has a Christmas specialty shop during November and December. The seed cleaning and processing plant cleans and stores seed for farmers and the company.

The wholesale store employs six outside salesmen. Walk-in customers are served by the dispatcher, wholesale purchasing agent, and wholesale secretary. The outside salesmen cover the entire state and parts of two bordering states. The retail store has a manager, a farm representative, and two full-time clerks. The seed cleaning and processing has a manager and two full-time helpers.

Salaried employees include the following: president/general manager, vice president/sales manager, seed cleaning and processing plant manager, accountant/ office manager, wholesale purchasing agent, dispatcher, retail store manager, and farm representative. All other employees are on an hourly basis with the exception of the outside salesmen who are on commission. The following statement was extracted from a company policy letter to new employees:

Promotions and Increases

We have no rigid salary classification system or arbitrary classing of employees and no automatic or periodic increases are given. Each employee is judged on individual merits of his work and increases in salary are made when in the opinion of management, they are warranted.

In 1972 Rollins and the sales manager, Arch Bolin, made an arrangement to buy out the other stockholders. The arrangement called for a five-year note plus interest. The note was to be paid in five equal installments. After completing the arrangement, the capital structure appeared as follows:

> 500   shares authorized
> 480   shares issued and outstanding
> 262   shares purchased and now in treasury
> ───
> 217   shares now outstanding (Rollins and Bolin)

After the arrangement was completed, Rollins was elected president and chairman of the board (owned 165 shares). Bolin was elected vice president (owned 52 shares).

In 1975 the company made a major investment in a new type of packaging machinery for the seed cleaning and processing plant. The machine, which cost almost $25,000, was to be used to package seed for the company and to do some packaging on a contract basis for other seed companies. Also, in 1976 the company entered a lease/purchase agreement on a small computer. The agreement called for 60 payments of $1,000. Title will pass to the company after all the payments. The computer has the capability of handling inventory, accounts receivable, payroll, accounts payable, and the general ledger. At present only the inventory and accounts receivable features of the computer are being utilized, although the other functions are expected to be operational soon.

Through the years Rollins has made most company decisions on his own — hiring, new products, etc. However, being 63 and approaching his retirement, he was keenly aware of the limitations in managerial skills of the other personnel in the business. Rollins would like to be able to sell his interest in the company to key employees upon his retirement and ensure that the company ownership would remain with the active employees. He was concerned that outsiders who know little about the business might gain control upon his retirement.

Figure A–1.
Chart of Organization.

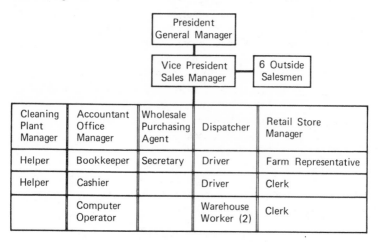

Cleaning Plant Manager	Accountant Office Manager	Wholesale Purchasing Agent	Dispatcher	Retail Store Manager
Helper	Bookkeeper	Secretary	Driver	Farm Representative
Helper	Cashier		Driver	Clerk
	Computer Operator		Warehouse Worker (2)	Clerk

Analysis of Personnel by Department

1. *Vice President*—college graduate in agriculture, extensive sales background, age mid-50's.

2. *Outside Salesmen*—all competent salesmen, all age mid-30's except one who is in 20's. The youngest salesman also serves as assistant purchaser for seeds.

3. *Cleaning Plant*—*Manager:* high school graduate, excellent mechanical aptitude, age mid-40's, 25 years on job.
   Helpers: both early 20's, the one with most time on job has been here 1 year.

4. *Office*—*Accountant:* college graduate in accounting, 2 years on job, formerly 3 years in consumer finance industry, age early 30's.
   Bookkeeper: high school graduate, highly experienced and efficient, 20 years on job, approaching retirement.
   Cashier: high school graduate, efficient, 1 1/2 years, age early 50's.
   Computer Operator: competent, 2 weeks on job, age late 20's.

5. *Wholesale*—*Purchasing Agent:* over 3 years college, efficient, conscientious, 20 years on job, age mid-40's.
   Secretary: junior college graduate, highly efficient, 2 years on job, age early 30's. (Acts as backup computer operator.)

6. *Delivery*—*Dispatcher:* high school graduate, hard worker, 2 years on job, age early 20's.
   Driver 1: good record, 2 years on job, age early 20's.
   Driver 2: good record, 1 year on job, age early 20's.
   Warehouse Worker 1: good steady worker, 11 years on job, age mid 50's.

TABLE A-2
Easy-Grow Seed Company: Comparative Income Statements

	1976	1975	1974	1973	1972
Sales	$2764227.70	$2965454.47	$2452087.23	$1912900.60	$1,873,671.65
Less:					
Cost of goods sold	2,224,303.55	2,374,919.71	1,853,678.25	1,449,179.14	1,424,133.72
Gross Profit	539,924.15	590,535.36	598,408.98	463,721.46	449,537.93
Operating Expenses	519,816.51	527,607.21	490,298.49	417,244.06	406,656.09
Net Income From					
Operations	20,107.64	62,928.15	108,110.49	46,477.40	42,881.84
Other Income	42,454.35	39,045.76	16,457.21	25,987.28	34,552.65
Other Expenses	23,377.03	17,741.82	25,709.53	19,602.57	17,292.63
Net Profit Before Taxes	$ 39,184.96	$ 84,232.09	$ 98,858.17	$ 52,862.11	$ 60,141.86

TABLE A-3
Easy-Grow Seed Company: Comparative Balance Sheets

	1976	1975	1974	1973	1972
CURRENT ASSETS					
Cash	$ 25,268.47	$ 10,879.38	$ 36,885.67	$ 958.07	$ 8,196.19
Accounts Receivable	241,220.77	288,758.49	222,365.06	208,484.01	201,392.65
Inventory	338,098.59	165,599.40	133,742.35	241,462.80	207,194.87
Prepaid Assets	25,951.62	19,827.88	19,019.92	22,109.85	16,495.55
Other Current Assets	38,592.10	32,797.71	32,077.53	32,692.37	27,513.08
TOTAL CURRENT ASSETS	$669,131.55	$517,862.86	$444,090.523	$505,707.10	$460,792.34
FIXED ASSETS					
Land	18,506.91	6,350.00	6,350.00		
Plant and Equipment	251,849.52	227,035.84	187,369.49	176,237.64	181,802.69
less Depreciation	-172,119.02	-156,300.29	-147,779.82	-153,590.87	-133,655.98
	79,730.50	70,735.55	39,589.67	22,646.77	48,146.71
TOTAL FIXED ASSETS	98,237.61	76,985.55	45,839.67	22,646.77	48,146.71
TOTAL ASSETS	$767,368.96	$594,848.41	$489,930.20	$528,353.87	$508,939.05
CURRENT LIABILITIES	$405,056.41	$209,665.49	$123,867.11	$211,607.61	$162,458.69
LONG-TERM LIABILITIES	39,156.00	61,542.00	82,056.00	102,570.00	
TOTAL LIABILITIES	$444,212.41	$271,207.49	$205,923.11	$314,177.61	$162,458.69
CAPITAL					
Capital Stock	48,000.00	48,000.00	48,000.00	48,000.00	48,000.00
Treasury Stock	-136,760.00	-136,760.00	-136,760.00	-136,760.00	
Addt'l Paid in Capital	2,760.00	2,760.00	2,760.00	2,760.00	2,760.00
Retained Earnings	409,156.55	409,640.92	370,007.09	300,176.26	295,720.36
TOTAL CAPITAL	323,156.55	323,640.92	284,007.09	214,176.26	346,480.36
TOTAL LIABILITIES AND CAPITAL	$767,368.96	$594,848.41	$489,930.20	$528,353.87	$508,939.05

Warehouse Worker 2: hard worker, 1 month on job, age early 20's.

7. *Retail—Store Manager:* junior college graduate, ambitious, 8 years on job, age late 20's.

Farm Representative: college graduate in agriculture, 9 years on job, expert in his field, age late 40's.

Clerk 1: high school graduate, good worker, 1 year on job, age early 20's.

Clerk 2: high school graduate, 6 months on job, age early 30's.

SUCCESS LUMBER COMPANY

Success Lumber Company was a relatively small, low-volume lumber supply house. Mr. Charles Wilson, manager and owner, had read in trade magazines that the metric system of measurement was becoming a dominant measuring stick for some U.S. companies. However, the metric system was still only used by the minority. Success Lumber had had a good track record of profits over the years. Although there were two major competitors in the immediate area whose volume exceeded that of Success Lumber's, the management felt its market share was holding steady and future sales looked good. Mr. Wilson felt that one reason for Success Lumber's success was their customers. He believed many of his customers were "repeats," people who had purchased there before. Store loyalty and location appeared to be strong motivators of sales.

Although a small amount of inventoried items were sold over the counter in the front of the store (fixtures, pipe fittings, tools, etc.), the main volume of the business stemmed from the sale of lumber itself.

Mr. Wilson knew that almost half of the nation's highest companies had either begun converting their manufacturing specification to the metric system or were inching into it; but many companies were dragging their feet. They questioned whether the costs of conversion (measured in everything from buying new tools to training workers) were worth the trouble and confusion. Manufacturers were reluctant to convert unless their vendors did, while suppliers did not want to make a move before their key customers did. Also, Mr. Wilson believed that this "trend" toward the metric system was being overshadowed by short-term economic considerations during the current recessionary period.

The metric system was scheduled to become mandatory in the Common Market by 1978, a prediction that appeared to be early. Congress finally passed the Metric Conversion Act of 1975. However, the act set no deadlines and stipulated that conversion should be voluntary. To give the new policy direction, it provided for the establishment of an independent U.S. Metric Board, consisting of seventeen members drawn from industry, small business, labor, education, science, and the consumer sector. The board's function was to plan, publicize, encourage, and coordinate programs for achieving national conversion.

Even though there were no deadlines for conversion, the remaining choices for Success Lumber, as seen by Mr. Wilson, related to timing and method and degree of metrication. Mr. Wilson discussed the effects of the metric changeover with an MBA student at a nearby university. The student researched the topic and made this following list of possible effects: most metric costs were intangible; productivity would dip slightly; proficiency would decline slightly due to thinking and working in a new system; there would be some duplication and errors while operating with two systems; and some results would amount to a nuisance factor. Metrication costs for a company could be expected to rise to a peak; but there would come a point, perhaps five to ten years after the start of metrication, when operations became so enmeshed in the changeover that what many viewed as costs would then be seen as savings.

One important decision that a business would have to make was whether their conversion should be "soft" or "hard." Soft conversion, which involved merely changing numbers but not dimensions, was fairly simple and inexpensive. A food processor, for example, could simply print labels that read 237.2 grams instead of eight ounces. Going soft was also relatively painless in industries where precision tolerances were low. The American Concrete Pipe Association, for instance, had proposed stadardizing thirty different pipe sizes to metric measurement. The typical twelve-inch (304.8 millimeters) American pipe would be well within the tolerance variation of 300 millimeter metric pipe. Hence, with soft metrication, new pipe would still fit everybody's old pipe, and the financial trauma should be small indeed.

Hard conversion, making products to metric specifications, entailed retooling, new machinery, and double inventories, and was considerably more costly. Nevertheless, if carried out as part of a coordinated industry effort, it could broaden markets and reduce costs.

Another point made by the student, specifically concerning the lumber industry, was that mechanics and carpenters would have particular problems with metrics. A lot of their decisions in measurements were instinctive, based on years of working with the customary system. This would have to be taken into consideration before a decision was made.

Projects
and
Resources

CHAPTER 1

Learning Experiences

1. Pursue an advertised or other known business opportunity. Obtain financial statements and determine the value of the business. Recommend whether or not to purchase the business, giving reasons in support of your decision.
2. Secure a franchise agreement. Analyze the pros and cons. Prepare a short report with recommendations for or against the franchise.
3. Report on the required steps for incorporation of a business in your state.
4. Discuss the possibility of Subchapter S Corporation with an existing small business company, and report on the attitude of the businessperson interviewed.

Bibliography

COLLEY DONALD G., "Buying a Small Going Concern," *Small Marketers' Aids Annual*, No. 2. Washington, D.C.: Small Business Administration, 1960.

DONNELEY ROBERT G., "The Family Business," *Harvard Business Review,* 42 (July–August 1964), 93–105.

GOULD G. H. B., AND DEAN C. CODDINGTON, "How Do You Know What Your Business Is Worth?" *Management Aids,* No. 166. Washington, D.C.: Small Business Administration, 1964.

"How to Buy or Sell a Business," *Small Business Reporter,* 8, no. 11. San Francisco: Bank of America, Small Business Advisory Service, 1969.

MANCUSO, JOSEPH, *Fun and Guts: The Entrepreneur's Philosophy.* Reading, Mass.: Addison-Wesley Pub. Co. Inc., 1973.

METCALF, WENDELL O., *Starting and Managing a Small Business of Your Own,* I (2nd ed.). Washington, D.C.: Small Business Administration, 1962.

PICKLE, HAL B., *Personality and Success: An Evaluation of Personal Characteristics of Successful Small Business Managers,* Small Business Research Series No. 4. Washington, D.C.: G.P.O., Small Business Administration, 1964.

CHAPTER 2

Learning Experiences

1. Visit with a small business entrepreneur about the profit objective for the business. Determine what the objective is and how it was set. If there are no profit objectives, discuss the advantages and report the reactions to your ideas.

2. Arrange with a small business for an opportunity to develop and present a "profit plan" for the business.

3. Prepare a break-even point for a business with Sales Income $500,000, Variable Expenses $250,000, Fixed Costs $50,000. Determine the marginal income, and marginal income per sales dollar as intermediate steps to the BEP.

4. Discuss with a small-business operator, how to increase profits, based on the suggestions offered in this chapter. Report the priority assessed by the business-person based on your interview.

Bibliography

DAVIS, RALPH CURRIER, *Industrial Organization and Management.* New York: Harper and Brothers, Publishers, 1940.

DRUCKER, PETER, *The Practice of Management.* New York: Harper and Row, Publishers, 1954.

S<small>ISK,</small> H<small>ENRY</small> L., *Management and Organization* (3rd ed.). Cincinnati, Ohio: South-Western Publishing Co., 1977.

CHAPTER 3

Learning Experiences

1. Contact an insurance representative and inquire what insurance package he would recommend for a beginning small business. Report the breakdown as to type of insurance and approximate costs per year.

2. Inquire of a small-business person what professional assistance he uses and on what basis they are employed. What are the reactions to these services?

3. From the last Census of Business in your library, report the number of businesses in your community, county, and state in a particular category. You select the category. Do you consider the competition excessive? Explain. What further information would you desire?

4. Select a kind of small business and prepare recommended sources of information of value to the entrepreneur and the cost of obtaining the materials.

Bibliography

B<small>AUER,</small> R<small>OBERT</small> J., "How Better Business Bureaus Help Small Business," *Small Marketers' Aids Annual,* No. 4. Washington, D.C.: Small Business Administration 1962, 83–90.

M<small>AYNE,</small> D<small>AVID</small> R., "Specialized Help for Small Business," *Small Marketers' Aids Annual.* No. 7. Washington, D.C.: Small Business Administration, 1965, 80–87.

P<small>ERRY,</small> K<small>ENNETH</small> W., *Accounting: An Introduction.* New York: McGraw-Hill Book Co., 1971.

P<small>OMERANZ,</small> J<small>ANET</small> M., <small>AND</small> L<small>EONARD</small> W. P<small>RESTWICH.</small> *Meeting the Problems of Very Small Enterprises,* Small Business Management Report, Small Business Administration. Washington, D.C.: George Washington University, 1962.

"Sources of Assistance and Information," Administrative Management Course Program, Topic 15. Washington, D.C.: Small Business Administration, 1965.

W<small>HITE,</small> L. T., "Management Assistance for Small Business," *Harvard Business Review,* XLIII (July–August, 1965), 67–74.

CHAPTER 4

Learning Experiences

1. Discuss with a small-business person the nature and extent of the company information system. Make an evaluation of the adequacy of the system. Include ideas for improvement.

2. Contact a small business for the purpose of evaluating specific use of the following types of information in the business: records of cash, purchases, equipment, depreciation, accounts receivable, production, materials, inventory, inspection, scheduling, sales, customers, competitors, advertising, publicity, personnel.

3. From either of the above learning experiences, suggest ways or means for economizing on the costs of information.

4. How can the information system contribute to profitable operations?

Bibliography

LASSER, J. K., *Handbook of Accounting Methods* (3rd ed.). New York: D. Van Nostrand Co., Inc., 1964.

MYER, JOHN N., *Accounting for Non-Accountants* (1st ed.). New York: New York University Press, 1947.

OVERMYER, W. S., "Picking an Auditor for Your Firm," *Small Marketers' Aids Annual,* No. 4. Washington, D.C.: Small Business Administration, 1962.

CHAPTER 5

Learning Experiences

1. Check and report on local ordinances that must be complied with by small business.

2. What state laws affect the operation of small business in your state?

3. Under what conditions do small businesses come under Federal legislation.

4. Arrange an interview with a small manufacturer to discuss the impact of OSHA. Report the attitudes pro and con about this legal provision.

5. Discuss the impact of taxes with a small-business owner and report the feelings of the small-business owner.

6. Interview a small-business operator about his experience with bad checks. Based on this information, what policy would you recommend?

7. Discuss the subject of "bankruptcy" in terms of justifiable use and also in terms of ethical considerations.

8. Obtain a lease agreement from a shopping center or landlord of business property, and evaluate from the standpoint of the business lease. Give the reasons why you would or would not sign the lease. If you have access to a lawyer you may also benefit from his opinion.

Bibliography

ALYEA, PAUL E., *Impact of Overlapping Sales Taxes on Small Business.* Small Business Management Research Report, Small Business Administration. University, Ala.: University of Alabama Press, 1961.

"Small Business Taxation," *Journal of Small Business Management,* 10 (April 1972).

Records to be Kept by Employers. Wage and Hour and Public Contracts Division, Washington, D.C.: U.S. Department of Labor, Federal Register, July 1, 1967.

Tax Guide for Small Business, A. Washington, D.C.: Internal Revenue Service Department of the Treasury (Published annually).

CHAPTER 6

Learning Experiences

1. Visit a banker and learn firsthand what his bank requires to make a loan to a small business as an initial source of capital or an ongoing operating capital loan.

2. Discuss with a small-business owner, the methods used to finance the business and what recommendations he would suggest to someone starting a business.

3. Investigate the possibilities of funding a small business in your community, and advise on the basis of a recommended priority which sources are best.

Bibliography

"Borrowing Money from Your Bank" (11). Washington, D.C.: Small Business Administration, Publication No. 1.10/2:2, Annual No. 2, No. 33.

KRENTZMAN, HARVEY C., *Managing for Profits*. Washington, D.C.: Small Business Administration, 1968.

ROBINSON, ROLAND I., *Financing a Dynamic Small Firm*. Belmont, Calif.: Wadsworth Pub. Co., Inc., 1966.

"What Kind of Money Do You Need?" Washington D.C.: Small Business Administration, Publication 1.10/2:11, Annual No. 11, No. 150.

ZWICK, JACK E., *A Handbook of Small Business Finance*. Washington, D.C.: Small Business Administration, 1965.

CHAPTER 7

Learning Experiences

1. Select a business property available in your community and do a locational analysis for a proposed small business listing the pros and cons and a final recommendation on the location.
2. Choose two communities and apply Reilly's law for the determination of an inter-city location.
3. Do a site history on a prospective business property location.
4. Conduct a comparison study of two or more available business sites in your community and recommend your choice with supportive reasons.

Bibliography

MERTES, JOHN E., *Creative Site Evaluation for the Small Retailer*. Norman, Okla: University of Oklahoma Press, 1962.

"Problems of Location and Real Estate," *Journal of Small Business Management* (January 1972).

WEBER, FRED J., JR., "Locating or Relocating Your Business." Management Aids for Small Manufacturers, No. 201. Washington, D.C.: Small Business Administration, 1969.

CHAPTER 8

Learning Experiences

1. Visit a selected small business, either retail, wholesale, or manufacturer and make a sketch of the existing layout. Based on the materials in this chapter

and information obtained elsewhere, prepare an improved layout giving reasons for changes. If you cannot recommend improvements, justify the existing layout.

2. Prepare a model or mock-up of an existing or prospective business layout.

3. Discuss store space values with a small business operator and compare the practice with the material presented in the chapter. Note differences and suggest improvements of space utilization for the store.

Bibliography

DAVIDSON, WILLIAM R., AND ALTON F. DOODY. *Retailing Management* (3rd ed.). New York: The Ronald Press Co., 1966. [See especially Chapter 7.]

IMMER, JOHN R., *Profitable Small Plant Layout* (2nd ed.). Small Business Management Series, No. 21. Washington, D.C.: Small Business Administration, 1964.

PINTEL, GERALD, AND J. DIAMOND. *Retailing.* Englewood Cliffs, N.J.: Prentice-Hall, Inc., 1971.

CHAPTER 9

Learning Experiences

1. Discuss risk with a small-business owner. Prepare a list of risks according to priority and what measures are being utilized to handle the risks.

2. Ascertain from a small business the insurance coverage and the expense involved. Then shop and see what savings you could obtain from other companies for the same coverage. Is the amount significant? Would you recommend a change? What factors should be considered before making any change in insurance companies?

3. Investigate the FAIR plan.

4. Evaluate the Federal Crime Insurance Program and discuss its feasibility for small business.

Bibliography

"Business Insurance." Washington, D.C.: Small Business Administration, Publication 1.10/2:1, Annual No. 1, No. 15.

"Commercial Crime and the Small Businessman," *Journal of Small Business Management,* 9 (July 1971).

GREENE, MARK R., "Insurance and Risk Management for Small Business" (2nd ed.). Small Business Management Series No. 3. Washington, D.C.: Small Business Administration, 1970.

"Insurance and Risk Management for Small Business." Washington, D.C.: Small Business Administration, Publication 1.12:30.

CHAPTER 10

Learning Experiences

1. Practice improving your use of time by making use of a daily time-utilization form. Report on improvements noted.
2. Ask a small business operator to tell you what is his major business problem. Is the alleged problem a problem? If not, pursue the matter until you can write the basic problem and explain the difference.
3. Take a reading test and find out your score. Do you need to improve your reading ability?
4. Take a listening test and find out your score. Do you need to improve your listening ability?
5. Report the availability of reading and listening courses in your community, and the cost of each.

Bibliography

MORRIS, JUD. *The Art of Listening.* Boston: Cahners Pub. Co., Inc., 1968.

NICHOLS, RALPH, AND LEONARD A. STEVENS. *Are You Listening?* New York: McGraw-Hill Book Co., 1957.

WEBBER, ROSS A., *Time and Management.* New York: Van Nostrand Reinhold Co., 1972.

CHAPTER 11

Learning Experiences

1. Write up an account of your most responsible managerial experience. Evaluate your performance based on the material presented in this chapter. Suggest ways you could have improved your performance.

2. Arrange and interview with a small-business owner and discuss with the person how the managerial functions (initiate, delegate, and evaluate) are accomplished. After the interview, prepare a written summary with recommendations for improving the managerial functions in the business.

3. Discuss with the operator of a small enterprise the greatest need in managing the business more effectively and more profitably.

4. After discussing organization with a small manufacturer, a wholesaler, or retailer, prepare an organization chart of the existing organization. Then prepare an improved version and state your reasons for the changes.

Bibliography

Hicks, Herbert G., and C. Ray Gullet, *Modern Business Management*. New York: McGraw-Hill Book Co., 1974.

Sisk, Henry L., *Management and Organization* (3rd ed.). Cincinnati, Ohio: South-Western Pub. Co., 1977.

Terry, George R., *Principles of Management* (7th ed.). Homewood, Illinois: Richard D. Irwin, Inc. 1977.

CHAPTER 12

Learning Experiences

1. Determine the Materials Management program for a small manufacturer and make a comparison with the seven phases suggested in this chapter. Do you see opportunities for improving the procedure used by the manufacturer? Did you learn something to supplement the material of this chapter?

2. Discuss the policies used by a small business engaged in purchasing raw materials, and compare with the subjects covered by policy in this chapter. How could the company situation be better implemented?

3. Review with an owner of a business the subject of inventory control, inventory valuation, and conducting a physical inventory. How do these inventory considerations affect profits?

Bibliography

Hedrick, Floyd D., *Purchasing Management in the Smaller Company*. New York: American Management Association, 1971.

HEINRITZ, STEWART F., AND PAUL V. FARRELL, *Purchasing Principles and Applications* (5th ed.). Englewood Cliffs, N.J.: Prentice-Hall, Inc., 1971.

CHAPTER 13

Learning Experiences

1. Ask a small-business person how the last employee was employed. What was the employing procedure? Was an application blank or test used? Evaluate the methods and procedures and suggest improvements you would adopt if it were your business.

2. Check with a small business on the "employee benefit" package offered employees. Compare with competitive businesses in the area and report differences between competitors on this facet of human resource management.

3. Select a non-union manufacturing plant and discuss methods of discipline and grievance procedures.

4. Discuss with a union plant the important details involved in negotiating their last union contract.

5. Ascertain from actual contact with a small business the type of "evaluation program" (performance appraisal) being utilized. How does it compare with suggested procedures outlined in this chapter? Does the program seem effective? Prepare comments for class discussion.

6. Outline a positive motivation program for improving morale in a small business. Then discuss with a small-business manager. Report the outcome of your discussion.

Bibliography

CARLIN G. S., *How to Motivate and Persuade People*. West Nyack, N.Y.: Parker Pub. Co., 1964.

CHRUDEN, HERBERT J. AND ARTHUR W. SHERMAN, JR., *Personnel Management* (5th ed.). Cincinnati, Ohio: South-Western Pub. Co., 1976.

MCQUAIG, JACK H., *How to Pick Men*. New York: Frederick Fell Publishers, Inc., 1973.

CHAPTER 14

Learning Experiences

1. Select from the following list of subject areas a subject of your interest and investigate the actual practices in a small manufacturing plant:

   a. Waste Control
   b. Work Simplification
   c. Work Standards
   d. Time Study
   e. Inspection
   f. Statistical Quality Control

2. Consult with a small manufacturing plant manager for practices of planning and controlling operations.

Bibliography

BARNES, R. M., *Motion and Time Study: Design and Measurement of Work* (6th ed.). New York: John Wiley and Sons, Inc., 1968.

BEGEMAN, M. L., *Manufacturing Processes* (5th ed.). New York: John Wiley and Sons, Inc., 1963.

GAVETT, WILLIAM J., AND JOHN H. ALLDERIGE, "Production Planning," *Operations Analysis in Small Manufacturing Companies*. Section 5, Small Business Management Research Report. Ithaca, N.Y.: Cornell University Press, 1963.

CHAPTER 15

Learning Experiences

1. Review the questions of the Marketing Information Checklist found in this chapter with the owner of a small business to find clues for possible increased profitability in operations. Report your experience.

2. Discuss pricing procedures with a small merchandiser. Is the merchandise being priced properly according to information of this chapter? Does the business use cost or retail as a basis for pricing? Discuss your findings.

3. Select a store with a "high quality" image and arrange an interview with the proprietor to learn the methods used to achieve the store image. Discuss your experience.

4. Contact a store merchandiser and discuss the concept of the price-volume relationship and ascertain the practical application and any limitations that may apply. Submit your answers to the class.

Bibliography

HAYNES, W. WARREN. *Pricing Decisions in Small Business.* Small Business Management Research Report, Small Business Administration. Lexington: University of Kentucky, 1961.

LEVITT, THEODORE. *The Marketing Mode—Pathways to Corporate Growth.* New York: McGraw-Hill Book Co., 1969.

MCCARTHY E. JEROME. *Basic Marketing: A Managerial Approach* (5th ed.). Homewood, Illinois: Richard D. Irwin, Inc., 1975.

STANTON, WILLIAM J., *Fundamentals of Marketing* (4th ed.). New York: McGraw-Hill Book Co., 1975.

CHAPTER 16

Learning Experiences

1. Evaluate the performance of three salespersons in three different small businesses, and decide if they qualify as "income producers" as used in the text. What, if anything, was lacking? How would you remedy if you were the manager?

2. Undertake a shopping tour of several stores to purchase the same item of merchandise, and identify the types of closing techniques asked by sales personnel. Report your findings.

3. Conduct a survey in the stores of your community, with a sufficient sample of particular kinds of stores to give you an indication of the amount of training given sales personnel, methods used, frequency, etc.. From your experience with sales personnel, is the training effective?

4. Contact a manufacturer, wholesaler, or retailer and discuss the basis for analyzing sales. Use the material provided in this chapter as a guide in preparing for your interview.

3. Discuss with a small-business operator the question of using ratio analysis as a control technique. Report the kinds of ratios in use. Otherwise, secure permission to prepare some ratios which would be useful for the operator. Report your learning experience.

4. Make arrangements to conduct a "profit audit" for a small business. Explain the merits to the owner and agree to furnish a report of the audit.

Bibliography

ALTMAN, E. I., *Corporate Bankruptcy in America*. Lexington, Mass.: D. C. Heath Company, 1971.

KUEHN, W. H., *The Pitfalls in Managing a Small Business*. New York: Dun and Bradstreet, Inc., 1969.

MA, J. C., AND H. D. HENNEY, "What It Takes to Come Out of Chapter XI," *Credit and Financial Management,* February 1962.

MAYER, KURT B., AND SIDNEY GOLDSTEIN, *The First Two Years: Problems of Small Firm Growth and Survival.* Small Business Research Series No. 2. Washington, D.C.: Small Business Administration, 1961.

PROXMIRE, WILLIAM, *Can Small Business Survive?* Chicago: Henry Regnery Company, 1964.

STANLEY, D. T., AND M. GIRTH. *Bankruptcy: Problem, Process, Reform.* Washington, D.C.: Brookings Institution, 1971.

CHAPTER 20

Learning Experiences

1. Interview a small-business owner about his plans for the continuity of the business in the event of unexpected death, semi-retirement, or full retirement. Report your findings.

2. Discuss with a small manufacturer, wholesaler, or retailer the various ways open for disposing of their business. Ascertain which method is preferred and the reasons.

3. In discussing the subject of estate planning with a small-businessperson, suggest the option of a family annuity. Note the reactions.

Bibliography

O'NEAL, F. H., *Expulsion of Oppression of Business Associates—Squeeze-Outs in Small Enterprises.* Durham, N.C.: Duke University Press, 1961.

STRANGE, M., *Acquisition and Merger Negotiating Strategy.* New York: Hawthorn Books, Inc., 1971.

Index

6667018

DATE DUE
